# SHIPS, ACCIDENTS & WORLD TRAVEL

## *How My Career Helped Me See The World*

## Bob Ojala

Published by A3Pi Services, LLC www.a3pi.comMilwaukee, WI



Color 979-8-8691-0332-1 Black and White 979-8-8691-0337-6
Color E-book 979-8-8691-0334-5
V03-01042024

# DEDICATION

To my family who put up with my frequent absences while I gallivanted all over the world. I missed a lot of birthdays and anniversaries but did my best to be home for major events. Thank you for being so understanding!

I think my parents and teachers made me an honest person and taught me to respect people of all races and origins. Some great bosses like Dennis Trone, Charlie Carsten, and Steve Hungness reinforced those traits and taught me to respect the people I worked with and those I audited. There were also great co-workers like Judit Kovacs and Susan Hoertt, who also reinforced those important traits. Thank you all!

# CONTENTS

# Acknowledgments

# ACKNOWLEDGMENTS

Special thanks to my wonderful editor, Amma Twum-Baah, for working with me on this updated edition. I had originally written this book as an Autobiography for my children, family, and friends, so they would understand what I did in my profession. It was not originally written for other readers to understand and enjoy. As usual, Amma made that happen!

Several people helped me to edit my original edition. Thanks to **Ann Braun** and **Teri Dupuis** for a lot of help in that regard. Then there were **Jan & John** Raymond, who took the time to read my entire draft and review its contents. I needed to know if technical areas needed more explanation and if there were sections that were just plain boring. They also provided positive feedback, which was important.

Then there were two men, both authors, who may not realize how much help they were: The first is Stephen King, author of Stephen King: On Writing. The second person is Dr. Arved Ojamma Ashby.

In his book, Stephen King: On Writing, Stephen said, "Write about what you know," and I have been guided by that in my writing.

Although I have never met him, we did communicate via e-mail before he passed away. Dr. Ashby wrote a book about his survival and eventual success, fighting the Russians in Estonia during World War II, and then coming to the United States, finishing Medical School, and becoming a very successful medical doctor. Someone recommended his book because Dr. Ashby had written about confusion with a man named OJALA (O-Yalla). His Estonian name OJAMMA (O-Yamma) sounded similar. Reading his Autobiography showed me how an unusual life can be interesting and worth writing about, although Dr. Ashby's survival story makes my life look like nothing!

Many people either knowingly or accidentally guided me throughout my life. To them, I am most grateful.

# INTRODUCTION

AT THE BOTTOM OF A DEWATERED LOCK CHAMBER, PANAMA CANAL, IN 1999

My first big decision in life came after high school. I was a decent student who had no clear direction for a career path, and college did not look like the right path for me. Education, however, was important to my dad, and he had already offered to help me pay for college, so I knew he would be upset if I refused to go. My dad had never finished grade school during the Depression because of his poor English skills. He came from a non-English speaking home, and his Swedish teacher did little to help this little Finnish kid learn any English. So, he sat in the back of his 1st-grade class for three years, until his younger sister came to school and helped him get to 2nd grade.

Although my dad lacked formal education, (he quit school after the third grade to work to help support the family) he was considered very successful for his generation. He was probably "self-educated," because we always saw him reading. Also, he passed his Coast Guard Engineer's Licensing Exams, which was certainly more than a 13-year-old, 3rd Grader would be able to accomplish. While I struggled with whether to go to college, I still had a thirst for knowledge, and always have. I was a curious child who asked questions about my surroundings. That trait came from my mother. She often traveled with me and my sister every summer to visit my dad, who was a Great Lakes Merchant Mariner. We usually took a car ferry to Michigan to see him, sometimes waiting on a deserted coal dock at 2:00 a.m. for his ship to arrive. We also visited my dad's relatives in Minnesota every summer. One of my first memories in life is of me clinging to my dad's back as he climbed a ladder up the side of his ship during a visit to Marinette, Wisconsin.

While my dad was away on the Great Lakes for long periods, my mother exposed me to the excitement of traveling. She once delivered clothing to an Indian Mission in North Dakota, with me and my sister in tow, while taking side trips to Mt. Rushmore and the Badlands. This was in the 1950s, with an old car that sometimes overheated, but she taught us to learn about things outside of our everyday experiences. I remember a visit to South Dakota with my mother and sister. We stopped to talk with a Native American gentleman who was selling souvenirs along the highway. My mother started the conversation, and I remember asking him a lot of questions about Native American history and current Native American life. This was during a time when movies and television portrayed Native Americans as aggressive, but somehow my mother had instilled in me a respect for that man, the sort of respect that has influenced my life to this day.

Because my mom exposed us to these experiences, I found myself choosing exciting paths when alternate ones presented themselves in my life and career. I was never foolhardy or curious enough to try life-threatening activities such as skydiving, bungy jumping, or mountain climbing. Travel, on the other hand, was exciting. It involved meeting new people and risking some embarrassment by experiencing unfamiliar things. This is why I considered a career in the Coast Guard instead of college.

My mom understood my concerns about going to college at seventeen. She also knew that I had no real interest in any specific field of study that was worth going to college for. So, when I suggested enlisting in the U.S. Coast Guard, she agreed. I was under the legal age of consent for entry, so my mother signed the papers on my behalf as my legal guardian.

Of course, my father was not happy about me joining the Coast Guard because he knew how hard life was as a mariner. He did not want that kind of life for me. But my exposure to his maritime life was exactly why the Coast Guard looked so interesting. This was several years before the Viet Nam Draft, so I was not looking for a way to stay out of Viet Nam (in fact, it nearly got me there).

## <u>Travels, Memories, and an Exciting Life</u>

This book is a compilation of many of my working trips around the world. All the stories are true. Looking back at the opportunities my career has given me, sometimes I have to "pinch myself" and ask, "Did I really do all of this?" Many traveling businesspeople hate their nomadic life, but not me. Other than a few minor glitches (and the increased airport security after 9/11/2001) here and there, I enjoyed my travels, my work, and the wonderful people I worked with and met because of these travels. I still enjoy it.

In cases where I've forgotten some details, I try to mention that in my narrative. My goal is to share insights about people and the cultures I witnessed and learned about during my travels, and not just to write a simple travelogue.

## HOW TO READ THIS BOOK

The book is arranged in a somewhat chronological order, but it is not necessary to read every page or chapter. The detailed Table of Contents will help you find chapters that interest you. Keep in mind, however, that reading things out of order may leave some unanswered questions in other chapters. My Cruise Ship audits extended more than 8 years, and my work in Ukraine was right in the middle of that, so not everything is chronological.

I just hope that you enjoy some, if not all, of my adventures, and that you find things that interest you. I truly had a great career and I think my life is interesting and worth sharing.

**For those readers in the Marine Industry**, you may notice some very simplified definitions of marine technical terms, or some I've simply ignored if I think the explanations might become too lengthy. This book was not meant to be read like a textbook! Some terms are defined, such as ABS, and Gas Free, as well as some riveting and welding terms, which were important to the stories. However, please understand that you may find some "layman" terms in many cases to avoid over-complicating the narrative. My other books about sailors' lives, Sweetwater Sailors, and Sweetwater Sailors – The Rest of the Story, are more technical. *Note: The indented paragraphs in Italics denote my definitions!*

If anyone is interested in how I got started in this crazy business, I also have an autobiography, Autobiography of a Ship's Marine Surveyor, which covers my formative years in the U.S. Coast Guard, gaining my degree in Naval Architecture at the University of Michigan, my first Engineering job at Dubuque Boat & Boiler Company, other intermediate jobs, and my long employment with the American Bureau of Shipping (ABS), before starting my own business. In that book, I also describe my dad's career as a merchant mariner and provide details about my years in the Coast Guard, my college experiences, and so much more about those first jobs before I started A3Pi Services. My Army Corps of Engineers experiences, near the end of my career, opened up an entirely new area in my life.

The details about how I prepared for this life of Marine Surveying and World Travel is a book in itself, and those subjects are covered in my **Autobiography.** However, the following is a summary of the experiences that led to my formation of A3Pi Services, Marine Consultants, and Surveyors:

- Enlisted in the United States Coast Guard for four years, working as an Engineman on two icebreakers. I also attended Fire Fighting and Damage Control School after a collision with a freighter on Lake Erie, during Search and Rescue Operations.

- Attended Parks Air College, and the University of Michigan, resulting in a Degree in Naval Architecture & Marine Engineering.

- Worked as the first (and only) Engineer at Dubuque Boat & Boiler Co., Dubuque Iowa, which had been in business since 1870, building river paddle wheelers, and even gunboats for the Navy during the Spanish-American War (though I was not there to witness those!)

- Worked as the first Marine Sales Engineer for Waukesha Engine Company, Waukesha, Wisconsin, installing engines in the U.S. and Mexico.

- Worked as a Field Surveyor with the American Bureau of Shipping, Chicago, Illinois, surveying both Great Lakes and foreign flag vessels, working in both Great Lakes and River shipyards, overseeing new ship construction and repairs, plus inspections at approximately 400 factories, inspecting both materials and equipment destined for shipbuilding. These factories included steel and aluminum mills, foundries, forge shops, engine manufacturers, reduction gear manufacturers, electrical equipment, pumps and valves, propeller manufacturers, boiler and pressure vessel manufacturers, and many more.

To say the least, I felt I was experienced and ready to strike off on my own!

# CHAPTER 1

## RULES OF THE ROAD:
## DO NOT BE AN UGLY AMERICAN

A coworker and friend at the American Bureau of Shipping (ABS), was stationed in Japan for over two years with his family. (I had tried to get one of those transfers overseas, but was thwarted because my family was too large for the Japanese housing owned by ABS.) When my friend returned to the United States, I went to visit him and wanted to know how he had enjoyed his time in Japan. He simply said, "It was fine." When I asked him what he saw in Japan and where he had traveled in Asia, he had little to share. Unbelievably, he had stayed in the "U.S. Compound" as he called it, ate only American food, and saved all of his vacation and comp time to travel home each year. He and his family had not experienced anything Japanese or Asian during his time there. Now mind you, I liked this guy. He was a great friend and professional resource. But I would have never wasted such an opportunity to experience Japanese culture. My family would have traveled as much as our budget would have allowed.

I did not like every place or every culture I experienced during my business travels, but I tried to learn as much as I could before those opinions were formed. For example, I did not like the Japanese culture on the main island of Honshu (I mostly spent time around Tokyo), yet felt Okinawa was very different, and the people there were much friendlier.

Luckily, I decided early on to look beyond the superficial things a "normal" tourist wants to experience and report on. I've seen enough museums and cathedrals, and have read travelogues describing them, so that was not my intention when writing this book. I may mention some details about cities, hotels, tours, and food quality, but only if they somehow affected my travels, (like my fantastic hotel dinner in Catania, Sicily!). I am not trying to compete with Rick Steves, whom I respect. I wanted to report those things that were different from my life back home and to share what I learned about the cultures of the people with whom I worked. In my original e-mails to my family, the details were supposed to be more than travelogues. They reported the deeper details of travel that I was lucky enough to experience.

Many people have traveled more than I have, and to more exotic destinations, but it's amazing, that when you ask them about their experiences, you often hear more about their hotels, tours, and food experiences than anything else. Occasionally, they might delve into the monetary problems they experienced and their disappointments with traveling schedules. They might even complain about the people they encountered, and their lack of English, but when asked what the people are like, they will give you a blank stare!

One **Rule of the Road** I've used since the beginning of my travels is this: **There are no problems when traveling, only unusual opportunities for new learning experiences.** Many of these experiences happen right at the airport! It is amazing how many interesting people you will meet when you are stranded in a strange airport for six hours. For example, having a cheerful attitude and the ability to laugh at your hopeless situation will attract the attention of those around you. Some might think you are a little crazy, but the ones who smile back will let you know that you've made an impact, in which case you can then start a conversation. No one wants to be miserable, but most can be made miserable by the negative people around them.

On more than one occasion, I walked up to the service desk, after witnessing irate travelers yelling at airline service agents about their missed, delayed, or canceled flights, and said, "I'm sorry for how that person treated you!" Even though it was done sincerely because nobody should be treated that way, I have found time and time again that service agents respond positively to such acknowledgments, and they will reward you by helping you with your problem. They have tough jobs; most of us could not do it for long without yelling back! So, it helps to remember that service persons are there to help you, and once you start yelling at them, they will not be as willing to help.

There was a young woman in the Warsaw Poland airport, working behind the service desk, who broke out in what appeared to be hives while trying to help an irate customer. Our flight had been canceled and she was doing her best to reschedule everyone, but this man berated her efforts. When we got to the head of the line, we apologized for how that man had treated her. We got a beautiful hotel for the night, a wonderful dinner and breakfast, and coupons for a taxi each way. We considered this a highlight of our trip. Now, I want to go back and see more of Warsaw!

I was stranded in Minneapolis one winter evening, while trying to return to Chicago after a job in Duluth, Minnesota. All of the flights to Chicago were either canceled or delayed. I started thinking, and by the time I got to the head of the line, I had an idea. "Can you still fly into Milwaukee?" I asked the ticket attendant. The lady said, "Yes, but you'd still have to wait until tomorrow for a Chicago flight." When I explained to her that it was easy to rent a car or take a bus to O'Hare, if she got me to Milwaukee, she was thrilled with my idea and passed it on to her fellow service agents. With her help, I got to Milwaukee, caught a bus to O'Hare where I retrieved my car, and was home four hours later instead of the next day.

The worst part of travel delays is that you will end up standing in long service lines for extended periods. Most of these service areas are filled with interesting people who are afraid to talk to the people around them. I see this, particularly in large international airports where language barriers may exist. What I usually do to get a conversation started is to identify the people around me, listen to the languages being spoken, and then try to determine where people are headed.

**Advice to Americans**: Remember that when traveling outside of the United States and Canada, *you* (the American) are the foreigner! Oftentimes, the Ugly American problem is alive and well in airports around the world. When Americans get frustrated, they tend to speak faster and louder, as if yelling will help people understand them better. Your loud voice and nasty attitude, even if you are not trying to be nasty, will commonly lead people to perceive you as American, which only proves that Americans are just as obnoxious as they had been led to believe.

After you have turned off the people around you, by being nasty, you will soon find yourself on your own in a foreign airport. But if you quickly convince the people in those service lines that you are "okay," they will begin to share their knowledge and experiences about that airport or airline with you. Don't act like an Ugly American, and you will possibly be able to find solutions to your problem through your fellow passengers and airline service agents.

I was once headed to Croatia from Chicago, with a change of planes in Frankfurt. My final destination was Trieste, Italy, where a driver from Croatia was going to meet me. The Chicago flight arrived late in Frankfurt, so the flight to Trieste had left without several of us. There was nearly a five-hour wait until the next flight to Trieste. While standing in that dreaded service line, I started talking to those around me, comparing our woes. "Aren't these service lines a great way to meet people?" I said. Once the ice was broken, another person in line told me to ask if the airline had an earlier flight to Venice. The Venice airport and Trieste airport are only a bit more than a one-hour driving distance apart. That plan worked out. The airline transferred my luggage, and I called my driver and asked him to meet me in Venice. He arrived there almost the same time as my flight. Soon, we were on our way to Croatia. All because of a smile and a simple, friendly statement! So, remember: when traveling, problems are just unusual opportunities for new learning experiences!

# CHAPTER 2

## THE BEGINNING OF MY COMPANY: A3PI SERVICES, INC.

While considering a partnership with a small group of investors in 1987 (where my services would be my investment), I befriended one of the potential partners from that purchase negotiation, and we decided to incorporate an inspection business in November 1988, called Associated Third-Party Inspection Services, Inc. I moved into my partner's office in Westchester, Illinois, near Chicago, where he ran his Manufacturer's Representative business. Luckily, we had a neighbor in the adjoining office who was in the advertising business. He laughed at the long company name when we gave him one of our brochures.

One morning, he walked into our office and handed us a sheet of paper. On the paper, there was a design he had put together for us, and he suggested that we use it as the concept for a LOGO. That LOGO was "A3Pi." We liked the idea and made it part of our letterhead, but we kept "Associated Third Party Inspection Services, Inc." as well. We later used that letterhead on a letter to our attorney, who was putting together our Corporate records. The attorney called shortly after, asking, "What is your Company name? Associated Third Party Inspection Services Inc., or A3Pi?" He said the confusion could cause problems, so we changed the name, and A3Pi Services, Inc. was born.

Although my partner, Alan Lyon, was a great help in getting me started, he never really became involved in any inspections or surveys. I needed him as my "crutch" to take the big step of starting a business although he did not understand the Marine Industry. My constant phone calls to potential clients and friends, trying to drum up new business, really irritated Alan, so he moved me into my own office just down the hall from his office. As my business grew, I realized that I needed help, so I hired a secretary. However, the secretary did not want to commute to Westchester, so we found a great location in a small shopping center in Willow Springs, Illinois. Through all of this, Alan and I remained friends.

After a few years, I offered to buy back his stock and repay his initial investment, including interest. The partnership was then dissolved, but we ended things on a friendly note.

The first few years were tough. My friends and acquaintances on the Great Lakes said they wanted me to become independent. They offered to give me survey jobs if and when I left the ABS position. Most did not follow through with that promise until 6 years, even 8 years later. I now understand that it would have been hard for those companies to give their service work to a new, small business. If A3Pi had failed, my clients would have had to return to their previous marine surveyors, which would have been an embarrassing situation for them. My first paying jobs were inspecting machine parts for the paper industry each week in Detroit, and inspecting cargo containers at factories and repair/testing facilities around Chicago. None of these were what I had intended to be doing, but they were a start, and I learned a lot about contracts and business relationships.

In business, I always ask myself. "Is this ethical?" "Will it eventually lead to making money?" "Is it interesting?" If the answer was yes, then I usually accepted that new job opportunity. Many times, taking small jobs for limited pay results in the first client's recommendation to a larger client. I also found that treating everyone fairly leads to a good reputation. Having a good reputation is priceless; it helps you skip the need to advertise for new clients. Over the years, word of mouth from satisfied clients has been the source of most of my business.

Because of my Naval Architecture background, I was able to pick up small design jobs, such as a small crane barge for a local marina, structural modifications for barges and tugboats, for submittal to ABS and the US Coast Guard, and other such work to keep some income flowing.

One very interesting job I performed over the first six months after I left ABS, was the one referenced above. The job involved traveling to Detroit every week to inspect large machine parts for the paper industry. Paper machine rolls are typically 30 feet wide, and the machining of these rolls was critical. I found innovative ways to check the accuracy of the machine parts and learned about the machining industry, where I previously had little or no experience.

Although I hated working on privately owned yachts, surveys for yacht insurance companies paid well, so I investigated damages, overheated engines, and other small insurance claims now and then. You will note later in this book, a chapter on more serious yacht surveys, which were very interesting. However, these initial small surveys typically included more work and travel time than the pay warranted. But they did keep some money coming in.

A major portion of my steady work during this early 1989 timeframe was the inspections of tank containers for several Classification Societies. Tank containers typically carry dangerous or toxic liquid cargo. The container must be pressure tested every five years, and a structural and internal inspection made every 2-½ years. Early in my career, I would perform five or ten of these inspections per week. (Note the tank container on the lower right of our first A3Pi Advertisement mailer, sent to clients, as shown below.)

Although most inspectors who were performing these container surveys were not experienced surveyors, my background not only helped me to obtain this work but also led to contacts within the marine industry. These new contacts occasionally developed into vessel survey work.

One of my first big breaks was to fly to Denmark, to install computer load sensors on the cranes of an Oil Drilling Rig in the North Sea. The job took two days but I was stuck on the rig longer due to fog. (I describe this trip in a later chapter). When I returned from Denmark, I started calling my friends to tell them about this interesting job in Europe. I didn't ask for work, but my "potential" clients began to realize how serious my efforts had become to stay in business. This eventually helped me to obtain their business.

One of the calls I made was to a man at the new ABS office in Houston. John Barr had been giving me small non-ABS classification work, such as new container design inspections and a few Great Lakes ship surveys. John remembered I had traveled to Europe and called me a few weeks later, asking if I would take a ship damage survey job in Kwajalein. I immediately said yes, and John asked if I even knew where Kwajalein was. I said it didn't matter because I wanted to go. (I also describe this trip in detail in a later chapter.) This started a long and great relationship between A3Pi and ABS Technical Services (ABSTech), which then became ABS Consulting.

One time, I asked John Barr if he ever called anyone else for those crazy jobs that he sent me on, and John said, "Hell no! Everyone else has an excuse for why they cannot go!" The only times I turned down overseas travel was if I was already booked on another job, and even then, I tried to adjust my schedule to take the ABSTech jobs. Once a surveyor starts making excuses, the job offers stop coming in. John Barr later retired, but his successor, Richard Goss, continued giving me fantastic adventures that kept my family fed, and ABSTech work helped to pay college bills for nearly 25 years.

Another man responsible for my early success was Dennis Egan, whom I cover in detail in Chapter 28.

This ends the more historical portion of my A3Pi business. In Chapter 27, you will read about some of the colorful people I came into contact with.

In the other chapters, you will read about some of the fascinating places I was privileged to visit and get paid for doing so. Most people have to pay to travel, but my clients paid for my adventures! Some countries were visited for only a day, but many were experienced several times (Korea, Singapore, New Zealand, Spain, Australia, etc.), and some for extended periods (seven weeks in Ukraine, three weeks in New Zealand plus a few shorter trips, numerous trips to Panama, etc.). Countries were not counted as visited if I never left the airport or even the airport hotel. I worked in 58 different countries (I kept track), but visited more than 70 countries in total. Maybe that number will increase, or I may return to some as a tourist, to better enjoy those countries. I hope you'll enjoy my narratives of my travel adventures!

# CHAPTER 3

## FIRST WORLD TRAVEL: NORTH SEA DRILL RIG

In 1988, I was doing small engineering projects from home, in addition to working for ABS. One needs to test the waters before leaving a full-time job like ABS. These small engineering projects involved helping a group of manufacturing representatives sell power-saving electronic controls to industrial applications. We even designed and proposed a "spy system" for McDonald's Corporation, which McDonald's then took and designed their own (that's another, long story about why I dislike McDonald's!)

The manufacturing representatives got a job from a small electronics company in Texas, looking for someone willing to travel to Europe to install a small load computer on several cranes mounted on a drill rig in the North Sea. They recommended me for the job and I used vacation time from ABS to make the trip. This was my early introduction to business world-travel long before A3Pi Services officially started.

First, I traveled to Houston, over a long weekend, to receive training on the installation and programming of these small computers and their sensing devices. This first trip to Europe was a learning experience, not only for my contemplated business plans but also for some of the problems I would later encounter during travel over the years that followed.

The trip started on a KLM flight to Amsterdam, my first experience on a 747 aircraft. "People watching" is a lot of fun, and a family of Hasidic Jews with small children was great to watch because they were fascinated with the stairway leading to the upper level of the 747. The flight attendants continually chased the children away from the stairway (my seat was adjacent, on the lower level), because only first-class passengers were allowed on the upper level. If the flight attendants had just taken the time to show the children what was up there, the children might have been satisfied and returned to their seats. These kids were well-behaved but just curious!

I arrived in Amsterdam and immediately noticed the difference between the two countries. Amsterdam's airport had more security than airports in the United States had at that time., with multiple luggage inspections and armed guards everywhere. While waiting to board my next flight to Esbjerg, a small coastal city in Denmark, where transport would be arranged to get me to the drill rig the next day by helicopter, I witnessed one of the worst "Ugly American" incidents I have ever seen! An American businessman, maybe 40 years old, came into the gated area. In addition to the main security screening to enter the concourse, a second random screening was being done at our gate, similar to what happened in the United States after 9/11! This happened to be not long after one of the early terrorist attacks at an airport in Germany, so security was tight.

This American complained because his baggage had already been screened once! *He didn't see why he was being inconvenienced again*! It probably only took ten seconds before a nearby soldier had this man on the floor with his foot on the back of the man's neck, and a machine gun pointed at the back of his head. The security team tore the man's carry-ons apart, including the lining of his briefcase. Finding nothing, they let the man up off the floor. He knelt there for ten minutes trying to put his stuff back together. Neither the security team, nor the soldier, and certainly not our "Ugly American" said a word afterwards. The man simply picked up his bags, found a back corner, and looked at the floor until the plane boarded. He deserved the humiliation. He should have understood the current tense atmosphere in Europe at that time.

The small, square-bodied, airplanes, built in Northern Ireland by the Shorts Company, were used for these short flights. Years later, while flying to Iowa regularly, these same square-bodied aircraft were used between O'Hare and places like Waterloo, Iowa. These aircraft were unpressurized due to the square body design, making them not good for flights in rough weather. They could not climb above 10,000 feet in rough weather.

Once, on our way to Iowa, we had to fly through a thunderstorm. About twenty-five of the passengers were sick, including me, upon arrival. I needed a few hours in a hotel room to recover before heading to my inspection job. No profits on that trip! However, my trip to Esbjerg was calm and beautiful. I saw numerous windmill generators along the coast, which we hadn't yet started to see in the United States.

Compared to the security at the airport in Amsterdam, arrival in Esbjerg was just the opposite. After leaving the airplane, there was no passport clearance, and after retrieving my baggage, there was nobody in the Customs area. I have no passport stamps to prove I was ever in Denmark on that first trip!

I took a taxi to the hotel which had been arranged, but there was nobody there to meet me. My first mistake was to nap when I got to the hotel. Even though the nap was just a couple of hours, I found it difficult to get a good night's sleep later that night. So I spent the night watching television on the Danish and German television stations, and this left me feeling exhausted the next morning. **Big Lesson Learned**: Resist the temptation to take a nap before the local, normal hour to go to sleep for the night.

The agent for the company that had chartered the drill rig, picked me up at the hotel the next morning and took me to the local airport, where a helicopter was waiting to transport me to the drill rig. After a very heated discussion between the agent and the helicopter company, all of which were in Danish, my trip that day was canceled. My American client had not given me the proper safety training before arrival, which was required by the Danish North Sea oil regulations. They agreed to give me the training at the airport before going to the rig, so I spent the rest of the day watching safety videos in Danish. Only then was a Safety Training Certificate issued. I was allowed to board the helicopter and head to the rig, the next morning.

While waiting at the airport, I saw a local newspaper that included an article about the company operating those helicopters. The article included a picture of the pilot on my helicopter. I kept a copy of the newspaper as a souvenir and, when I returned home, I was able to get a translation. This pilot had trained American helicopter pilots during the Vietnam War, and the article was praising him because he was also known for flying to the rigs in emergencies, even in bad, North Sea weather. Although such flights were normally canceled, he would agree to fly out to a rig alone, if an injured worker needed to be transported to a hospital. He was well respected worldwide, and certainly in the North Sea!

This pilot was the only person aboard the helicopter who spoke English. He was very helpful to me once he realized he had a "newbie," who had never flown in a helicopter before. It was a bit unnerving when we all had to wear a maritime flotation/survival suit during the flight. At that point, it was becoming obvious that this environment was unfamiliar to me, and this was serious business!

The helicopter was a large, 20-passenger type, which turned out to be surprisingly calm, despite the very windy weather. We first landed at a large oil platform in the middle of the Danish North Sea oil fields. Some of us were asked to get off the helicopter and wait on the platform for further instructions. The platform was large and had all of the facilities necessary to service the smaller platforms and drill rigs in the area, which operated in Danish waters. There was even a small hospital on the platform. Reading the signs in the lounge was interesting. I read some of them while waiting for further instructions. Some were warnings about sexually transmitted diseases because the rigs had both male and female workers aboard. This was in 1988, we were not having such open discussions of such things in the United States.

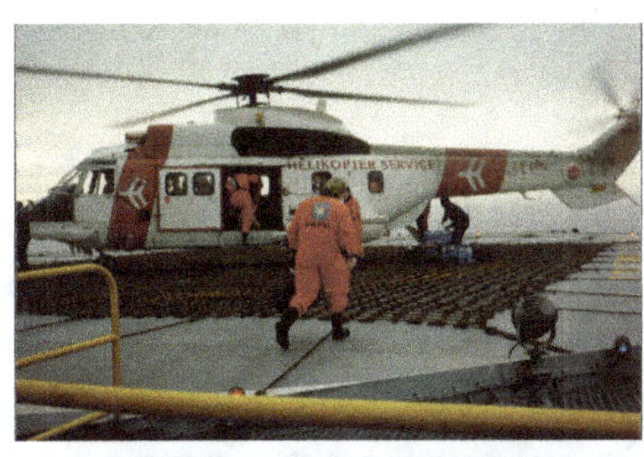

**HELICOPTER LANDING ON PLATFORM**

After about one hour of waiting on the large platform, a smaller helicopter landed and several of us boarded for transport to the various rigs on which we would be working. Although this flight was also quite smooth, the wind was very severe upon arrival, and it felt like you would be blown over the side if it were not for the traction provided by the heavy rope netting that covered the steel deck. We landed on a large helicopter platform. The platform was the type that hung over the side of the drill rig (as shown on the last page of this chapter), and we were immediately guided down to a safer position.

Once inside the rig, two Captains introduced themselves. One was the Maritime Captain, in charge when the drill rig was floating, and the second

SMALLER HELICOPTER ARRIVING AT
PLATFORM TO TAKE ME TO THE OIL RIG

captain was in charge once the legs of the jack-up rig were secured to the ocean bottom. This second captain was responsible for the drilling operation, and he was totally in charge of the drill rig at that point. Both captains were American. It quickly became obvious that this was an American drill rig out of Houston, Texas. The captains were very helpful and explained that the cranes on this drill rig did not currently need the load sensing equipment for American regulations, however, the Danish government did require such safety equipment. The drill rig crew had been anxiously awaiting my arrival. The rig had come to the North Sea without this important crane safety equipment installed, and they were about to be sent home if they didn't have the equipment installed soon.

In my room, I was finally able to remove the hot, rubber survival suit ("Gumby suit"). However, the suit had to be kept easily available on a chair alongside my bed, due to the ever-present possibility of an emergency evacuation.

There was an orange, Danish oilfield safety vessel stationed within eyesight of every drill rig. New arrivals were instructed on how to enter the evacuation vessel on our rig, which looked more like a space capsule mounted

at a 45° angle on the rear of the drill rig. Again, it was clear this was a different world and serious business! Those evacuation vessels are now common on most ocean vessels. However, I had not seen one of them before this one.

DANISH OILFIELD EMERGENCY VESSEL ALWAYS ON STANDBY

My roommate on the rig was a technician from Schlumberger, who would be called out at all times of the day and night to take readings relative to the drilling operation. This drill rig was mounted adjacent to a large oil production platform, and several of the oil production lines had become plugged. The Texas drill rig had been hired to "re-drill" these oil lines to break the plugs and allow the oil to flow properly. Being unfamiliar with the oil business, this description may not be completely accurate.

After breakfast the following morning, we were provided with more safety information. The Captain inspected my camera and placed tape over the flash. He explained that the tape had to remain there until I was outside the oil field because "flash sensors" were installed on all the rigs and platforms to automatically shut down the entire oil field in case of an explosion. Again, a reminder that this was serious business!

The chief engineer and the drill rig electrician worked with me to install the sensing devices at the proper positions so that the load on the crane and the angle of the crane boom would be sensed. This information was then used by the minicomputer to calculate the safe load for the crane at that boom angle. Cranes have occasionally been pulled off a drill rig when lifting supplies from the supply vessels bringing equipment and materials out to the rigs. The sensing equipment and computers we were installing would prevent this from happening. The installation went well, and the training I received

LOAD SENSOR ON CABLE END

from the manufacturer in Houston worked perfectly to program the computer. This all went like clockwork and everyone was happy. The helicopter was scheduled to leave the rig the next morning and take me back to Esbjerg.

Before taking that job, I stressed to the computer manufacturer that this had better NOT be an ABS rig. That was because it could create a conflict of interest if I worked on a rig certified by my employer. While working with the chief engineer on the rig, he mentioned to me that my name sounded familiar.

ANGLE SENSOR ON BOOM

On the second day, he told me he remembered where he had seen my name and took me to his office. There, he showed me certificates for generators, on board the rig, I had certified at Electro-Motive in LaGrange, Illinois. At that point, I had to tell him that I was an ABS employee. I asked if that would be a problem and he assured me that most people in the maritime business also moonlight on the side so he would keep my secret.

MINI-COMPUTER IN CAB

It would be terrible to end this part of the story without mentioning that the food aboard this drill rig was fantastic. They had three different galleys serving food around the clock. Actual mealtimes were at 6 AM, 12 noon, 6 PM, and midnight. However, food was available whenever you were hungry. One galley served American food and a second galley served Muslims on board the rig. The third galley served European-style foods. If you ever get on a rig, make a habit of eating from all three. The food was wonderful, you will hear this repeatedly throughout the book! It certainly explains my expanded waistline!

MY RIG AS SEEN FROM PLATFORM

When the job was done and it was time to go home, calm winds and a calm sea prevented me from leaving. One would expect winds and high seas to be the reasons for a delay, but it turned out to be quite the opposite. Because the wind had died down, the rig was fogged in, making the helicopter unsafe to fly off the rig. The delay was only one day, but missing my flight home meant I had to call my boss at ABS in Chicago to tell him I needed an extra day for my "vacation." When the winds picked up again, one of the smaller helicopters was able to fetch me off the rig.

**WE FLEW ON ONE OF THE SMALLER HELICOPTERS BACK TO ESBJERG**

# CHAPTER 4

## WHERE THE HELL IS KWAJALEIN ISLAND?

After I resigned from my job at ABS and started my own business, ABS began using me for small projects in the Chicago area, including condition surveys on several Great Lakes ore carriers and witnessing cargo container prototype tests. These jobs were arranged through the main office in Houston since my old boss in Chicago was upset when I resigned. ABS did not fill my vacant position in Chicago when I resigned, although they asked me to stay for an extra month, even though I gave them two weeks' notice. My duties as the Quality Control Auditor for engine and steel factories were hard to replace, I guessed, and I had to help my old boss take over the Quality Control work. (I had some good bosses at ABS, but not the last one). These people are described in more detail in my autobiography.

Mr. John Barr was one of the program managers in the ABS Technical Services Division (ABSTech), which performed marine surveys outside of the normal scope of their classification surveys. John was looking for a Naval Architect with a surveying background; someone who was willing to travel to Kwajalein Island to look at an NOAA research vessel that had been damaged during a typhoon in the South Pacific. The crew did not want to proceed unless the vessel was inspected and approved by a Naval Architect and repairs made if required. John Barr was surprised when I accepted the job without any questions. He had made calls to other Naval Architects and surveyors, all of whom had made excuses for why they could not take such a long trip. John told me I would need a security clearance to visit the island because there was US Military work being done there. He said he wanted to get that process started, so my quick acceptance was appreciated.

I need to give a lot of credit to my travel agent, Lilian Bannach, at National Tours & Travel, formerly in Westchester, Illinois. I walked into their agency on this first project, not knowing Lilian or her partner, and they booked my flights. Because they were always willing to go above and beyond, spending a lot of time researching my weird destinations, I continued using them until they retired and closed their agency in 2008. Booking trips on the internet put them out of business, but without their help, my travel planning would have been pure hell!

So, my first stop was a visit to my previously unknown travel agent, Lilian, to ask her to arrange airfare to Kwajalein Island. She asked me where that was located and I told her she was the travel agent, and I was hoping *she* knew. I had accepted this job without really knowing where John Barr was sending me. Luckily, the airlines knew where Kwajalein was located, and we scheduled a flight from Chicago to Honolulu via Houston. Even the airline informed Lilian about the need for me to have a security clearance for this destination. Lilian was impressed.

After I booked my flight, John Barr told me I would be staying overnight in Honolulu and meeting several U.S. Government employees, who would accompany me to Kwajalein.

On the flight to Honolulu, the crew upgraded me to First Class, which seemed like a blessing at the time. However, the shrimp dinner in First Class was tainted and, within an hour, I became violently ill. After disembarking the plane, I had to lie on one of the airport benches for over 15 minutes before gaining enough composure to walk to baggage claim. My taxi ride to the hotel was spent lying in the back seat.

I hoped that a short nap in the hotel would be enough for me to recover, but the situation eventually required that I ask the hotel to contact a doctor because my condition was getting worse. Without medication, I was afraid that the trip scheduled for the following morning might never happen. I couldn't eat or even move around without becoming nauseous. Fortunately, I got the medication I needed and felt well enough the following morning to return to the airport and meet the Government officials who were waiting for me.

The flight to Kwajalein included a stop at Johnson Island, which is another top-secret U.S. military base. At the time, it was being used to store nerve gas and other chemical warfare weapons which were slowly being outlawed and destroyed. Passengers were not allowed to leave the plane at

Johnson Island, and it appeared we only stopped to drop off mail and picked up a few packages, then took off again.

From Johnson Island, we flew to Majuro Atoll, which is the capital of the Marshall Islands. There, we dropped off passengers and picked up a few new ones. The airport on Majuro was built into the lagoon of the island, so when we were landing, we saw nothing but water. Until the wheels touched down, there was no runway in sight. The entire island is only a few feet above the level of the ocean and, although it has been recently improved, the original landing strip was built by the Japanese during WWII.

From Majuro Atoll, we landed in Kwajalein during a driving rainstorm which made the trip even more eerie than it had been up to that time. When we entered the airport, we were confronted by a large military-looking man with a Marine-type haircut. He spoke with a Southern U.S. accent and said he was with the Marshall Islands Police Force. It was obvious to me that he was a U.S. Marine, and that he was there to be sure we obeyed the "rules." All of our luggage was x-rayed upon arrival. He warned us that we had to follow the "rules," which included carrying a Military ID card at all times. He then went on to state that the next island was over 100 miles away and that the island was surrounded by shark-infested waters, in case we had any crazy ideas. This all seemed to be a "little over the top," seeing that we all had to have a security clearance to even get on the plane.

We were driven to our hotel, which looked like a military, bachelor officers' quarters, and in fact, that is exactly what it was. We were given a map of the island and told that we would be contacted first thing in the morning to attend to the damaged NOAA research vessel.

OUR 'HOTEL' ON KWAJALEIN

The map had notations on the reefs reading, "Japanese drowning pools" and also "American drowning pools." I found those notations strange. The following day we were told these large holes in the reef were dug first by the Japanese to prevent an American invasion of the island. Soldiers would land by jumping from landing craft and, while walking to the shore, they would fall into these holes (pools) and drown. After the United States successfully invaded the island, they dug similar pools at different locations because the Japanese would have avoided the pools they dug, but would not know where the American pools were located. We were advised not to swim in those reef waters. War is Hell!

My inspection of the NOAA research vessel, which was a re-purposed tuna seiner, showed that there was no actual damage. The crew had noticed the ballast tank bulkheads flexing as the ship rolled during the storm. The ballast tanks aboard the ship had been overfilled, causing the bulkheads to flex as the vessel rolled in heavy seas. I proved to the crew that if they did not overfill the tanks by overflowing the vent pipes (which were more than 20 feet above the deck), the bulkheads would not flex and the vessel would be safe. There were also numerous pre-existing damages which were detailed in my report. Later, I traveled to Virginia to make a presentation to NOAA's engineers. I'll share more on that later.

**DAMAGED NOAA RESEARCH VESSEL**

While walking around the island, I noticed several, familiar-looking army-green containers with unusual side doors. Several months earlier, I had attended tests of a newly designed military container in Kansas City, which was going to be used as a portable hospital unit, the modern version of what we saw on the MASH TV show. MASH had tents for their hospitals during the Korean War, but the Army had graduated to using steel containers. The containers did not look like they were being used as a hospital when I saw them in Kwajalein, however, it turns out they were practicing the procedure needed to connect the containers properly to a working hospital. I was amazed to realize that these exact containers in Kwajalein were the ones I had approved just several months earlier.

One day, with nothing left to do, I rode the only bus that traveled from one end of the island to the other, to pass the time while waiting for my flight home. The entire round-trip bus ride took little more than 10 minutes, and I rode it for several trips. When I tried to talk with some of the bus passengers, they stood up and walked to the other end of the bus without speaking to me. I asked the native bus driver about this and he explained that most of the residents on the island were scientists working for various American military contractors, and they took their instructions seriously. Their work was top-secret, so silence was required. The big Marine-looking fella we met upon arrival came to mind!

THE 'MAIN STREET' ON KWAJALEIN

There were natives on the island working in construction, as well as women who appeared to be house cleaners and gardeners. Most of the women had children with them, and the children had sores on their legs, some bleeding. The natives arrived by boat early in the morning and had to leave the island by boat before sunset. I later learned that all of these natives were living on a neighboring island, part of the Kwajalein Atoll, and they seemed to be treated poorly by the military and civilian scientists on the island. The excuse was that the natives did not have security clearances.

The island where the natives lived was filled with concrete apartment buildings. They were said to have the highest alcoholism and suicide rates in the world at the time. This was in 1990. Thirty-five years earlier, the natives were living happily in grass huts, gathering coconuts, fishing, and just enjoying life. When I was there, I thought they were being treated like indentured servants. It was shocking to see this going on. I obtained most of this background information on my return flight, from a civilian nurse who was flying home after visiting his friends on the various islands. He had worked there with the natives for several years, and he never forgot the terrible conditions confronting them.

The United States has a 100-year lease on Kwajalein Atoll to conduct missile tests. Missiles are fired from a California Air Force Base, and they land in the shallow Kwajalein Lagoon, which they call the "world's biggest catcher's mitt." The scientists on Kwajalein are there to study the missile tests, including missile parts retrieved from the lagoon.

I thought it was interesting that people could get clearance to come to the island to scuba dive on the WWII wrecks in the lagoon of the atoll. In addition to American and Japanese fighter planes, there were several ships in the lagoon, including a German warship that had been used as a target during the Bikini Island, atomic bomb tests after WWII. The ship did not sink during the tests, and it was towed to Kwajalein for safekeeping because it was contaminated by radioactive debris.

This also brings up a terrible situation that was caused during the Bikini tests. The natives on Bikini, who stayed during the tests, were placed on a remote island in the Kwajalein Atoll because they all came down with radiation sickness. Who in the world decided to let them stay in Bikini during those tests?

The night before we left to return home, our inspection team planned to meet for dinner and a few drinks at the military Officers Club. We had eaten our other meals on board the NOAA ship, and it was time for a change. I arrived on time and ordered a drink at the bar. The bartender asked to see my ID card. After changing clothes at the "hotel," I left my ID card on the dresser. The bartender refused to serve me unless I returned to the hotel, retrieved my ID, and came back to "prove I was supposed to be there." By this time, everyone on the island knew who we were and why we were there, and this ID card was just a useless military requirement. But I still had to comply with the rules if I wanted to socialize.

The flight home was much less eventful, but I did have that interesting conversation with the civilian nurse mentioned above. At our stopover in Honolulu, not being sick, I attended a Hula Dance contest at the local shopping mall before heading to the airport for my flight home.

HULA CONTEST IN HONOLULU, BEFORE MY FLIGHT HOME

After returning home and producing my written report on what I found, I mentioned all of the pre-existing damages I had noted on the ship. This was an old, re-purposed tuna seiner, and those vessels are lightly constructed and have short life spans. NOAA noticed my comment about old damages in my report and asked me to travel to Maryland, just outside Washington, D.C., to discuss what I had found.

I am not a good public speaker; I get nervous under those conditions. I thought this would just be a small meeting in a conference room, but upon arrival at the NOAA offices, they told me my presentation would be in their Conference Center, and they had loaded my report and photographs onto a projection system. That got me worried! In their Conference Center, I was on a stage with an audience of maybe twenty-five NOAA Officers and civilian engineers. My voice was breaking from nervousness for the first few minutes, but they were extremely gracious and helped put me at ease.

The NOAA engineers were very interested in my comment about the over-pressuring of those ballast tanks, because the normal procedure for ballasting a cargo ship (which is typical), and apparently for a research vessel, is to fill the tanks until the water flows out of the vent pipes. However, tuna seiners have no ballast tanks, because the entire hull between the collision bulkhead and the engine room is considered to be fish tanks. There are either 6 or 8 on each side of a centerline refrigeration piping tunnel, depending on the vessel size. The ship leaves at the beginning of the voyage with those tanks filled with salt water, and as they catch fish, they start filling one tank at a time with fish, and then the ship's engineers start the refrigeration system to cool the water in that tank. As the fish are dumped into the tank, the water runs out the top, onto the deck, and drains over the side of the vessel. When more fish or a different variety of fish are caught, they start filling another tank, and so on, until the ship is full. Because of this, the ship generally maintains the same draft from the start of the voyage, full of water, until it returns at the end of the voyage, full of fish.

Because the ship owner (not NOAA) had turned these fish well tanks into ballast tanks, and the main deck was now full of laboratories and living quarters, the fish tanks (now ballast tanks) had vent pipes added. The vents were led up through the exhaust stack, more than 20 feet above the main deck, to then flow out onto the weather deck. This extra "head" of water created a serious pressure increase. Although the ship's crew and even the scientists on the ship did not understand this, the NOAA Engineers in Maryland understood, and they thanked me for my finding.

We also discussed my comment regarding pre-existing damages. I explained why the damages appeared old, pre-dating the NOAA charter of the vessel, and then asked them if they had performed an On-Charter Condition Survey to document these pre-existing conditions. They answered, "No, this owner would never try to cheat us. We are a U.S. Government Agency!" The owner was a very "Prestigious University," so I thought, maybe NOAA was correct!

About two years later, NOAA contacted ABSTech and asked if we could write an "after the fact" report about those pre-existing conditions, which we did. The "Prestigious University" had decided to sue NOAA to repair those damages at the end of the charter, just as I had predicted. I hope my report helped them, but we never heard the result of the lawsuit (which happens a lot in my business).

# CHAPTER 5

## QUICK TRIP TO ECUADOR

Following the Kwajalein trip, John Barr at ABSTech, now realizing that I was willing to travel, started calling me regularly. I once asked John if he ever called anyone else and he said, "Only if you are busy!" He went on to explain that everyone else seemed to have an excuse for not traveling, such as commitments for coaching their son's baseball team or that it was someone's birthday or their wedding anniversary. Although I did my best to be home for such family events, many were missed because of these jobs. However, when you start turning down assignments in this business, the clients stop calling.

The following true story may explain how my family dealt with my frequent travels.

I tried to attend Boy Scout meetings and camp-outs with my son, David, as often as possible. As my business began to grow, it became hard to make a lot of those meetings, as well as other family events, and I was feeling very guilty about it. At one of David's Scout meetings, he was talking to a friend, the son of a doctor. The friend commented that I had made it to this meeting and asked David why I was missing more meetings than in previous years. David answered, "My dad is sort of like your dad. When his pager goes off, he has to go to see his patients. But my dad's patients are ships."

Hearing this made me glad to know that David understood why many family events were missed, although I still feel guilty about the dance recitals, sporting events, Tae-Kwon-Do meets, and other events I missed. Comparing my ships to patients meant David knew how important some of my "patients' needs" might be. Certainly, a ship was not as important as a human patient, but there once was a comment from a ship owner early in my career, when I apologized about the "After Hours Fees" being charged by ABS, my employer at the time. He said, "This ship costs the owner $30,000 per day in fuel, crew cost, and lost revenue while sitting idle at the dock. Not waiting until tomorrow and paying your 'After Hours' Fees saves us a lot of money!"

**IGUANAS IN THE PARK**

You will find during my stories in this book that I was often asked to drop everything or even reshuffle my life schedule, to "attend to patients" all over the world. On one occasion, I left the table during Thanksgiving dinner and headed to a ship that had an engine crankcase explosion.

I certainly am not implying that I fixed or repaired the ships I worked on in my career. As the "Third Party" Marine Surveyor, I recommended repairs, oversaw the quality of repairs, reviewed and approved repair costs, and advised my clients on the conditions of the ships I inspected.

Anyway, John Barr called me soon after my Kwajalein trip and asked me how much I knew about aluminum hull corrosion. He said the ship would be on drydock one week from the time of the call, and I told him, "I can be an expert with that amount of time." The Society of Naval Architects and Marine Engineers was my source of such documentation, and I ordered every research paper available on aluminum hull corrosion, paying extra for fast, Fed-Ex delivery.

This job involved an aluminum passenger vessel that operated in the Galapagos Islands. They had found several types of unusual corrosion on the ship's hull, and seeing that they had built the aluminum vessel hoping to avoid such corrosion problems, they needed help to stop the corrosion.

My research was completed, and I felt well-prepared upon arrival. There was no agent of the ship, or owner, to meet me at the Guayaquil, Ecuador, airport, so I took a taxi to my hotel. The hotel was across the street from a beautiful park. With a couple of hours left before nightfall, a leisurely walk in the park seemed like a good way to chill out, after checking in to my hotel. During the walk through the park, little things hit me in the head and shoulders. It turns out that the trees were full of very large iguanas, and they were dropping nuts on me. *At least I hope they were nuts*! I'm not sure if it was accidental or on purpose, to get me out of their territory. At the end of the park, there was a beautiful white church. The church had a distinctive feature, which was very interesting. There was a fairly large tree growing out of the bell tower. Guayaquil, Ecuador, impressed me a lot!

Later that evening, I noticed that there was no bottled water in my room. I was hesitant to drink the tap water, so I called the front desk to ask for water. My minimal knowledge of Spanish at least included "agua," the word for water. However, the person on the phone did not understand the rest of my request and may have thought there was a plumbing issue. Finally, he got one of the hotel's restaurant staff on the phone who understood a little English, and he brought the bottled water to my room. We both had a little chuckle over my inability to communicate in Spanish. I vowed to learn Spanish and bought books and tapes to help me. However, my trips to Latin America were few and far between at that time, and I could never learn the languages of all the countries I began traveling to. High School Spanish would have been much better than the Latin we studied!

**TREE IN THE CHURCH STEEPLE**

Anyway, the vessel's owner, a very pleasant German gentleman, picked me up in the morning and we went to inspect the vessel at the local shipyard, where it was drydocked. One of the corrosion problems was easily diagnosed; caused by the blue chemical used in the stainless-steel sewage system. The chemical had spilled out of the stainless-steel tank onto the aluminum hull plating, and the chemical was reacting with aluminum.

There were lots of dissimilar metal conditions causing corrosion, as well as an electrical grounding problem which was blowing chunks of metal off of the propeller shaft log (cutlass bearing housing), near the propeller. Although the crew had thought the engine was isolated by rubber mounts, they had hard-piped a waterline between the hull and engine.

All of these problems were easily solved, and we were done with my inspection in just a few hours. Worth being well-prepared!

*You may wonder about the dissimilar metal corrosion conditions referenced in the above paragraph. This corrosion occurs when aluminum and steel or some other such combinations of dissimilar metals are physically connected, or both submerged in an electrolyte, such as salt water. If you think of a lead-acid car battery, having plates submerged in acid, it produces an electric current. Also think of the corrosion (the green/white powder) that occurs around the battery cable connection on your car battery, which is caused by connecting the metal cable clamp to the lead battery post. Many battery cables are also stranded copper, and the copper also corrodes. These same reactions can occur when steel and aluminum are submerged in salt water, or when a copper pipe is inadvertently connected to a steel pipe fitting.*

*It is too long of a discussion for this book, but sacrificial zinc (for steel hulls) or magnesium (for aluminum hulls) anodes are connected to the outer hull of most ocean vessels, and those sacrificial anodes are first depleted by these reactions, thus protecting the steel or aluminum hull plating. Further discussion of corrosion is included in a later chapter about fishing vessels.*

The ship's owner later offered to give me a tour of Guayaquil, and we spent the rest of the day touring and having a great lunch. Old men were walking back and forth on the streets with rifles and shotguns. I must have shown concern, because the ship's owner said, "Don't worry the guns are never loaded." Then he explained to me that this was how the local businesses ward off potential thieves and robbers who might intend to rob their stores. It was like paying protection to the Mafia. The old men were not part of the mob but the mobsters respected the old men, and would not rob a store being protected in this manner. Strange!

Next on the agenda, the ship's owner took me to a store to buy souvenirs for my family. We stopped at a very nice store with nicely made replicas of antique native artworks, which I still have to this day. In almost every store, they had large stocks of glue cans on the shelf. It soon became obvious what these glue cans were for. The children on the street had their hands out asking for money. They all held a brown paper bag in the other hand, which they would hold up under their nose and sniff. This was my first experience with glue-sniffing children, who all had a glassy-eyed, blank stare. My tour guide (the ship's owner) asked me not to give them money because it would all be used for glue.

The company name on those glue cans stuck in my memory. Several years later, I saw an exposé on television, with a reporter visiting that company in Minneapolis, Minnesota. The reporter was asking why they were selling glue in South America, which was only being used for sniffing. The company official stated that they were selling the glue for shoe repair and that the company was not aware of the glue sniffing problem. However, the reporter was well-prepared and stated that in the United States, similar glue was required to have an additive that caused nausea which prevented the glue from being sniffed. The company official said that would be too expensive for their South American clients, who could not afford the added cost. Again, the news reporter was well-prepared, she showed him that the cost of the additive was less than one-half cent per can. I don't know if the practice stopped, but glue-sniffing children were seen again in Peru on a subsequent trip.

# CHAPTER 6

## LONG-TERM PROJECTS: BEEN TO HELL TWICE!

Starting in 1998, there were two very unusual projects, which allowed me to travel the world and experience very short snippets of various cultures, sometimes repeatedly. Although this was physically challenging at times, making family plans difficult, these jobs were steady and paid the bills. Between the two jobs, it required over 60 days out of the country each year, plus another 20 or more days of travel. Later, I began a third contract which added 15 more ships, requiring about 35 more days overseas and another 25 travel days. These projects kept me very busy from 1998 through 2008.

The first project was an environmental audit inspection of a tanker fleet, which started with seven ships that eventually became five after two were sold (more on that in a later chapter). These ships had to be inspected twice annually, and for the first two years, I made all 14 inspections myself. ABSTech eventually hired a staff surveyor to assist me with some of these projects, cutting my travel time to about one-third of what I was doing before. This help allowed me to take on a third project, which otherwise could not have been properly covered. That amounted to 32 ship audits in a year, over 120 working days, plus travel, while also trying to keep my Great Lakes clients happy.

Here's a list of some of the great trips I took as a result of these tanker audits:

- Norway. This trip included a night in Hell (no kidding). I later returned to Hell, this time in the Grand Cayman Islands.
- Greece. Athens and Piraeus specifically.
- Spain. In the Cadiz area.
- One amazing around-the-world trip for four ships, which took me to Sicily, Singapore, Korea, and San Diego, before returning to Chicago.

- Another around-the-world trip from Norway to Spain, and then to Singapore and Okinawa.
- Guam, our loyal Pacific outpost. I went there on several trips, and it is one of my favorite places.
- Japan; Tokyo and Okinawa (several trips).
- Korea; Ulsan and Pohang, two different trips
- Many US ports such as Baltimore, Mobile, San Diego, Long Beach, San Francisco, Portland, Seattle (Anacortes), Honolulu, and Galveston.

'HELL' GRAND CAYMAN

After several years on this project, there were also return trips to some of these destinations. There was even a chance to ride on one of those tankers to Antarctica after the project ended. The tanker company offered to let me make the trip to Antarctica, but it was difficult to justify giving up five or six weeks of my life with no pay. One of the tankers went to Antarctica each year to refuel the American operations there. It would have been great to make the trip. If circumstances allowed it, the ship started in New Zealand and returned to New Zealand at the end of the six-week voyage. I had this crazy idea to see Antarctica after listening to a tape of a book written about Shackleton's one-year Antarctic survival story. In this story, his ship, the Endurance, was caught in the ice and finally sank during the 1890s. I recommend "Endurance: Shackleton's Incredible Voyage," as a great survival story if anyone wants to read it.

In the next chapter, I will describe a few exceptional stories about some of the trips listed above. Some of the destinations were frustrating, because they involved little more than airports and hotels, with most of my time spent working. Each trip required recovery from jet lag several times, with little time to do so. And there was usually very little heads up about the trips, which left no time to properly prepare. Ship schedules changed continually, causing delays in travel plans, which prompted changed itineraries while

'HELL' NORWAY, NEAR TRONDHEIM

overseas. There were many long waits at hotels, waiting for phone calls from the ship's agent, instead of being able to sightsee or enjoy myself. Traveling alone on most of these trips was boring, but, occasionally meeting one of the tanker owner's representatives, Jeremy White, was a pleasant diversion. He is a fine gentleman, originally from Great Britain, who enjoyed showing me the best restaurants in town, wherever we met. I looked forward to trips when Jeremy was going to be there.

When there were long waits during my trips overseas, (for example, when a ship was delayed or diverted), I was on my own for several hours, or sometimes even a day or two. The ship's agents were locals, so they were not interested in sightseeing. On those occasions, I enjoyed walking or touring on my own. Most cargo ship owners and their representatives did not want to act like a tourist, although they occasionally gave me recommendations for what I should do or see. And because I was working on their behalf, they dictated the amount of free time I had, as well as when my working hours would be. Being alone was sometimes a good thing because it gave me time to see those things that interested me, without worrying about the ship agents. It just didn't happen as often as I might have liked. But then I remembered: I was being paid well to see the world, with nearly no cost to me. Not a bad gig!

# CHAPTER 7

## AROUND THE WORLD IN 8 DAYS

### Catania, Sicily, and Then Delays!

During one unusual "tanker" auditing trip filled with delays, I was scheduled to do inspections of four ships, possibly five; one in Catania Sicily, one in Singapore, one in Okinawa, and one in Tokyo. If the schedule worked out, there was also another one to inspect in San Diego.

One of the frequent adventures on these trips was being assigned a local agent from the tanker company to meet me at the airport. They would arrange for my hotel and assist as needed to get me to and from the ship, and then back to the airport. This process could take as little as 30 hours from arrival to departure or up to 3 or 4 days if the ship was delayed or diverted. If the ship's arrival was delayed, I was on my own until I received a message from the agent. Sometimes the agent himself never appeared but would send a driver.

Sometimes, the drivers spoke little or no English. These trips usually were off to a challenging start. I would arrive at the airport to find a stranger holding a sign with my name, or the name of the ship, on it. Many times, the driver would also be picking up crew members for my ship or another ship, so we could have a van full of people, or I could be the only person. Most times there were no instructions for me, because of the language barrier.

The driver would typically drop me at my hotel, tell the hotel desk that the agent was paying my bills, and then leave me to wait for the agent to call the hotel.

To start this four, possibly five, inspections trip, I departed Chicago for Catania, via Milan, and arrived with no problems. In Catania Sicily, my driver spoke excellent English, because he'd spent about 15 years in Buffalo, New York until his wife became homesick, and they returned to Sicily. This was my first experience with the famous Italian drivers we see in the movies, and it was all true. My driver was somewhat under control, probably due to his 15 years in the United States, and also because he was probably paid by the hour. The drivers on the open highway never slowed their speed and cut in front of the cars they passed with only a few feet to spare. Even at high speeds, they kept little more than two car lengths between cars.

But the white-knuckle part of this Sicilian/Italian traffic experience was the narrow, one-way streets of the inner city. Most of the streets in Catania were probably built 500 years ago, with no idea of what future auto traffic would become. There was usually room for one car and maybe a narrow sidewalk, with no room for parking, yet the streets were full of parked cars pulled up on the sidewalks. Despite the close quarters, drivers sped through the streets at 30 to 35 mph, blowing their horns constantly as people stuck their heads dangerously out of the building doorways or tried to enter parked cars. Turning corners was a two or three-step Y-turn process, so you can imagine how tight the quarters were. The only other place where I've seen such streets is in San Juan, Puerto Rico, but there they don't speed like they do in Catania. Puerto Ricans love big 4 x 4 jeep-type vehicles and they drive in their streets with only two or 3 inches on each side, requiring 5 to 6 step Y- turns to turn a corner. At least they do so at 5 mph. But in Catania, a 12-inch clearance seemed to be a license to speed even if it was only at 25 to 30 mph. Policemen seemed not to be upset by the high speeds and they also ignored the parked cars which obstructed the speeding cars, even though there were "No Parking" signs posted.

The trip from the airport to the hotel was quite exciting, and luckily not to be duplicated again on this trip. However, dodging speeding cars as a pedestrian was normal the entire time I was in Catania. The agent's driver informed me that the ship was a day late so there would be a free day to rest and see the town. He then requested my airline tickets so the agent could get them changed. Airline tickets are a difficult part of these trips, which my travel agent had slowly become accustomed to handling. She was told *not* to look for non-changeable, non-refundable bargain fares, because they would probably be changed, possibly two or three times on a long trip like this one. Just book a skeleton itinerary and then I'm usually the guy on the airplane with the most expensive fare. Sometimes sitting next to people with a $200 ticket, mine could be as much as $1700, due to a last-minute change.

When the driver, Sal, pulled up to the hotel, I asked him where I could find a sports store to purchase a soccer jersey, for my son, David, who is a big fan of the INTER Soccer team from Milan. Sal said I'd be lucky to find an INTER jersey in all of Sicily because they hated that team. Even so, he pointed me to a couple of sportswear stores on the main street.

The hotel where Sal was dropping me off was a beautiful sight. It was a huge building right out of a 1940s movie. It had large pillars and a beautiful fountain in a plaza out front, shaded by large trees. Sal took me inside, assured the hotel that all charges were to be paid by the ship's agent, and told me to expect a call from the agent the next day, giving me plans for the ship's arrival.

Those types of instructions are terrible because one cannot plan long excursions. The agent could call to tell me the ship was diverted and I was flying elsewhere to meet it. Because of that, my only option was a short two to three-hour walk around town to see the sights. I would then return to the hotel for meals and check for messages. It's better now that Americans have good cell phone service in Europe, but my cell phone was useless on that trip. As a result, there were no trips to Mount Etna or other local sites because they could take 6 to 8 hours. I share this just in case you thought my trips were all fun and games and were envying my escapades. I usually sat there while watching others doing what I wanted to do. There was seldom an opportunity to be a tourist, other than those short walks.

Anyway, on that first walk the afternoon I arrived, I ended up down the main street of Catania. I soon realized that the Italians were unhelpful to tourists, at least in Catania. When I asked for directions, they would point at a rack of maps and brochures on the lobby wall. But I could hardly find north or south on those tourist maps, much less the streets. Each building had street names on them, but most of the streets ran just one or two blocks, sometimes only a few hundred feet. The next street was at a 10° angle to the first, and then the street name changed. Only a few of the major streets ran continuously.

Eventually, I found the ocean, but I soon learned about the Italian siesta time. Whatever it is called in Italian (I assume still siesta), they take it very seriously. Stores close at 2 PM and don't reopen until 4 or even 5 PM, and then stay open until 8 PM, or even 10 PM. I found out about the siesta when I returned to a sports store on my way back to the hotel from the ocean but it was closed.

Restaurants, too, keep a very tight schedule, one opposite that of the stores. If you're hungry at 4 PM in Catania, you will starve. Restaurants close between 4 and 8 PM and stay open until after midnight. All of this is very upsetting to a hungry American suffering from jet lag, who is used to eating dinner at 6 PM. With my stomach growling, I decided to go on another walk to the sports store I had spotted earlier, to ask about that INTER jersey for David. Fortunately, after a lot of sign language and the help of a customer who spoke a little bit of English, we were able to find an INTER jersey, but there was only one left and not the right size. I bought it anyway, even if David could only hang it on his wall as a souvenir, which he did (I later found a larger size on a subsequent trip to Genoa).

After I left the store, I took in the scenery and took photos of areas I missed on my earlier walk. I was mostly looking for interesting pictures to take for my "calendar shots." (Every year, my Aunt and I printed souvenir calendars for family and friends). The age of everything in Catania amazed me. In the United States, we think anything over 50, is old and over 100 years is an antique. The typical ages of the buildings in Catania, according to the dates on the buildings, were 150 to 200 years. Historic buildings were 300 to 500 years old.

I walked back to the ocean. There was a park that had the remains of an old Spanish Fort built in 1300 and was now covered in lava from a previous eruption of Mount Etna. Compared to things seen on later trips to Greece, Croatia, and Cadiz, Spain, even 700 years old is modern, but this old fort was still impressive.

On the return trip to the hotel, I discovered a beautiful, ornate building across the street, which had a polished bronze statue on each side of the main entrance. I stood in front of the entrance and began taking photographs. Not very long after I took my first few shots, I felt something

**LAVA COVERED SPANISH FORT IN CATANIA**

poking me in my back. I turned around to see what it was, only to find a machine gun in my ribs, held by a very upset soldier or policeman. He started screaming at me in Italian. I must have looked very dumbfounded, because he called over another man, presumably his sergeant, or superior officer, and the screaming continued. Maybe they were asking for my ID, but I was just babbling in English, so finally, they just pointed for me to leave. As I left, I heard one of them say, "Stupido Americano," or something that sounded like that. At that point, who would disagree with them? Certainly not me! What would they have thought if they inspected the contents of my bag? Finding the INTER jersey, they might have arrested me for that! I can joke about it now, but trust me, this was not a funny event at the time!

I returned to the hotel with a couple of small pastries I was able to buy at a coffee shop. Coffee shops are very popular and they remain open on store schedules, not on restaurant schedules. This should have tided me over until the hotel restaurant opened for dinner, but I hadn't yet experienced a typical Italian dinner.

At the hotel, I told the desk clerk about my experience with the armed men and he slapped his forehead in disbelief! Apparently, I had taken photos of the entrance to the Courthouse where one of the judges had recently been murdered on those steps during the trial of a local Mafia boss. The soldiers probably thought that someone was taking photos for another "hit". Luckily, my English made me look stupid; it could have resulted in a lot of trouble or worse!

I arrived at the hotel restaurant door at 7:45 that evening and waited until it opened at 8 o'clock. There was activity inside, but the lights were not turned on until 8 o'clock sharp. My stomach was growling persistently the entire time. Stomachs get into the habit of being filled at the times we train them to expect it, so I was not surprised to be that hungry at that time. The manager of the restaurant seemed to be though.

I walked into the restaurant the moment the doors were opened and asked for dinner. The manager looked at me like I was an idiot for wanting to eat dinner that early. He sat me at a table to wait while the waiters arranged all of the tables, silverware, and dishes and finally decided to look at me. That was 15 minutes! As was starting to be the standard in Catania, none of the waiters spoke a word of English and the menu was in Italian. Luckily the food names of most Italian foods are what we call them in the United States, so ordering was not too terrible, but it was obvious that some mistakes had been made with the food combinations or other Italian etiquette because the waiters seemed upset by my order.

The waiters, who looked like they had walked off the set of the "Godfather," if you remember the Italian waiters in the New York restaurants as they were depicted in that movie, wore what looked like a starched white tablecloth as an apron, nearly reaching the floor. The Headwaiter wore a black formal jacket and the table waiters wore white waistcoats above those long aprons. My first thought was that I was underdressed, but once other patrons finally arrived at about 9 PM, it was apparent that my attire was just fine. The waiters just happened to take their job seriously and dressed the part.

I found out later that the waiters were indeed upset about my order because I had not ordered any pasta. Americans think of pasta as a full meal, but to Italians, it is only one course of the meal, and apparently, it cannot be skipped in Italy. Watching the waiters serve my meal, and eventually those of the other patrons, it became obvious that these employees treated their duties very seriously. Even though they were upset by my lack of ordering and eating etiquette, they seemed to be treating me to a real show of waiter skills, to make a good impression. Each course was served to my table by a rolling cart with food loaded from a larger, central table, which had all of the cold foods laid out beforehand (as witnessed during my 7:45 arrival).

My order, which arrived on a rolling table, included an appetizer and prosciutto which I was already familiar with, except that it was served with a variety of garnishes and sauces which I probably used incorrectly during my meal. The waiter proceeded to take each slice of prosciutto from a larger plate on the table and use two spoons in one hand to arrange the slices on another plate by folding each slice into neatly bundled rolls. He then deftly used the pair of spoons to grab individual olives, tomatoes, and parsley, and finally, he cut lime into a decorative garnish. The plate was arranged like a work of art in a matter of two minutes. When he placed it in front of me, he pointed to his stock of sauces. I was confused. Why were they needed with prosciutto? We eat that by itself or in a sandwich back home! Seeing the look of confusion on my face, he disgustedly spooned several sauces onto the edge of my plate and left. He soon returned with the plate of Italian bread and I devoured my prosciutto. None of the sauces seemed to be something to be used with prosciutto, so I left them untouched, something I'm sure upset the restaurant staff greatly.

Next came the pasta! The waiter seemed to be saying, "You forgot to order pasta, but you are getting some anyway," even though I did not understand. The head waiter was animatedly telling my waiter something before he served me the pasta, probably that he must explain the necessity of ordering pasta to this unsophisticated American. And, it was bowtie pasta, which you wouldn't think of getting as pasta in Sicily, but as it turns out, it is not just an American novelty but came from Italy.

The pasta was simple and very al dente. The sauce was also simple and very tasty. Parmesan cheese was grated with a tool I'd never seen before. After being served, I then proceeded to eat every bowtie pasta – which turned out to be a mistake from watching the other patrons in the restaurant. Over the next two evenings (the ship was further delayed), I watched the other patrons eat, and not one person, other than me, ate more than half of their pasta. The Italians seemed to leave a lot of food on their plates, so my clean plates did not impress the wait staff. But it tasted too good to leave unfinished!

The main course was veal in a heavenly cream sauce. I remember being surprised because I did not know the Italian word for veal and did not know that that was what I had ordered. That mistake probably impressed the staff!

It would have been nice to tell the waiters how much I appreciated the education they had provided, as well as how much I enjoyed the meal, but I'm sure it would not have changed their opinion of me in the least. It was one of the best "shows" of artistry I have ever witnessed in a restaurant!

The ship finally arrived and my Environmental audit went as planned. The agent gave me my new airline tickets, to my next stop in Singapore, where I had hoped to meet Jeremy, the Englishman who worked for the tanker company. Because of the delay in Catania, the Englishman had to leave Singapore, so I was going to be alone there as well. My last trip to Singapore had been with Jeremy, and he knew where to find all the good food (drunken shrimp in Singapore was unusual and great!), but he was not interested in sightseeing, so this was going to be my opportunity to see the sights.

I soon found out that Singapore would have to wait because my trip was once again changed to a Catania-Rome-Frankfurt-Singapore itinerary. The original schedule was for me to meet the second ship in Singapore, then the third ship in Okinawa, then Tokyo for a fourth ship, with possibly another in San Diego, and finally home to Chicago. I was familiar with these long trips, with several bouts of jet lag, and I was not looking forward to that aspect of this trip, but the delay in Catania had changed the itinerary and another delay was "in the cards" for me on this trip.

The new flight schedule was with Alitalia from Catania to Rome, then another Alitalia flight to Frankfurt, where I was looking forward to my first flight on Singapore Airlines. Singapore Airlines was reported to have the best service in the air at that time. To make things even better, they had booked me in Business Class for the rest of this "Around the World" trip. The ship's agent must have felt sorry for me, or maybe Coach was just sold out!

When I arrived in Rome, I went directly to my gate to check the status of the Frankfurt flight, which is always a smart thing to do. The flight said "DELAYED" but the plane was at our gate, so everyone at the gate was puzzled. Nearly three hours later, we boarded the plane, with no explanation. However, my boarding pass for the Frankfurt to Singapore flight had been changed to Lufthansa. I had missed my chance to experience Singapore Airlines! During the flight from Frankfurt to Singapore, I sat next to two young gentlemen from Singapore and explained to them that due to the delay in Rome, I had missed the Singapore Airlines flight. I asked them if I had missed out on something good, and the two men first looked at each other, then looked back at me, and both nodded their heads and exclaimed, "YES!"

When the two men asked if I realized why the flight from Rome had been delayed, I told them we received no explanation. Because they had not been on that Rome to Frankfurt flight, I wondered how they would know anything about it. History, or the "making of history" can affect your life in unexpected ways. As it turned out, that night was the first bombing in Kosovo and Serbia by American planes, and many of the planes involved came from American air bases in Italy, with additional military planes flying over Italy from bases elsewhere in Europe. To avoid any danger to civilian aircraft, with all of that extra military air traffic, they decided to hold all domestic flights for a couple of hours, and my Rome to Frankfurt flight fell within that window of time.

## **<u>Singapore was Great, and Then Great Again!</u>**

When I finally arrived in Singapore, my British friend had already departed and headed to the next ship in Okinawa. However, he had left instructions for me at the hotel so I knew to pick up where he left off on the inspection.

I took a taxi to the hotel. I was given an envelope with instructions at the front desk. Their company's local agent would call me in the morning to arrange transportation to the ship. This was my second bout of jet lag on this trip, so after a quick dinner, I was off to bed.

The next morning, the ship's agent called and told me to meet him at the hotel entrance before lunch. He arrived by car, and we traveled to the local ferry terminal where we ate lunch. We then took a launch to the ship which was anchored in the harbor.

The food in Singapore is very good but other than some ethnic dishes from China and India, there was nothing very unusual. However, I have vivid memories from my first trip to Singapore when Jeremy introduced me to "drunken shrimp." Drunken shrimp are shrimps that have been marinated, while alive, in an alcohol bath and then cooked. The shrimp ingest alcohol which enhances their flavor.

Our lunch at the ferry terminal was not quite as exotic, but every meal in Singapore was very tasty. The agent hired a launch (water taxi) for a 30-minute ride to the ship. The sights of the harbor alone were worth the trip. Singapore Harbor is huge and very busy. Ships were anchored or moored everywhere! We finally got to our tanker where I recognized both the Captain and the Chief Engineer from previous environmental audits. Most of my time on these audits was spent reviewing records, testing some equipment, and interviewing the crew.

SINGAPORE FERRY TERMINAL

The following paragraphs will give you a brief overview of what ship crewmembers around the world have to deal with daily. You can skip this if you are not interested, but non-maritime people rarely understand how much responsibility sailors have:

THE OIL TANKER INSPECTED IN SINGAPORE

## <u>A Brief Discussion of MARPOL Regulations</u>

*The cargo records of oil operations must be kept separately from the engineroom oil records. This company had originally gotten in trouble because of an incident where the engineroom slop oil tanks were full, and the Captain had refused to allow the Chief Engineer to put his slop oil in the cargo slop oil tank, stating that this was not allowed by MARPOL Regulations. The Chief then discharged oil into the ocean, which is even more illegal. He lost his license for this and the company was issued a huge fine. In addition, they needed to be audited for three years by a Third Party Inspector, which was my job.*

*I eventually explained to each crew, that in an emergency such as the one this crew experienced, the engineroom slop oil could have been pumped into one of the two cargo slop tanks. That cargo slop tank would then need to be isolated for the rest of that voyage, so none of that oil could be discharged until the ship reached port. Log Book entries would also need to be made in both the Engineroom Oil Record Book and the Cargo Oil Record Book, with details of these actions, and why they had to be done.*

*When the vessel reached its next port, the cargo oil slop tank would then be pumped ashore and that tank would require a full cleaning to remove all engineroom oil residues.*

*The reason for all of this is that the Cargo Oil Regulations and the Engineroom Bilge Oil Regulations are totally different. The cargo slop tanks can be pumped overboard after the water settles out from the oil, and that discharge is monitored by a 100 PPM (parts per million) device, which stops the discharge if the 100 PPM is exceeded. The engineroom bilge water is collected and runs through a much more complex "Oily Water Separator" (OWS), which is then discharged through a 15 PPM monitor.*

*The cargo slop oil comes from washing the cargo tanks, whereas the engineroom slop oil comes from machinery water leakage into the engineroom bilges. So, the source of the two oil wastes is very different, and two different International Treaties were agreed upon to deal with those oil sources.*

in my opinion, there should be a less complicated set of regulations for these sailors to follow. Numerous sailors have ended up in trouble, some with prison terms, for violating MARPOL. Yes, some were willful, and those crewmen should be punished. But many, if not most pollution incidents were just plain mistakes or poor record keeping. All records must be kept in English or French (to show how political it all was), yet most of the world does not consider either of those languages their first language.

*MARPOL is the International Marine Pollution Agreement, signed by all of the maritime countries in the world. It is part of OPA-90 and is complicated because each country tried to include its own agenda.*

With all the regulations covering oil pollution, if a tanker is carrying certain chemical cargo, those cleaning residues can be legally discharged directly into the ocean without being separated, if they are non-toxic. We heap a lot of responsibility onto these sailors, so don't always think the worst when you hear about a shipboard pollution incident.

*In addition to oily waste, the ships are regulated for garbage as well. Food waste can be discharged overboard if ground up into small pieces. Paper and wood can be discharged also, but almost every ship in the world now has an incinerator, so most ships now burn all wood, paper, and non-recyclable plastic. Some ships also burn their large food wastes (bones, lobster shells, etc.). Glass, aluminum, and tin cans are saved and recycled ashore. The other big headache is sewage, but the newer ships all have sewage systems that can treat all wastewater on board to a drinkable state (not by me, however!) and the solid residue is then incinerated.*

In this particular tanker's case, the captain on the offending vessel was probably trying to avoid the delay and cleaning cost of his Cargo Slop tank, if he even thought of that (some captains refuse to agree with anything the engineers ask). However, the cost of that cleaning, maybe $10-20,000, was nothing compared to the multi-million dollar fine paid by the company. The ships' crews live in fear of company managers criticizing expenses but, on the other hand, they need to fear the possibility of losing their license, or even going to prison! Sailors have a tough job!

So, back to my Around the World Trip!

The tanker survey in Singapore was now finished, but having already missed the ship in Okinawa, because of my delays in Catania, my next ship was scheduled to be in Tokyo. I love Okinawa, but not wild about Tokyo. At least this time, the trip would be on Singapore Airlines. Finally!

The agent picked me up the next morning and dropped me off at the airport. I had hoped to play tourist for a day in Singapore, but again, the ships' schedules determined my plans, not my "tourist desires."

The flight from Singapore to Tokyo was approximately seven hours long. About three hours into the flight, the Captain came on the loudspeaker and told us a warning light had come on his instrument panel. He assured us that it was nothing mechanical since the alarm was defective. He asked us not to be alarmed. However, the airline regulations told him that because we were at the halfway point of the flight, he had to return to Singapore. He also stated that Singapore Airlines was already working on new flights for us.

The ship in Tokyo was scheduled for less than a 24-hour stop there, so it was assumed I would miss the ship again. I had been at the Yokosuka ship terminal in Tokyo once before and was now secretly happy to be missing it on this trip. My favorite thing about Tokyo was the great sushi at Narita Airport on my trip home. It would be too bad to miss that, but I would not miss not Yokosuka.

When we arrived in Singapore, I called the ship's agent and explained the situation to him. He instructed me to return to the same hotel while he worked with the airline to redirect my flight, which now appeared to be in Korea. I had already visited Korea on one of my previous tanker audits while working with Jeremy, the British tanker company rep, and it was very impressive. I was happy to be returning to Korea!

At my hotel, there was a message from the agent saying that he had arranged my flight to Korea for the next day. He apologized for the flight being an evening flight which would arrive in Seoul the following morning.

The agent asked me if I was okay taking care of myself the following day. I was secretly thrilled and told him it would be just fine. He said he would pick me up at the hotel the following afternoon to take me to the airport.

SINGAPORE'S HINDU TEMPLE

I made the most of my free day in Singapore by visiting the Hindu Temple and walking through all of the famous sights found nearby.

## Then On to Korea!

The next day, the agent picked me up and dropped me off at the airport again. This time the flight to Seoul, Korea went as planned. And yes! Singapore Airlines was great! I was meeting the ship in Ulsan, which required a domestic flight after arrival in Seoul. Our final descent into Seoul was a bit eerie. The Captain told us the DMZ (demilitarized zone) between North & South Korea was just out our left-side windows.

In Seoul, I changed planes and arrived in Ulsan, where the company agent met me. He said the ship was delayed again and there would be a two-day wait in Ulsan. I was happy to be left alone and, again, decided to play tourist. My hotel had several good English-speaking staff, and they gave me some ideas for sightseeing.

Because of the tiring nighttime flight, I decided to stay close to the hotel by walking the neighborhood and eating at the numerous food stands on the streets for lunch. I am a brave eater and have seldom turned down any food offered to me, but I was cautioned to avoid any white items in a red sauce if those were seen on the street vendors' carts. Apparently, these were raw grub worms, something the Koreans consider a delicacy. I did not see any of those but saw one suspicious item that I tried. It turned out they were grilled, flattened chicken hearts on a stick. The chicken hearts and all of the other food from those vendors were excellent.

After a nap that afternoon (just from flying; no jet lag flying North-South), the hotel recommended a good neighborhood restaurant for dinner. I walked into the restaurant alone and immediately saw the "look of fear" on the poor lady's face. She spoke no English. I smiled and gestured with my fingers (holding several to my mouth) in sign language and she smiled in return. Most Asian menus have pictures of the food, and occasionally some English, but this menu was entirely in Korean. Luckily the pictures were very descriptive, and by pointing to pictures and signing, the food began to arrive. After trying three or four dishes, I put up both hands, which in sign language meant I had enough and they could stop. The bill was very reasonable. She bowed and smiled, so we were both happy. No need to communicate using words, as long as both people are friendly and work together to understand one another.

The next day, the hotel arranged a bus tour, which had an English-speaking tour guide. We drove out to a beautiful Temple, far outside of Ulsan.

**KOREAN TEMPLE OUTSIDE ULSAN**

**LADIES RENTING KOREAN DRESSES FOR PHOTOS OUTSIDE THE TEMPLE GROUNDS**

**BEAUTIFUL POND AT THE TEMPLE**

That evening, the company agent joined me for dinner at a Korean barbecue restaurant. This style of Korean cooking was a new experience for me. Meat is cooked on a small charcoal grill at your table. I have since seen several such restaurants located in the Chicago area. I go there whenever possible. Needless to say, the agent was surprised by my familiarity with kimchi, and even more, surprised because I liked it. I explained to him that I had spent years in Chicago, surveying Korean crewed ships and trying and liking the kimchi on those ships. He was impressed with my love for different foods. The Captain on one of those ships sent me home with a pint jar of kimchi, and my wife and children also developed a liking for it.

The next day, we met the ship at Ulsan harbor and the survey was completed without problems. Later the same day, I was able to get a flight to San Diego, where the fourth ship on this journey was scheduled to arrive. Nothing exciting happened on this last leg of the journey, and I finally made it back to Chicago after an 8-day around-the-world journey. Other than suffering from the third case of jet lag in eight days, that is!

## Trondheim, Norway

Later that year, another around-the-world trip for the tanker audits later that year took me first to Trondheim, Norway, then from there, I flew to Cadiz, Spain, for another ship in Rota, Spain, and then finally to Okinawa, Japan.

HELL IS THE CITY FOR THE TRONDHEIM AIRPORT

As with many of these trips, little more was seen of Norway than the airport, my hotel, a quick drive to the ship, back to my hotel, and flying out again the next morning. Particularly due to my jet lag, I found it difficult to enjoy the short time I had in Trondheim, although this picture of the sign for the town where I landed has gotten a lot of comments. The airport at Trondheim is located in Hell, Norway. Hell means "flat land" which is a good place for an airport, with all the mountains in Norway!

Until just recently, my short stop in Norway was my only trip there. I ate a quick dinner, slept the first night, and then the company's agent picked me up after an even quicker breakfast. The tanker was moored in an old, WWII Submarine Base located inside a mountain. Yes, you read that right, 'inside a mountain'. The base stored fuel for NATO, but I had learned not to ask too many questions, by this time, about the bases I visited on these trips.

After about a two-hour drive from Trondheim, we pulled up at a huge steel door on the side of the mountain. There was no water or ship in sight! The agent made a phone call and the door started to open. Very eerie! We drove through a tunnel, which had been hewn through the rock, and entered a large bay inside the fjord. There was my tanker! The audit was the same as described in the above scenarios. Nothing exciting!

The only unusual thing in Norway was the fantastic cell phone service out in the middle of the forest. Although there were no cell towers visible and seldom a building in sight, my agent's phone worked perfectly. Apparently, he was planning my next leg of this journey throughout our time in the mountains, so he was on the phone a lot. I asked the agent about the good cell phone service in Norway and compared it to the United States, where we had limited or no service at all in rural areas at that time. The agent explained to me that the European cell phone system (at least at that time) was very different from that of the United States and that they had small towers or repeaters located along the roadways, rather than the huge towers we used in the United States. I'm not an electronics expert, but based on what I saw, their system was far superior to ours at that time. Based upon a recent history of dropped calls, our U.S. service does not seem to have improved much outside of largely populated areas!

After that audit, we returned to the hotel where I ate a quick dinner and was off to bed. My next flight was an early one to Spain the next morning.

## <u>Cadiz, Spain</u>

This time, the itinerary was from Trondheim to Oslo, then to Madrid, and finally to Cadiz, Spain, which was near my destination of Rota, Spain. This was another NATO Base, they told me. I arrived in Cadiz in the late afternoon but took the opportunity to do a quick walking tour. There was a lot of Roman history in Cadiz, and they were starting to unearth a Roman Theater at that time. It sure seems funny that I saw a Roman Theater in Cadiz, Spain, and a Spanish Fort in Catania, Sicily.

There seemed to be very few English speakers in Cadiz, but everyone acted friendly, even when they learned I could not speak Spanish.

**CADIZ CITY WATERFRONT**

ROMAN THEATER RUINS IN CADIZ

Being an active NATO Base, this base at Rota was much more secure than the others on my trip. My visit had been pre-approved for entry, but it was a little more formal than usual; checking documents and identification. The audit was uneventful, and I was soon back at my hotel in Cadiz for one more evening.

GOOD PORT & SHERRY IN CADIZ

I must be honest; as of this writing, I have no recollection of how I flew from Cadiz to Okinawa. Some of these lengthy trips started running together. This explains why I have skipped details of what had to have been a long flight.

I do remember stopping in Taiwan and changing planes for Naha, and Okinawa, so I assume we may also have stopped in Singapore. This was my second trip to Okinawa, and I had been looking forward to getting back. Despite my dislike for Tokyo, Okinawa was pleasant on my first visit.

## Naha, Okinawa, Japan

Since my first trip to Okinawa, the US Navy had closed its base on the island due to a sexual abuse scandal. The agent in Naha told me that the Japanese Government did not realize how much the Americans' departure would hurt the local economy. This same thing occurred in Panama when the U.S. Army and Marines left their bases around the Panama Canal. Many of the stores and restaurants near the base in Naha, Okinawa, were now closed, just like the restaurants in Panama City. On my previous trip to Okinawa, I had purchased pearls at a store just outside the base at Naha and was going to buy more, but that store was now gone too. Good quality pearls were surprisingly inexpensive in Okinawa. They appraised well at home, so I had hoped to buy more on this second trip. No such luck.

The agent in Naha spoke openly about how the residents in Naha did not appreciate the U.S. Military because of ongoing sexual assaults. I remembered hearing about this on the news back home. It seems the Okinawa residents were much different from those on the main island of Honshu, where Tokyo is located. He said many of the Honshu residents were no longer "pure-blooded" Japanese because many had intermarried with the Chinese and Koreans. In his mind, the Okinawans were "more Japanese" than those on the other islands. It seemed to be a little more than the pride of being Okinawan, and it appeared he disliked the mainland Japanese, particularly in Tokyo.

Japanese breakfasts were very enjoyable, particularly in Okinawa. They always served miso soup, rice, a raw egg, a piece of cooked fish, and seaweed salad. I always mixed my raw egg into my hot miso soup, along with half of my rice. The restaurant staff did not seem to think highly of me mixing them, but I didn't want to eat the raw egg. Miso soup alone at other meals is great, but this method made better use of that raw egg. Sushi and sashimi in Japan are wonderful, and the cooked fish at breakfast is a good sign that the sashimi in the evening will be fresh. Leftover fish from one day was cooked and eaten for breakfast the following morning.

There was always an "American Breakfast" on the menu, but being unable to ask what it included, I decided to just be brave one day and try it. The Japanese must figure Americans eat the same combination of items the Japanese eat for breakfast, so here is what you get:

- Cream of Mushroom soup; instead of miso
- Mashed potatoes or French fries, instead of rice
- Two eggs, cooked hard as leather
- Still had a piece of cooked fish (thank God!)
- Lettuce salad with Thousand Island dressing (I prefer the seaweed!)

I tried it twice at two different hotels (hence the mashed vs. French fried potatoes) but after those two experiences, the Japanese breakfasts were the best choice. I loved them.

Again, the tanker was anchored offshore, so we went out to the ship on a small tug and boarded using the gangway (no Pilot's Ladder, I was happy to see). Things went well and I headed home to Chicago via Haneda and Narita airports in Tokyo.

On the way from Naha to Tokyo, there was an announcement in Japanese and all of the passengers crowded to the left side and looked out the windows. I was sitting on the right side of the plane. The stewardess may have seen the look of concern on my face (was the left wing on fire?), so she came to my seat and bowed, saying, "We fly over Mount Fuji!" I had not realized the Japanese love for Mount Fuji, which must be similar to Americans passing the Statue of Liberty.

## My First Trip to Okinawa

While on the subject of Okinawa, I should relate a quick story about my first trip to Okinawa, which was from Chicago to Tokyo, then on to Naha, Okinawa. Because this was my first trip to Okinawa (only flown to Tokyo before), neither I nor my travel agent realized that Tokyo had an international airport, Narita, and a different domestic airport, Haneda. The two airports are about 50 miles apart, which is a good 90-minute drive using the shuttle bus. During my flight from Chicago to Narita, one of the flight attendants came to my seat to confirm that my destination was Okinawa. She politely explained that there were only 2-1/2 hours between my flights. This meant that clearing customs, getting on the shuttle bus, traveling to Haneda, clearing Haneda security, and trying to make my flight would be difficult. She said she would come and get me before arrival and explain what I could do instead. Of course, I was worried during the rest of the flight.

About ten minutes before arrival, the flight attendant came back and told me to take my carry-on luggage and follow her. She reseated me in First Class for the remainder of the flight. When the plane door opened at Narita, another young woman met me at the plane door and we boarded an electric cart and drove to Immigration and then on to baggage claim. My bags had somehow been prioritized and were waiting for me. She easily cleared me through customs, took me to a window to buy a shuttle bus ticket, and walked me outside to the shuttle bus. The bus must have been held for me because it left as soon as I boarded. I thanked her profusely!

When we arrived at Haneda, another young lady met me at the bus and walked me through security and then to my flight, with nearly fifteen minutes to spare. Each of those young Japanese women was so polite and helpful. Each of them continually bowed to me each time they asked a question. I understand that bowing is just part of their culture, but service people in Japan show much more respect than in other places in the world, particularly to older people. Even the airline ground crews in Japan line up as the airplane leaves the gate. They all look at the Captain first and bow, then they turn toward the cabin and bow to the passengers. I do not like the general Tokyo "atmosphere" which seems cold, but this airport experience was fantastic!

I had previously been to the large Naval base in Tokyo, Yokosuka, to visit one of these tankers. It was not a great experience. Maybe, it had something to do with all the American Navy personnel in the area, but people were not as warm as those I experienced at the airport, and certainly not like Okinawa. Japanese food is fantastic, but when the ship's crew made a dinner recommendation near Yokosuka, they referred me to a street full of Chinese restaurants near the shipyard. I'm not sure why they suggested those restaurants, but I assume they had encountered some anti-American sentiment in Japanese establishments and wanted me to avoid them. The Chinese meal was still delicious.

Later, for dinner, the ship's agent in Okinawa recommended a good restaurant for me to try. The directions took me just outside the Navy Base. The dinner menu was great that evening, but it was still not a traditional Japanese menu. The agent had sent me to a place much like the Beni-Hana restaurants here in the United States. The food was good but I was disappointed in the lack of traditional Japanese options. I vowed then to be more specific about which types of restaurants I preferred to eat at.

# CHAPTER 8

## SUE AND BOB'S EUROPEAN ADVENTURE

I wrote the following narrative to my family while returning home from a lengthy trip to Europe in 2003. I will leave the narrative as written, in "present tense," so you can understand my feelings at the time. The chapter is divided into a *Business Trip Section*, and the *European Adventure Section*, but both happened during the same trip. I will comment at the end about how my perspective may have changed. My references to Susan (Susan Hoertt) will eventually become clear, but to save confusion, Susan became our lead auditor on the Cruise Ship Environmental Compliance Plan Audit program, which will be discussed further in a subsequent Chapter on Cruise Ships. The following is my letter to my family:

I'm sitting in Row 45 of a 46-Row Airbus on my way home, after my 15-day trip in Europe. At least I have an aisle seat and an empty seat next to me, so I have some room to work.

I've always heard that coming home from a vacation, and wishing you could stay away longer, are signs that the vacation was too short. Well, I was ready to head home two days ago, so this must have been a great vacation. Reaching the saturation point near the end must be a good sign.

### Business Trip

The first half of the trip was business, including two cruise ship environmental audits. Although the work on the ships was business, I have worked with these people for six years now, so they are friends, which makes the "job" enjoyable until we have a problem. Luckily, on these two ships, we found nothing to spoil the pleasant conversations and nice dinners we had on board.

The first cruise was from Civitavecchia, Italy, (the Port for Rome) to Barcelona, Spain. We flew into Rome and were met by a driver sent by the ship's agent, so we saw nothing but the Italian countryside on the drive to the ship. (Luckily, I had other chances to see Civitavecchia and Rome, which I will cover later in this book). After a quick breakfast, our audit team was on the ship by 9:30 AM and working by 11:00. However, we quit working early because jet lag caught up with us quickly. Instead, we had an early dinner and decided to get a good night's sleep and start again the next morning.

The purpose of these Environmental Compliance Plan audits is to oversee the U.S. Government's probation for these two cruise ship lines. They had violated International laws and this audit team was chosen to oversee their changes during the five-year probation period. As you might expect, there was originally a lot of tension, but their improvement has been great, and that tension has disappeared. We are now accepted as people there to help rather than being a punishment. It is very rewarding!

We only had two full days to finish this first ship audit, so we could not take any time off in Naples, which was our only stop before Barcelona. I've been to Naples four times, but still have not been to Pompei, which was covered by ash and lava from Mt. Vesuvius in that famous eruption. It is supposed to be amazing, and maybe someday I will get to see it. Mt. Vesuvius towers over Naples Harbor, so I've seen the mountain (though not close). During one flight I took out of Naples several years ago, you could smell the sulfur from the smoke that still belches out of the active volcano. I wonder if, someday, Naples could be covered, just like Pompei!

Naples is not one of my favorite Italian cities. The drivers are crazy, on the narrow, winding streets. Even the cruise ship crews do not like coming to Naples because the stevedores and other dock workers give them a hard time. The crew assumes that they are Mafia-controlled.

Our first ship landed in Barcelona, one of my favorite cities in the world. The sights are wonderful, the food is fantastic, and the people are quite friendly and helpful. The majority of service-related people speak good

English, but I've never found a cab driver who speaks English, so that can be exciting!

I've been to Barcelona every year for the last six years for these cruise ship audits, and I have usually spent about half to three-quarters of a day there, either before or after an audit, sometimes with one night in a hotel.

Two years ago, David (my son) and I spent three days there after our trip to visit relatives in Finland, and we were able to see much more, including the GAUDI tour, a sports tour (soccer and Olympic related) and we did our own city tour, in addition to a short bus tour.

Until this trip (see the Budapest section below), I think I would have recommended Barcelona as the one city worth seeing if someone only had a couple of days in Europe. I know that everyone wants to see London, Paris, or Rome, but a couple of days is not enough for those cities, and if you want something different, Barcelona is it! In addition, it is a safe city (watch out for pick-pockets, however) and you can get by just fine without speaking Spanish. The language in Barcelona is Catalan, not Spanish, though the locals understand Spanish if you speak it. I'd recommend that you first apologize for not speaking in Catalan if you decide to use your Spanish. David found that out during one of our taxi rides in Barcelona.

This year, because the ship schedules had been changed, we had no time to enjoy Barcelona. One of the auditors was meeting a friend in Barcelona (just a fluke chance, brought on by an E-Mail). We had her friend meet us at the ship where the Hotel Director had organized an early, 11:00 AM lunch. We headed to the airport immediately afterwards to catch our flight to Munich, then connect to Rome and on to Dubrovnik, Croatia, where we were meeting our next ship.

Another one of our auditors, from the first ship, was flying home due to another commitment, and we were to meet his "replacement" in Dubrovnik. We were disappointed, because the Barcelona to Rome to Dubrovnik plane connection was sold out, and because of the extra Munich leg in our itinerary, we were now scheduled to get into Dubrovnik at 8:30 PM, missing a chance to see the city. Dubrovnik is one of the most dramatic and friendly cities in Eastern Europe. Last year, during a stop on an audit, we had time for a quick lunch and a walk through the old walled city (built around 900 years ago). We had hoped to see more on this trip if we had arrived at 3:30, as originally planned. However, we were resigned to our late arrival and no dinner – just airline snacks.

The other auditor traveling with me, Susan, and I, left Barcelona for Munich. Luckily, we went to check on our gate location as soon as we arrived and found our Munich-Rome flight had been delayed for one hour. We only had 45 minutes between flights in Rome, so we knew we would miss that connection. The Lufthansa service people were great and rescheduled us on Croatian Airlines through Frankfurt, then to Zagreb, and finally to Dubrovnik, where we were to arrive at about midnight. At least we were over our jet lag by this time, so we would only miss a good night of sleep.

We were very impressed by Croatian Airlines, which we flew from Frankfurt, for both of these "replacement" flights. Despite the time of day and short flights, both flights included a sandwich, coffee, and free alcohol. Do you know what we would have received on American Airlines or United these days? Peanuts without a smile!

When we rearranged our itinerary in Munich, the service agent called the baggage area to have our bags pulled from our Rome flight and put on our Frankfurt – Zagreb – Dubrovnik flights. However, poor Susan, who has had lost baggage problems on these audit flights before, had her luggage lost again. My bag showed up just fine, but nothing for Susan. Reporting her lost baggage, etc. took nearly one hour at the Dubrovnik airport, so our night of sleep got even shorter.

We began to see the friendly nature of the Croatians at this point. The taxi drivers heard that we had a lost bag as we stood around in the baggage claim area. They asked me if we would need a taxi. It turned out that the airport was closing for the night and all the taxis were leaving, but one could wait for us if we needed one. The driver was quite nice, did not charge us any extra for his wait, and gave us a narrated tour through town. He told us about the history of what we were passing, even though it was after midnight.

We stayed in a beautiful hotel. Dubrovnik was Marshal Tito's "playground" in the old Yugoslavia, and the hotels all overlook the Adriatic Sea. Croatia is very narrow in this southern region (maybe three miles, at the narrowest point), with the cities built on the rough rock cliffs overlooking the sea. This is why Dubrovnik was so badly damaged by shelling during their war with Serbia in the 1980s, with Serbian-controlled Bosnia just over those hills.

All of the hotels are built with most of the rooms having a sea-view balcony, though my room was on the inside. We had a nice breakfast buffet (always included in the room price in Eastern Europe) and then headed to the ship. Our new "replacement" auditor was "rubbing it in" about his wonderful afternoon touring the old city and his great dinner in Dubrovnik, but we were working on board by 11:00 AM, again! (Thanks, Hans, for making us feel bad!)

This second ship was a real beauty! The cruise line has four sister ships and each has wonderful, "normal" food, as well as a "Specialty" Restaurant, known as The Liners Restaurant. These restaurants are decorated using original woodwork and memorabilia from old "ocean liners," such as the "Oceanic" (owned by White Star Line, also the owner of the "Titanic"), the S.S. "United States," the "Ile De France," and another which I cannot remember. They serve a 4-course gourmet meal, which we usually turn into a 5 or 6-course by getting extra appetizers. I've now eaten at The Liners on each ship several times and the meals are extraordinary! Just the cheese tray alone is amazing, with choices from 12-15 different gourmet kinds of cheese. I have ordered the Crepes-Suzettes for dessert (made by hand at the table-side) for at least 8 of my ten meals in these restaurants – TO DIE FOR! Now you can understand my waistline!

BOB, SUE & HANS IN VENICE

This second cruise ended in Venice. We were in Venice last year, but only had 15 minutes ashore, and saw almost nothing, except for the cruise out of the harbor, which was amazing. But this year, we spent two afternoons in Venice, walked for over 4 hours, and took a water taxi ride on the Grand Canal to get some great pictures. We had a great time roaming Venice. We had no time to do the "inside tours" of the churches and museums, but we spoke to a lot of interesting people. Susan is a mask collector, so we found a great shop with all the typical Venetian masks, and the saleswoman gave us detailed explanations of the masks, who wore them in the old Venetian masked balls, and why! It was quite interesting. We found out that this woman had a degree in Environmental Science, and had just lost her job on a wildlife preservation project when the funds were cut by the Italian government. It may be a lucky thing for her, as my audit colleagues were able to give her the name of an Environmental Consulting firm in Milan, and we hoped she would have success in finding a new job in her chosen field.

## **European Adventure Part of the Trip**

After completing our work on the cruise ships, Susan and I continued on a European Holiday in Eastern Europe. Last year, the previous lead auditor (Judi), whose mother lived in Budapest, had planned a trip to visit her mother this year, and had invited Susan and me to "tag along." Judi quit her job with this auditing company (went to work for a major entertainment company as their Safety and Environmental Director), and we thought our European adventure might be canceled. But in July, Susan and I worked together on another audit, and we decided to go ahead with the plans. We had kept our plans very flexible, originally planning to take a train from Venice to Trieste, then Trieste to Budapest, and then Budapest to Zagreb. We found the train schedules and times were bad for our proposed tourist plans, so we changed to an air flight from Venice to Budapest. We skipped Trieste until another day and found another flight from Budapest to Ljubljana, Slovenia. From Ljubljana, we rented a car and drove to Rijeka, Croatia, and then to Zagreb for our flight home. The following is a summary of our adventures in Eastern Europe.

## <u>Trip to Budapest</u>

Our flight from Venice to Budapest was uneventful, which was very unusual, based on our poor experiences on the previous air flights between Barcelona and Dubrovnik. We flew an airline that neither of us had flown or even heard of before – MALEV, the Hungarian Airline (the "MA" is from MAGYAR, the real name of Hungary).

As an aside, why do English-speaking people always change the names of countries and cities into names that are not even close to the names used by the actual residents? MAGYAR vs. Hungary, SUOMI vs. Finland, HRVATSKA vs. Croatia, and so forth! Maybe it is understandable when the alphabet varies drastically, such as Arabic, Cyrillic, and some other obvious ones, but what was the reasoning for changing country names to English names that don't even sound like the original? But I've digressed, though on purpose!

Back to MALEV Airlines – they were a really nice surprise! The first flight (only 75 minutes) served a small, but tasty meal, with drinks (free alcohol) and coffee. The crew was courteous and spoke excellent English. The Budapest airport was also very nice and well laid out.

Susan had bought a book on touring Eastern Europe, and it had a recently revised section (2003) on Budapest. The author (Rick Steves) recommended two "personal guides" to use for walking tours of Budapest. We called one and booked him for the afternoon of our arrival day, and it was a great decision. Peter Polczman was a nice, young man of about 30 – 32 years, well-spoken, and born in Budapest, where he had attended University. He loved Budapest and knew all the sights and the history behind them. (Just a note from long after this trip, Peter Polczman is featured in Rick Steves' Travel videos, walking in Budapest with Rick Steves.)

The first thing Peter did was have us buy a 3-day pass for the Budapest Transit System, which included the four METRO lines (underground and elevated), all the street cars, buses, and several other modes of transport. It also includes free access or discounts to many attractions. The total cost was $11.00 for a 3-day pass.

Hungary is not yet in the "EU" but already uses the EURO, as well as the Floren (about 200/$ or 250/Euro). We thought the prices were about the same as in Chicago, except for the large open market, where food and some craft items were a bit less expensive. (Hungary has since joined the EU, which was probably a mistake! More on that later!)

Budapest has now been added to my list of "Favorite cities to visit, but don't want to live there!" My top favorites include:

- Barcelona
- Budapest
- Stockholm
- New Orleans
- San Francisco

There are more favorites but let's not get too detailed for now! There are my favorite small cities on my list, but you don't need two days to see them. Then there are cities like Chicago, but you need two weeks there to do it justice. That is why the list does not include great places like Rovinj, Croatia, Bardolino, Italy, etc. Then there is New Zealand, where you'd need a month or more!

To make my list, the city must be safe (New Orleans is "iffy" on safety), have great food, good music, and other entertainment, have good sight-seeing for a two-day trip, and the people must speak English (I'm lazy on languages, and again, New Orleans is "iffy" on English, considering the Cajun).

We found the sightseeing in Budapest was great, easily accessible, inexpensive, and usually well described with signs in English. The Danube (Dunay) River divides "Buda," the old city where the castle sits on a high hill with mountains behind, from "PEST," the newer city, which is flat, with shopping, markets, hotels, restaurants, and the airport.

We wanted to try the public Hot Spring Bath in the park in Pest, but Susan had lost her luggage, and her swimsuit was in her bag. When we asked if she could buy a suit at the baths (the book said yes) we found they only rented swimsuits, and Susan was a bit worried about the health aspects, so we decided to take a pass on that experience. Maybe it is worth a try next time. A 2-hour bath and 30-minute massage were only about $25.00.

We had one other disappointment when we wanted to visit the "House of Terror." The House of Terror was the headquarters of the German Gestapo during World War II and the Russian KGB-Hungarian Secret Service during the Communist years. The Hungarians are very anti-Communist at this time (that sure has changed among their leaders) and seem ashamed of this history. They seem to want to preserve this "Monument" as a warning against what might happen in the future. Peter, our guide, told us to return to this place on our own, but when we returned the following day, some "skin-head" Neo-Nazi group had planned a demonstration, and an Anti-Nazi group was also there, so the Museum of Terror was closed for the day. (Eventually saw the museum on a subsequent trip. It is quite dramatic!)

**BEAUTIFUL BUDAPEST BRIDGES**

We experienced some other great sites, including the gallery and museum of an artist called Imre Varga. Imre Varga's art was different, it consisted of mostly large sculptures, but his original sculptures for street art, including the Jewish Memorial at the Budapest Synagogue, were in the museum on a smaller scale. His work was mostly 'tolerated" by the Communists. I'm not an "artsy" person, but I was impressed by his work. (I returned to this gallery again on a later trip, and the new "almost-Communist" regime in Hungary seems to have shunned Varga's work again!)

**VARGA'S JEWISH MEMORIAL, WEEPING WILLOW**

We had a great dinner at a floating restaurant, "Spoons," on the Danube, and then took a night tour of all the buildings we had walked to see the previous day.

We also experienced some great music at a small Blues Club called "Alcatraz." One of the performers, a great Chicago Blues Artist called Tino Rodriquez, had one of the best Blues-guitar sounds I've ever heard. The walls were covered with Chicago memorabilia, as well as newspaper articles about Al Capone, Dillinger, etc.

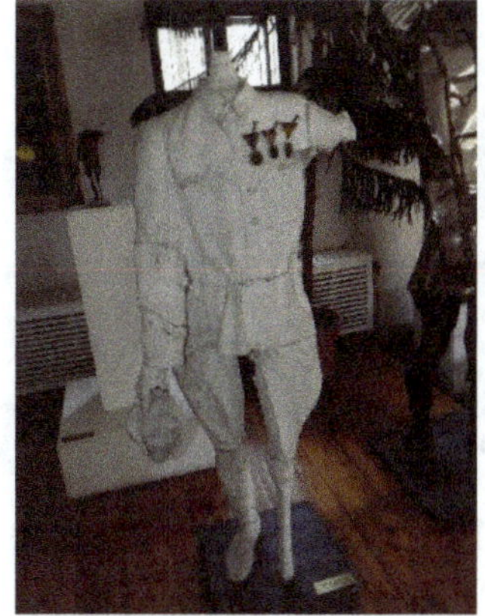
VARGA'S ANTI-WAR SCULPTURES

On our last night in Budapest, we found a festival at a Greek Orthodox Church, only four blocks from our hotel. The festival had a combination of Greek and Hungarian food, a great drink that tasted like spiced hot wine, Greek music, jazz music, and Greek and Hungarian dancers. This was a nice change from our busy three days in Budapest.

## Ljubljana, Slovenia

CLUB ALCATRAZ SECOND VISIT

The Eastern European travel book said Slovenia was an often missed "treasure" in Eastern Europe, particularly its capital city, Ljubljana. Ljubljana is highly recommended as a one-day stop since it is only a 1.5 to 2-hour drive from Rijeka (1.5 for the locals and 2 hours for Americans). We were originally going to fly to Zagreb to Rijeka but realized we would then have to drive back to Zagreb to fly home. On the map, Ljubljana was just as close to Rijeka and had good flight connections, plus additional stops on our tour, so we decided to try going that route – from Budapest to Ljubljana. Our flight on MALEV was only a short turbo propeller plane ride and was great.

We found Ljubljana to be a beautiful old town with a nice, small castle on a hill, a beautiful town square, and a scenic river with unusual-looking bridges. The Slovenian food was very good (a mixture of Austrian and Croatian dishes), with prices cheaper than what I found in Budapest. Their English skills were also good, but not as great as those in Croatia.

DRAGON BRIDGE AND THE BEAUTIFUL LJUBLJANA CASTLE

The people were very nice, and they liked Americans. Another reason to visit Slovenia is a trip to Vrhnika, a town between Ljubljana and Rijeka, where a leather factory is located (*closed in 2018*). Susan was looking for a leather coat for her husband and asked about it at the airport. The lady immediately mentioned this factory outlet store that made coats and other leather products, so we drove out there. We could not believe the prices! Susan bought two suede jackets for under $125.00 each, and a jacket for herself (on sale as color rejects, but we didn't notice any problems on any we saw) for $30.00. I bought a beautiful polished Lamb-skin leather jacket for about $250.00, which would have been over $800.00 in the U.S.

## The Drive from Ljubljana to Rijeka

We left Vrhnika around dusk and headed for Rijeka. Funny how the maps don't show how steep the mountains and curves are in those areas! I'm sure this is a great drive in the summer, or even in daylight, but your first drive should not be at night. With the little we could see, it was a beautiful drive, but you could already see the snow on the higher mountains.

About 30 minutes into the drive, with me driving 110 kph, and being passed by locals driving 150 kph, we hit a coating of hail and sleet on the highway. Within a short distance, several of the guys who had passed me were all tangled up on the highway. It didn't appear that anyone was killed, but several cars were nearly totaled. After only a few kilometers, the locals' speeds were back to 140 KPH, so they apparently don't learn! During the drive, we hit sleet and hail several more times, and over the next few days, we found that evening rain was typical, and sleet at higher elevations was also common at night.

Another interesting part of our drive from Slovenia to Croatia was the border crossing. It is the typical border with an inspection station on each side, and although our passports were inspected, the U.S. Passport obviously made our passage easy. The Slovenians were inspecting Croatian cars and vice-versa, so the tension we had heard about was certainly evident.

There is some government tension between the Slovenian and Croatian governments due to an unsettled treaty, giving Slovenia the port city of Koper, which Croatia historically had claimed. This complicates the border access for Croatians going to Italy. (Slovenia has free access to Italy after joining the EU. However, Croatians must still be checked at the Slovenian and Italian borders. (Even though Croatia was accepted into the EU recently, the Slovenian border checks continue.)

## **House Hunting in Rijeka**

Part of the purpose of this trip was to see Croatia in general, and Rijeka in particular because I was looking for a place to buy as a possible retirement home.

When we arrived in Rijeka, we had problems finding our hotel, which is common in Croatia, as we would soon learn. We called the hotel during our drive from Slovenia, and the clerk told us to ask anyone when we arrived in Rijeka because everyone knew where the Bonavja was located. We did what he told us, tried to follow the instructions, and after many one-way and dead-end streets, going by the hotel or its signs maybe five times, we finally pulled up in front of it.

We came to love this hotel and its great location, just off the huge walking street that extended a total of six or seven full city blocks. It is like the many attempts at downtown shopping areas in the United States, formed by blocking off streets. They were tried in the '70s and '80s in the States, but most had failed back home. But in Croatia, they really work and are full of people, 20 hours a day. Pubs, sidewalk cafes, specialty shops, and large department stores are all prospering. There is part of an old Roman arch built into the side of a modern building, just off this walking street. The Croatians believe in saving the old architecture and do not tear it down to make way for the new buildings.

We found the local beer and food in Rijeka to be very good and the prices reasonable. On the outskirts of the city and in smaller villages, prices were even lower, with coffee about 4 Kuna, or approximately $.75, and a large meal about $10.00, a fancy meal $20.00. Wine is also reasonable and local wines are quite good. (Croatia reportedly has the highest wine consumption per Capita, in the world. Most Croatians, with even small plots of land, will grow wine grapes and make their own family wine.)

Croatians, particularly those along the Adriatic Coast, seemed unusually friendly. Even those who did not have great English skills would call someone over to help with a conversation. You can be shunned in restaurants in Miami because you cannot speak Spanish, yet Croatian waiters and store clerks will "work with you" and smile about the challenge. Some are friendlier and more helpful than others, as would be expected anywhere, but their general attitude is great.

While walking the historical part of Rijeka one day, we saw a sign for the local "ABS" office, my old employer. I still worked for ABS as a contractor (on these cruise ship audits, for example) at the time, so we went over to the building and asked the general lobby receptionist if anyone was in the ABS office. She called to find out, and a wonderful man named Boris Pirjak came down and invited us to their office upstairs. We even met his boss, George Gardiakos, who had recently been transferred to Rijeka from Greece. That was a wonderful experience as well.

During one of our tours of Rijeka, we visited the airport. The airport in Rijeka is on KrK Island (no, I did not forget any vowels! It's pronounced KERK), a large resort area about 5 miles south of Rijeka. Access to the island is by a toll bridge called the KrK Bridge. The KrK Bridge used to be the longest, concrete arch bridge in the world, until recently, when the United States built a larger one over the Hoover Dam. In fact, Croatian Engineering is well respected around the world for bridges, tunnels, and highways. They designed and built most of those impenetrable tunnels in Baghdad, which the U.S. bombers could not destroy during the Gulf War.

At the airport, we were told by the policewoman at the gate that the airport was closed and that the closest airport was PULA. We didn't understand, as we thought this was an active airport. Even our hotel clerks thought it was active, however, the ABS Surveyor had told us the airport was closed until the next Spring, due to poor revenue during the winter. If a house in Croatia was to work for me, it needed to be near an active airport, so the Rijeka area was not looking like it would be my place. I also found that high winds in that area often caused a closure on that bridge, so living on Krk Island was not going to be good for my travels, in addition to the airport problem.

THE KRK BRIDGE, NEAR RIJEKA TO KRK ISLAND. SEE THE SMALL BOAT?

Since we were already on Krk Island, we used the opportunity to drive into some of the resort areas to look around. The island is very nice but would be too much of an expensive place to live. It is also, apparently, inaccessible on some winter days, due to the high winds on that bridge.

## Driving in Croatia

We did a lot of driving around Rijeka and one day decided to drive to Pula, the southernmost city on the Istrian peninsula. The drive there includes some dramatic cliffside roads and numerous tunnels. The major tunnel through Mount Ucka (pronounced OOCH-KA), which is over 5 kilometers long, has a toll of about $4.00. You can take the coastal route to avoid the toll, which is very beautiful, but it would probably add one hour or more to the ride because of the numerous curves.

Pula is known for its 2000-year-old Roman amphitheater, which is the fifth-largest Roman amphitheater in the world. Part of the seating has been restored and it is used for music concerts during the summer. Pula also has a Roman Forum and a large, ancient Roman arch in the middle of the city, in quite good repair.

ROMAN AMPHITHEATER IN PULA ROMAN FORUM IN PULA

I learned a good lesson about Eastern European drivers, and motorcyclists in particular, during the drive to Pula. We had stopped to make a left turn into a scenic turnout, the coastline was on our left the entire trip, and it took quite a while for the oncoming cars to clear so I could turn left. Right when I was about to do so, two motorcycles pulled around the line of cars behind me and tried to pass everyone at once. The bikers swerved wildly to miss hitting me broadside, causing them to come alongside our car to give me a 2-3 minute tongue-lashing in Serb-Croatian (turned out they were from Bosnia). I didn't understand them and if they understood my English, they never responded. Although my left turn may have been "legal," I learned that I needed to be a little more defensive when driving in other countries, particularly in Southern and Eastern Europe. It reminded me of my experience with Russian drivers in Finland.

All the drivers in Slovenia and Croatia seemed to be very impatient. They pass other cars on curves and hills where Americans would never try to pass. They also exceed the speed limits by a much greater margin than we do in America. We were usually the slowest car on the road, even though we drove 10 – 20% over the limit, with 25 – 35% over the limit being common for locals and 40 – 50% not unusual.

I could "hold my own" in city traffic, probably due to my experience in Chicago, but the one-way streets drove us crazy, largely because they were old, narrow streets. America has its own cities with that problem.

## Zagreb

On the last day of our stay in Croatia, we drove to Zagreb to find a hotel near the airport for our early departure. The highway between Rijeka and Zagreb is a toll road, in very good condition, with many tunnels and dramatic bridges over large gorges. Unlike US toll roads, the road changes from 2-lane to 3-lane (passing lane) and 4-lane (both divided and undivided) several times during the trip, even when tunnels were involved. The trip is about 80 miles, and the Croatians told me it was a 65-minute trip, so you can tell how fast they drive. It took me nearly two hours because morning fog slowed the trip a little (but not much for the Croatians who passed me).

We stopped at a small village outside Zagreb, near the border of Slovenia (Zagreb is in far North-Central Croatia, near the border). These small villages have interesting open markets, and old churches, and all of them seem to have a small river with an interesting bridge. The old buildings are amazing, and well-kept, unlike the ones in Budapest. We did see a lot of renovations and new construction too.

However, our arrival in Zagreb was very frustrating. We wanted to find the airport, and then find a hotel near the airport. Our intent was then to drive into the old city center to see the sights. We soon found out why our reference book on Zagreb had little to say about the city. We could not find the airport, even after several attempts over two hours. We then tried to find the city center. Despite following the signs, we never found the city center while driving. We seemed to be wandering and then decided to try and find a hotel that had been recommended by our hotel in Rijeka.

We saw a sign for the hotel, several miles away, and followed the signs toward the hotel. During this adventure, including numerous wrong turns (signs give no warning, so invariably we were in the wrong lane to make the turn) we suddenly started seeing signs for the Aerodrome (airport). Unlike our airports, with large freeways leading to them, and surrounded by numerous hotels and other services, Zagreb airport is accessed by a two-lane road with the closest hotel several miles away. The airport is small and parking is awful, so Susan ran in to ask our Budget Rental Car office how we should return the car the following morning. None of the car rentals opened before 7:00 AM and our flight left at 7:40, so we were a bit worried. However, the return went quickly the next morning, and it turned out fine.

We had seen the sign for the U.S. Embassy near the airport, so we went there to ask some questions about American ownership of property in Croatia, etc. We arrived during their lunch break, so we were unable to see anyone. We thought we would return after lunch, but our hotel search became "very interesting," and allowed no time to return to the Embassy.

We finally located the hotel recommended by our hotel in Rijeka and found it was over $150.00/night for each of us. We only needed the rooms for an early check-out, so we decided to find a cheaper option. The hotel clerk in Zagreb recommended the Zagreb Hotel, which we found after three tries, due to bad signs and wrong turns. This turned out to be a very depressing, 1950s-looking place, in poor repair, with some foreign soccer team standing out front. We never even got out of the car at this place! We saw signs for another hotel, (Laguna), made several attempts to find it and never located it. However, during our search, we made a wrong turn. While trying to make a U-Turn (got very good at these) we found ourselves in front of the International Hotel. This was a ten-story hotel that was on none of our hotel lists, and we never saw the typical street signs that pointed out its location. In desperation, we checked in for $90.00 per night, the same rate as our beautiful hotel in Rijeka. The hotel was old, the carpet was very worn, and the furnishings were from the Socialist era, but it was clean, friendly, and smelled good.

After getting organized, we found that there was a street trolley at the corner of our hotel, which would take us to the Zagreb City Center. The cost was 8 Kuna ($1.35), but we needed local coins to pay, and we did not have the correct change. The street cars in Budapest and Zagreb are on the "honor system," and most people buy a monthly or yearly pass. There are "fare inspectors," but we never saw one in either city. We just cheated, and hoped we could explain our dilemma if questioned. Nobody ever asked!

**MAIN SQUARE IN DOWNTOWN ZAGREB, CROATIA**

So, we finally made it to the City Center and passed the area of one-way streets where we had gotten lost earlier in the day. We were probably only three blocks away while driving, but after seeing the parking situation, we were glad we didn't find it while driving earlier, particularly with all the street cars sharing the same roads. These beautiful rail cars cannot move to avoid you and would easily total a car in an accident.

We spent one last night walking around, seeing the sights close to the main city square and found a nice local "Pizza Pub" where we had a good meal and drank my new "favorite" beer (Tomislav). After all that, we returned early to the hotel to rest up for our flight home.

## <u>Buying a House</u>

On my next trip to Croatia, I concentrated on looking for property on the Istrian Peninsula. During my previous trip to Croatia, we stopped in a small town in Istria, along the Adriatic Sea, just southwest of Opatija, called Moscenicka Draga.

**MOSCENICKA DRAGA AND A SMALL FISHING VILLAGE, WHERE I CONSIDERED BUYING**

It was a beautiful view, high up in the hills, overlooking the Adriatic Sea. On subsequent trips to Croatia, I found the seacoast property, just like in any country, to be very expensive. Plus, many of the homes had been bought by German, Austrian, English, and Italian nationals. I liked the Croatian people and did not want to live amongst non-Croatian landowners.

My guide, during this trip, Davor Jurum, took me to places near Pula, Rovijn, Porec, and other seaside areas. By chance, the man who owned the B&B where I stayed, overheard our discussions and asked if we had looked in the mountainous region near the Slovenian border.

**CROATIAN HOUSE BEFORE REPAIRS     RENOVATED GETAWAY IN BUZET, CROATIA**

It just so happened that his bookkeeper's daughter was trying to sell her house in the small town of Buzet. He drove me to the house in Buzet later that day, and I fell in love with it. The house, which I bought, was situated looking down on the hilltop city of Buzet, with 3000-foot mountains in Slovenia behind me. That's another, long story for later in this book.

**NATURAL BEAUTY NEAR MY HOME CITY OF BUZET, SEEN FROM ABOVE MY HOUSE**

## My Comments on the EU and Changes in Europe

After many subsequent trips to Europe since the above trip, I am personally convinced that joining the European Union (EU) was a huge mistake for the continent's smaller countries. The EU Rules appear to have been drafted to only benefit large countries like Germany, France, Italy, and others. The small countries were promised an infusion of money for improvements, but while the EU fulfilled part of that deal by improving their highways, these highways are now used by the larger countries to transport goods and natural resources from and through those countries, not to help them. At least that is my opinion!

Croatia has been told to stop subsidizing its shipyards, which will essentially shut the shipyards down after they lose contracts (*By 2018, all but one shipyard had closed*). Croatia builds excellent ships, such as car carriers and bulk carriers. They cannot compete with China without those subsidies. The shipyards in Finland, Germany, Italy, and France will continue building cruise ships, but Croatia's shipyards cannot compete on that level of shipbuilding. Finland was told their fish did not meet EU standards, so Finland's fishing fleet is getting smaller. But Germany and other countries have increased their fishing fleets.

In 2016, while visiting Romania, we heard the EU had promised them a lot. However, the rights to their iron ore, oil reserves, and precious metal ores were bought up by large EU corporations. The Romanians thought this would improve the Romanian steel mills (once the largest steel producer in Europe) and oil refineries, but instead, those EU corporations are closing many of those factories down, to eliminate competition.

Beware! Communism still exists in these Eastern European countries, under a "Socialist Democratic" name. The EU is punishing these small countries and may eventually drive them back to communism. As one Romanian tour guide told us, "Nothing has changed in Romania except we now have freedom of speech, and we will continue to use it."

After numerous trips to Croatia, I now realize that the coastal regions along the Adriatic Sea have learned how to better cater to the needs of tourists, therefore, the signage is much better. Many signs are in Croatian, Italian, and English. In Eastern Croatia, even in the Capital, Zagreb, there are fewer numbers of foreign tourists, so the signage is still terrible. Our experience in Zagreb, looking for the airport, was so frustrating it was almost funny! The signs pointing to the airport were located on the street AFTER you made the turn. Until I had Sue look both ways at each intersection, we could not see any signs.

## ◄— AERODROME

There was never this type of sign anywhere on that main road. The signs only made sense if you already knew how to get to the airport. Eastern Europe has a lot to learn, but the EU is the wrong teacher!

# CHAPTER 9

## SURVEYS WHILE RIDING SHIP

Other than the numerous cruise ship environmental audits that required me to ride a ship each time, I was seldom required to ride a ship during my surveys. Cruise ship surveys will be discussed in a separate chapter of this book, meanwhile, my apprehension about ship-riding surveys stemmed from my history with motion sickness. Early on, in my Coast Guard career, I would become ill on ships when they were in heavy seas. There were, however, occasions where I had no choice but to perform a survey while the ship was underway from one port to another.

### Norgas Tanker Survey

John Barr, at ABS Worldwide Technical Services, called me again with an interesting survey of an LPG (Liquified Petroleum Gas) tanker preparing for its Classification Renewal Survey (required every 4-5 years to maintain International Maritime Certificates and Insurance coverage). The owner of this tanker knew they had unusual corrosion occurring in the void spaces between the ship's hull and the cargo tanks. They required an in-depth inspection, involving ultrasonic thickness gauging of the internal structure, and detailed drawings of the steel which would need to be removed and replaced during their shipyard period.

The ship was loading LPG gas in Coatzacoalcos, Mexico, and the ship would be met there, and then I would sail with them to Houston, Texas. Coatzacoalcos is not a tourist town and my flight there was very interesting. Most of the people on my flight appeared to be oilfield workers.

When we arrived at the airport in Coatzacoalcos, my first challenge was to find a taxi driver who spoke English. Even the gentleman who was directing travelers to the various taxis did not speak English, so I began walking down the line of taxis and asking the drivers if they spoke English. At one of the cars, the driver appeared confused by my request. A lady was sitting in the front passenger seat who said she spoke English. After telling her the location of my ship, she said she could direct her husband, and asked me to get into the taxi. Our drive was well over an hour and my conversation with my driver's wife was very interesting and informative. Although this was well after sunset, she was an excellent tour guide and explained what I would have seen if the trip had been done in daylight. We arrived at a large refinery complex a little over an hour later, and I asked the taxi to wait until the security guard confirmed we were at the right location. My lady guide had done a good job, and the security guard called the ship to tell them of my arrival. I said goodbye to my driver and his wife and thanked them for the good service and her great conversation.

One of the ship's crew came to the security gate and escorted me through the refinery to the ship. It was already close to midnight at this point, so they gave me a bed in the ship's hospital. This is quite common when contractors are riding ships because the crew cabins are normally quite small and shared by two people. The ships are gracious to their guests, and we are usually given the Pilot's cabin, but, in this case, they already had a Pilot aboard who was using that cabin. For that reason, several times I have slept in the ship's infirmary, which is normally large and comfortable.

When I woke up the next morning, we were at sea. The crew member who greeted me guided me to the Captain's cabin where I met the Captain. The Captain was a very gracious Norwegian who greeted me with a fresh pot of coffee. We then proceeded to the ship's mess deck for breakfast. The Captain introduced me to the 1st Mate and the Chief Engineer, both of whom would be assisting me during my survey. Although the ship's crew understood the purpose of my survey, we held a lengthy meeting after breakfast to discuss the work to be accomplished and the safety requirements involved.

I had brought my personal ultrasonic thickness gauger, and the Captain and Chief Engineer inspected it to be sure that it was intrinsically safe. This is required when working aboard tankers carrying any flammable liquids or gases, due to the possibility of an explosion if a spark should occur near the cargo. Luckily, all of the paperwork and certificates for my gauger were in the carrying case, and the Captain allowed me to use my own equipment during the survey.

Following the safety briefing, the 1st Mate brought me out on deck and showed me the entrance hatches to the 12 voids we would be inspecting. All of the voids had been tested for fumes and sufficient oxygen, and all were found to be safe for entry. The 1st Mate assigned a junior officer to accompany me during my inspections, and we spent the next three days in the heat of these voids, taking thickness readings, recording measurements of plates needing repairs, and making rough sketches of our findings.

I ate and slept well (now in the Pilot's cabin) due to my physical exertion during the survey, and my interactions with the crew members were thoroughly enjoyable. An interesting item I saw on this ship was my first tube of mayonnaise! The United States had not seen things like catsup, mustard, and mayonnaise in plastic tubes at that time (like toothpaste), so the crew thought my reaction to those condiment packages was comical.

Luckily on this trip, we did not encounter any rough weather, so there was no motion sickness this time. We arrived in Houston where I took the opportunity to visit the ABS office to discuss the results of the survey, as well as several upcoming projects that John Barr was planning. Then I was off to Chicago where I completed my written report and prepared drawings for the areas of repair, found during my survey.

## **<u>Atlantic Crossing</u>**

One of the more grueling surveys performed in my career was on a new, double hull, crude oil tanker, which was undergoing its first year, Shipyard Acceptance Survey. It was originally planned for me to meet the ship at its loading port in Africa, however, the tanker owner decided it was not safe at that time, due to political unrest in Western Africa. Instead, they had me meet the ship while it was unloading near Freeport, Bahamas, and then ride the ship to the Suez Canal.

**TANKER UNLOADING AT FREEPORT, BAHAMAS**

A Shipyard Acceptance Survey is similar to an inspection at the end of a Warranty period and is carried out by the ship owner with shipyard personnel also in attendance. The survey is to determine if the ship still meets the contract requirements that were in effect during construction. In this particular case, the tanker owner had a young relief Captain on board who represented the owner, and the Japanese shipyard had two representatives on board, plus another Japanese gentleman representing the paint company. ABS had been hired by the ship's owner to provide my services as an "Independent Third Party" inspector and mediator. The main scope of this survey was to inspect every ballast tank and every cargo tank on the ship. The ballast tanks were to be inspected during the unloading process in the Bahamas, and the cargo tanks while underway across the Atlantic.

We soon realized the empty ballast tanks were extremely hot because the cargo tanks, which were directly above our heads, were filled with crude oil which was being kept hot in order to pump it ashore. This ship was 1200 feet in length and 210 feet in breadth. The distance from the deck to the bottom of the ballast tanks was 85 feet. There is a stairway leading about halfway into the ballast tanks, but then vertical ladders were used to access each of the areas between the large transverse girders. We were looking for any structural deformation, as well as any failure of the paint coatings. Each tank inspection took approximately 90 minutes, which in the 100+ degree heat and 100% humidity, was exhausting!

Because of the heat and the continual use of ladders, we would emerge from the tank soaking wet and thoroughly drained of energy. The climb up the ladders and stairway to the deck was dreaded by every one of us, after inspecting just one tank. We would crawl out on the deck and lay in the hot Bahamas sunlight, which at this point seemed much cooler than the atmosphere in the tank we had just inspected. The ship's crew gave us a large container of iced water while we lay on the deck trying to recover. We would then return to our staterooms, take a shower, and meet in the dining room for lunch. The same procedure occurred after lunch and, because of the extreme heat and exhaustion we were experiencing, we were only able to inspect two ballast tanks a day. On the second day, one of the Japanese shipyard representatives became so exhausted during the inspection that we had to have iced water brought down into the ballast tank for him, and needed to assist him out of the tank and up to the deck.

While we were eating dinner on that second evening, the Japanese shipyard representatives came to me and stated they had gained trust in my "third party" status, so they would not be riding the ship to the Suez Canal. They would trust my opinion on any conditions found and would request a copy of my report from the ship's owner. The young Captain and I had noticed that all of the Japanese were heavy smokers and were very small in stature. The combination of their smoking, and not having sufficient body weight to lose, apparently made it too difficult for them to deal with the heat and the exertion level needed to inspect those hot tanks. The three Japanese representatives left the next morning, thanking me for being so honest in resolving our findings up to that point during the survey.

We found only minor paint problems, which the shipyard was quick to point out were not covered by the contract signed by the tanker owner. When steel is cut or sheared, there are sharp edges that do not easily hold paint. The contract had specified that if the plate edges were to receive a 2-pass grinding to round off those sharp edges, the paint was guaranteed not to fail on those edges. However, the owner had crossed out and signed off on that portion of the contract, because that extra pass by a grinder would have cost well over $1 million extra. You can imagine the number of cut steel edges in a ship that size, and the amount of time required to grind all those edges.

We had a total of 42 tanks to be inspected on board this vessel, including ballast tanks and cargo tanks, plus two large cargo slop tanks, used when cleaning. We were able to inspect all of the ballast tanks and slop tanks before we departed from the Bahamas, and the crew cleaned each of the cargo tanks as they were unloaded, making them safe for our entry while crossing the Atlantic. To be sure that all of the ballast tanks were inspected before we left, the young Captain and I pushed ourselves to inspect three tanks per day. It was easier because the cargo tanks were cooling down after the cargo was discharged, and I also think we were getting more efficient in our inspection techniques.

**CARGO PIPING ON THE DECK OF THE TANKER**

We departed Freeport and set out across the Atlantic, headed for the Mediterranean. Although the cargo tanks were large, the cleaning process had cooled them substantially, and we were able to make these inspections with much less physical torture than the ballast tanks had caused to our bodies. The young Captain, John Horgan, and I became fast friends during this job, and we still communicate via E-mail and Facebook to this day. It's interesting how experiencing something together, something as difficult as this job, can form some sort of lasting kinship.

While crossing the Atlantic, my free time was spent in the pilot house asking questions and watching the horizon. One day I joked with the Deck Officer about what kind of chart he would have on the chart table, and it probably was just a large sheet of white paper because there was nothing to be seen in the middle of the Atlantic. He told me to take a closer look at the chart, where there was a diversion in our course, which was to be executed that evening. I asked him why this had to occur, and he explained that a ship had sighted an unusual disturbance in the water near that area many years earlier, and it was determined that a large underwater mountain or volcano was present in the area. Although the exact location had never been determined, all large ships, such as this tanker, always avoided that spot in the Atlantic Ocean.

One day, while standing on the bridge wing, I noticed a small boat on the horizon. We were going to closely pass it. I told the Deck Officer what I had seen and he checked out the boat with his binoculars and told me that it was a small fishing boat from the Canary Islands. Looking at the chart to see where the Canary Islands were located concerning our position, it was amazing to find that the small two-man fishing boat had ventured nearly 300

SMALL FISHING BOAT, 300 MILES FROM THE CANARY ISLANDS

miles from home. I expressed concern over this, but the Deck Officer told me that these fishermen have been known to sail as much as 500 miles and still return safely to their home island. As we passed them, they only waved!

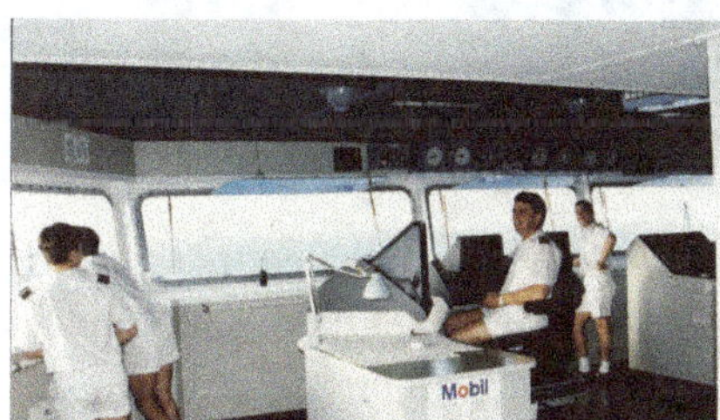 

WATCH OFFICERS ON THE BRIDGE AND I AM TAKING "MY TURN" ON WATCH

Although I normally ate my meals with the officers on board the ship, I also enjoyed visiting the crew galley to see what they were eating. The officers were English and the majority of the crew was from the Philippines. I found Filipino food to be fantastic and tastier than the British meals, so occasionally a side dish of Filipino food would magically appear with my dinner.

DINNER IN THE OFFICER'S DINING ROOM 1

There was a lot of respect shown between the officers and crew members, and one evening we had a karaoke session after dinner, to celebrate the birthday of one of the ship's officers. The entertainment by the Filipino crew members, who were actually part of a band back home in the Philippines, was very enjoyable. My enjoyment turned to terror when I was "required" to sing a song in honor of the officer's birthday. Try to think of a song and know all the words! Not being really "into" music, the only song I could think of other than Happy Birthday, was Take Me Out to the Ballgame. My singing debut passed without too much difficulty, and the officers and crew were very gracious.

**OUR GREAT FILIPINO BAND    SINGING 'TAKE ME OUT TO THE BALLGAME'**

While crossing the Atlantic, our Captain had been notified that fighting had occurred in Egypt and several Europeans had been killed. The Captain called me to his office to inform me of this situation, and because of this problem, we both would be departing the vessel at Gibraltar. The Captain's son was getting married back home in England, and the young Captain, who had worked with me inspecting tanks, would be taking over the ship when we left. The Captain asked if we could finish our work before reaching Gibraltar, losing the two days sailing time by not going to Suez. Because we had been able to do three tank inspections per day, we were able to finish the survey in time.

**VIEWS OF THE TANKER AS WE DEPARTED IN GIBRALTAR**

We approached Gibraltar in the early evening and a tugboat had been ordered to take me and the Captain to shore. After nearly 10 days aboard the ship, and having experienced some tough challenges together, the young Captain and I hugged each other before I left. The tug brought us to the cruise ship terminal, where we entered an empty building. Because the Gibraltar Immigration and Customs had not expected anyone to arrive, we entered Gibraltar with no questions, and therefore, no passport stamp to prove that I was ever in Gibraltar.

**OLD STYLE GUARDS**

The older Captain who left the ship with me, said we would meet for dinner after we checked into our hotel, and he took me to a very traditional English pub. Jokes are plentiful about the English drinking warm beer, but this pub only served beer at room temperature. That first Boddington's Ale went down like a tasty, rich cream. I am certainly not a big drinker, but that evening, I drank six large tankards of ale without feeling any effects. In fact, when we left the pub, the Captain appeared quite inebriated. After reaching our hotel, my conversation with my wife stated, "I just drank an English sea Captain under the table!"

The next morning, the phone rang in my hotel room at 6:30 AM, and the Captain told me to meet him in the lobby for breakfast. My hangover had kicked in, so I learned that English beer goes down very easily, but it punishes you the next morning. The Captain showed absolutely no ill effects of his drinking during breakfast. When I told him about my

hangover headache, he just chuckled.

The captain had been in Gibraltar before, and we proceeded to take a tour of some of the highlights. One of the great sights in Gibraltar is the airport runway, that crosses the road which is the access point between Spain and Gibraltar. We watched a plane land, which was interesting to see because only a railroad crossing-style arm came down to block traffic on the road, while the plane landed on the runway. Once the plane had landed, the arm was raised and auto traffic continued to cross the runway.

Numerous monkeys inhabit Gibraltar. It is said that as long as these monkeys survive there, the English will control Gibraltar. Most of the fresh water in Gibraltar is captured on large panels installed on one side of the large "Rock of Gibraltar."

If you remember the Prudential Insurance advertisements on television, they always showed the Rock of Gibraltar (Like a Rock!). That very distinctive profile from those TV ads was hidden from view during our time in Gibraltar, but after boarding the plane to London, looking out the window, there was a distinctive profile from the Prudential ad! The advertising agency for Prudential had seen that profile from the airport, as shown in my photo. As mentioned above, the Gibraltar airport sits on the border between Spain & Gibraltar, with the road crossing the runway.

VIEW OF 'THE ROCK' FROM RUNWAY

We were served a beautiful dinner on the plane, including shrimp. Having an anticipated overnight layover at London Heathrow Airport, the ship's crew had recommended several tourist locations for me to visit after arriving in London. The shrimp on the airplane was not fresh, (didn't I learn from my trip to Kwajalein?) and I became ill as soon as the plane landed in London. Checking into the airport hotel, there was no way to recover in time to make my sightseeing trip to London. To this day, although I have traveled through Heathrow and Gatwick airports many times, I have still never been in England, because I do not count an airport as visiting a country. So, Great Britain remains one of the countries on my bucket list.

The ship's owner asked me to divert my trip to visit their headquarters in Virginia to discuss my findings from the survey. There was a weight scale in my hotel room in Virginia and that is when I realized how tough this job had been. Despite eating all that good food on the ship, I had lost over 20 pounds from the time I arrived in the Bahamas to the time I returned to the United States. Although the food poisoning on the airplane certainly contributed, most of the weight loss was due to the heat and exertion during those tank inspections. With no extra body fat to be lost, it is no wonder that the Japanese gentlemen were unable to continue.

# CHAPTER 10

## PANAMA CANAL LOCK PROJECT

**THE THREE-STEP GATUN LOCKS ON THE 'ATLANTIC SIDE' OF THE PANAMA CANAL**

In 1999, John Barr again called from ABS Worldwide Technical Services and asked me to perform a survey of the emergency caisson at the Panama Canal. Of course, I was interested, and ABS sent me drawings and a scope of work covering the inspection of the caisson. The caisson is like a floating gate, which can be brought into a notched section on either end of a lock chamber, so the chamber can be pumped dry for either emergency repairs or normal maintenance.

The Panama Canal had two emergency caissons at the time I arrived there. Both of the caissons were of riveted construction, with the oldest one about to be scrapped. This made it very important that the second caisson

When the United States signed the agreement to return the Panama Canal to the country of Panama in 1975, they agreed to make repairs to the Canal and Locks before the Canal was returned. Panama had been dewatering the lock chambers for repairs, and this required that the caisson be used to hold back the water on one end of the lock chamber to remove the Lock Gates for overhaul. The Panamanians had attempted to make numerous repairs to the caisson by using welded inserts in the riveted structure. This welding had caused surrounding rivets to leak and they were asking ABS for assistance.

Because of my riveting experience on the Great Lakes, where numerous riveted vessels were still in operation, my name was suggested as the possible surveyor to attend in Panama. My previous ABS background and my Naval Architecture experience made me the perfect candidate for this project.

Excuse my first attempt at map-making, but these are the places in my story:

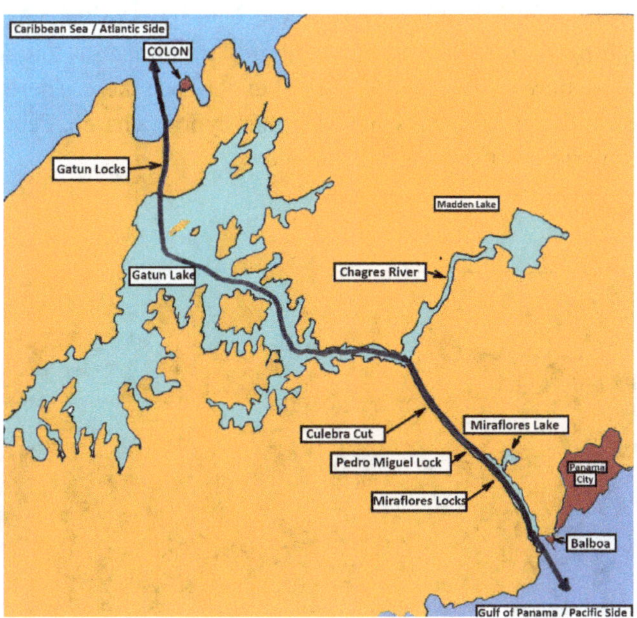

My first trip to Panama was very stressful but interesting. Although my work "mates" at the Panama Canal Commission spoke very good English, I found it necessary to learn the cultural differences quickly to gain their trust and cooperation. English is the primary language at the Panama Canal. Every employee was Panamanian, except for some of the American tug pilots. Some of the people working there were also Panama citizens of European descent. It was great to make some very good, lasting friendships, which made the job both fun and rewarding.

One of the early problems I encountered in Panama was dealing with the extremely hot and humid weather. My quarters on the first few trips were in the old Panama Canal employee apartments, and as soon as you walked out the door in the morning, you broke into a full-body sweat. At first, I found this very disconcerting, but I was soon able to just take it in stride. After all, the day was going to be spent sweaty from head to toe anyway, so why let it ruin my day?

The food was great. During my first visit, my workmates introduced me to the various types of Panamanian and South American food available in the Canal Zone. I also had a college friend who lived in Panama with his wife. Spending some time at their home, I learned a lot about the Panamanian culture from their 25 years of experience there. There was also a local ABS office in Balboa, where the Surveyor in charge, Pete Midboe, was an old friend from my ABS Chicago days.

**MIRAFLORES MOORING SITE FOR CAISSON AND PCC CREW TOWING CAISSON TO DRYDOCK**

My first inspection of the caisson was done afloat in Miraflores Lake, which is near the Pacific side of the Canal (see the map above). We performed a full structural, mechanical, and operational survey of the caisson. The welded inserts and other welded repairs were noted, which had been made before my arrival, and they were causing problems. Those repairs needed to be removed and proper repairs completed. This would require the caisson to be placed in drydock.

There was a drydock on the Pacific end of the Canal, which was a graving dock. Their Graving Dock was built the same way as the lock chambers but only had a gate on one end. Because the drydock gates were also in need of repairs to the seals around the gates, the caisson was going to be used to seal off the drydock while these minor repairs could be made.

*For those who are not familiar with drydocks, there are two major types: Floating Docks and Graving Docks. When a ship is to be drydocked, concrete or wood blocks are pre-set on the bottom of the dock with the graving dock pumped dry. The blocks are laid out to fit the shape of the ship's bottom and then the ship enters the flooded graving dock. Once the ship is centered over those pre-set blocks, the drydock is pumped out again and the ship settles on the blocks. Repairs can then be accomplished in a dry environment, and once completed, the dock is reflooded and the ship sails away. The drydock in Panama was built at the same time as the Lock Chambers and it looked identical to a lock chamber, with the same gates on one end but solid concrete on the other end. Floating Docks are quite different, and more details will be given on those in my Chapter on my trips to Guam. There are also inclined railway docks and some others, but not as many of those exist, and they are usually smaller.*

The drydocking of our caisson could not take place immediately, so I returned to the United States, wrote my report, and made my recommendations to ABS.

The first photo below shows the Panama graving dock, blocked for the tanker that was in the dock with us and the second photo shows the caisson installed at the Gatun Locks, but it was used in the same manner, to close off the drydock for repairs.

**BLOCKS SET AT BOTTOM OF GRAVING DOCK CAISSON INSTALLED AT GATUN LOCK**

## Drydocking the Caisson

A few weeks after returning to the United States, ABS called me to return to Panama for the drydocking of the caisson. On this visit, most of the time was spent at the shipyard, working with my new Panamanian friends, as well as shipyard personnel. Many of the shipyard managers were American. The shipyard had been sold by the Canal to an American firm from Norfolk, Virginia, and they were operating the shipyard independently from the Panama Canal. During this visit to the shipyard, we shared the drydock with a small oil tanker that was in for repairs. The shipyard also had a smaller graving dock, and a Colombian submarine was in that dock.

**CAISSON IN THE PANAMA GRAVING DOCK**

My personal ultrasonic thickness gauging instrument came to Panama for this portion of the job. We performed numerous ultrasonic gauging and documented all of the areas that required repairs. Repairs would be required where wastage of the steel had occurred, as well as the improper welded repairs of rivets, which had been previously made to the caisson. This time, my report included numerous drawings of the caisson structure, showing the areas that needed repair.

COLUMBIAN SUBMARINE IN ADJACENT DRYDOCK

During that visit to Panama, I told my workmates that some riveting needed to be done because welding on the riveted structure had only resulted in leakage of adjacent rivets. The Panamanians told me that they thought riveting was no longer done and that the riveters the Canal had employed were all gone, including their factory which had made rivets since back in 1915. On the Great Lakes, we still had nearly 100 riveted ships at that time, and three of our shipyards on the Great Lakes had one or even two riveting teams (rivet gangs).

I asked ABS for permission to contact the shipyard in Toledo, Ohio, to ask if they would be interested in sending one of their riveting gangs to Panama, to train the Panamanians in making riveted repairs again. The Toledo shipyard expressed interest as long as we would use the team during the summer months when they did very few riveted repairs. Arrangements were made between the Toledo shipyard and the Panama Canal Commission, and my third visit to Panama was to greet the riveting team from Toledo. The Toledo riveting team remained in Panama for approximately 3 months, doing many of the repairs on the caisson, but also training the new Panamanian crew. When they left, they said that the Panamanian crew had learned well and were very capable of performing their own riveted repairs in the future.

During this third visit, much of my work was performed at the Canal-owned shipyard at Colon, on the Atlantic side of the Canal. I had impressed my workmates while working on the caisson, so they introduced me to the repair supervisor at the Colon shipyard. This was where they were drydocking the Canal's lock gates for repairs. The gates on the Panama Canal float, and are ballasted so that there is minimal weight held by the hinges on each gate. During these drydock inspections, the repair supervisor, who was born in Yugoslavia, had noticed many of the rivet heads on the riveted gates were heavily corroded. Because all of the gates had been built in 1915, the Canal Engineers thought that the gates were in poor condition. The Yugoslav supervisor had heard about my riveting experience and wanted my opinion on how to make repairs to the lock gates because he knew that the welding was not working.

While at the shipyard in Colon, my new Yugoslav friend asked me if I also had a good background in weld repairs. I had been an AWS (American Welding Society) Certified Welding Inspector while working full-time for ABS and could offer advice, although I told him I was not a welder myself. He showed me some large welded structural members he called bulkheads, but he did not explain their use. Then he asked me to look at the welds of the structural members to the outer plate and give him my opinion. While looking at the smooth side of the plate, which is on the other side from where the structural members are located, I did not see any heat discoloration caused by the welding. Then, when looking at the welds on the structural members, it appeared the welds had been applied "cold" and that good penetration had not been obtained between the plate and structural member. I explained these observations to him. He thanked me for my advice and nothing more was said at that time.

The Canal Commission Engineers were concerned because some of the rivet heads on the lock gates had large portions of the head missing due to pitting of the steel rivet. These rivets were large, 1-¼" in diameter, so the heads in the countersunk area were approximately 2" in diameter.

The rough sketches below (I am not a great artist...Sorry!) show why riveted joints are so resilient. The driving of hot, cherry-red metal into the

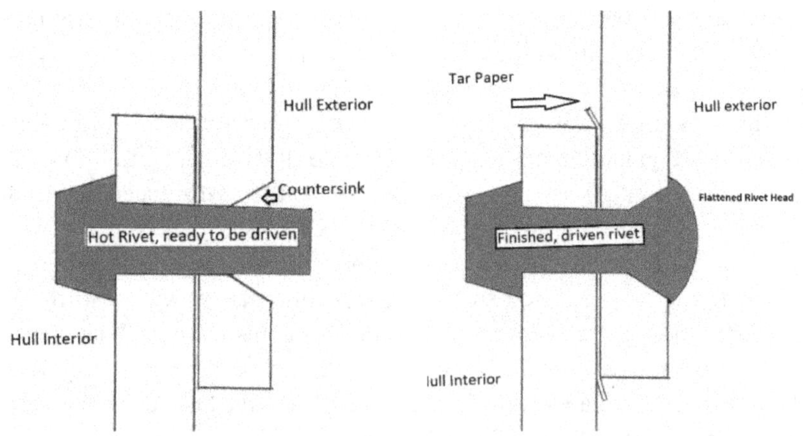


**NOTE THAT 'WATERTIGHT' RIVETED JOINTS USUALLY USE TARPAPER BETWEEN THE PLATES**

holes in those plates, creates a 100% sealed joint, keeping out water, thus avoiding corrosion around the shank. The length of the heated rivet shank is important, to provide enough metal to fill the countersunk hole, yet not so much as to have a large protrusion on the outside of the hull, which might catch on a dock or lock wall.

The way a rivet gang works is like watching a well-rehearsed ballet. The rivets are heated outside the ship in a small, portable furnace. A small, round hole, approximately 4-6 inches is cut in the hull, and the man heating the rivets grabs a heated one with tongs and throws it to a man outside that hole in the hull. He catches it in a sheet metal can, usually funnel-shaped, and then the catcher uses tongs to place the hot rivet through the hole. Another man inside the hull grabs the hot rivet with tongs and shoves the hot rivet into the rivet hole. A second man inside the hull has a heavy backing hammer, which he places against the "cone head" of the rivet. The "driver" is outside the hull, using a pneumatic hammer to flatten and round off the rivet shank into the countersunk hole. Therefore, a typical rivet gang consists of five men, three outside and two inside the ship.

It may seem that it would be easier, and use fewer men, to place the rivet from the outside (four men instead of five), but that would leave the cone head on the exterior of the vessel more exposed to possible damage to both the ship and the docks, dolphins or lock walls, which are typically rubbed by passing ships. Ships generally use the "cone head" rivets as shown in my sketches, although there are button heads, and round, and semi-round heads used in some internal structures. Bridges use others, like flat heads, round heads, etc.

The engineers at the Panama Canal believed all of the corroded rivets needed to be removed to make a proper repair. I told the field repair personnel that the rivet shanks seldom corrode despite the heavy pitting of the rivet head, and to prove my point, we removed several rivets and were able to see the original mill scale between the rivet shank and the shell plates of the lock gate. It was extremely difficult to remove those rivets because they were still so tight after 85 years. Although the point had been proven to the field personnel, I was asked to attend a meeting at the main engineering offices for the Panama Canal, in Balboa.

The next morning, approximately forty engineers gathered for the Panama Canal Engineers meeting in a large meeting room, listening intently to my presentation. There was a lot of quizzing by the Chief Engineer. However, the field repair engineers had done a good job of presenting my conclusions to the office engineers. The engineers were quizzing me to be sure that I really "knew my stuff." The office engineers suggested the use of bolts to replace the damaged rivets because they had used bolts successfully in their railroad bridge repairs. I explained to them that we had tried bolted repairs on several Great Lakes ships and found the bolts became corroded very quickly when submerged in water, and their salt and brackish water in Panama would quickly corrode such bolted repairs. The reason for this was that a bolt is stretched when it is tightened, allowing water to get into the space between the bolt and the plate. On the other hand, a rivet is driven into the hole while hot, and the metal fills the cavity. We showed them the results of the sample rivets we had removed the previous day, showing the original mill scale from when they were installed in 1915. The engineers then asked how they should make repairs to the corroded rivet heads and I explained the method of "Frenching and caulking," which tightens and fills the area near the plate.

*Frenching & Caulking Rivets: This repair method uses a curved chisel head on a pneumatic (air) operated chisel. This pulls the rivet head upwards and tightens it, however, this also leaves an empty gap between the rivet head and the hull plate. The caulking is then accomplished by driving more metal into that open gap. This was once accomplished by driving some of the hull plates into the gap, but that practice caused damage to the hull plate, reducing its thickness. The more accepted method was to place a "cold" weld bead around that open gap and then drive that weld metal in, to fill the space.*

This same "cold weld" was also used to repair rivet heads, refilling the area which had been lost due to pitting. Although they were skeptical, I told the engineers they should get a demonstration of this technique from the Toledo shipyard riveters before they left Panama. The Chief Engineer for the Panama Canal seemed quite critical during my presentation, however, I found out later that he was very impressed by my show of confidence during my presentation. He even told his field staff to follow my instructions.

Apparently, the Chief Engineer's staff had told him that bolts were a bad idea, but he needed to hear it from an outsider, like me.

**BEAUTIFUL MURALS IN THE ROTUNDA OF THE PANAMA CANAL OFFICE BUILDING**

During this visit, two weekends were spent in Panama, with very little work to be done. The shipyard had been instructed not to work overtime, therefore most of my weekends were free. On one of these occasions, the shipyard manager asked if I liked to fish. I love fishing but have never done any ocean fishing. He said that was no problem, and he also asked me to invite my "Panamanian boss" along on the fishing trip.

Fernando agreed to come along on the fishing trip, and he seemed very excited. We found out the next day that he had never held a fishing rod in his entire life. As is typical for ocean fishing, each person aboard takes turns landing a fish. My turn was first and we landed just a small tuna, and I was unhappy to see that my fish was just cut up and used as bait. The next fish was for Fernando, who was nervous because he had never fished before. The boat crew was very helpful and constantly coached Fernando on landing the fish. We could not believe our eyes when we saw a beautiful, dark blue sailfish break the surface of the water. Sailfish are not large but are much more beautiful than swordfish.

The fish was landed but never actually removed from the water. They installed a tag in the sailfish's sail and released him after pictures were taken. The records of that tag were sent to a conservation organization with Fernando's name, and the picture that was taken of the fish. If that fish is caught again, the tag number is reported to that organization, and Fernando will be notified that his fish was caught a second time, with the current size of the fish and the location where the fish was caught. I took numerous photos of Fernando while fighting the fish. I was just as excited for him as he was, but also a bit jealous!

**FERNANDO AND HIS BEAUTIFUL SAILFISH**

## Chamber dewatering and lock gate repairs

My next visit to Panama was to witness a dewatering of one of the lock chambers. This was one of the most exciting and interesting jobs in my entire career. My freshly repaired emergency caisson was being used for the first time to seal off one end of the chamber (lock gates still in place on the other end), and then they removed and replaced both existing lock gates with two refurbished gates. The old lock gates were then transferred to the shipyard in Colon to be rebuilt. After witnessing the installation of the caisson, the dewatering of the lock chamber, and the removal of the old gates, we examined the pintle balls (lower hinge) at the bottom of each gate when they were removed.

The pintle ball is mounted solidly in the concrete at the bottom of the lock gate, and the gate has a mating socket that fits perfectly over the pintle ball. Because much of the weight of these lock gates is supported by flotation, the pressure on the pintle is greatly reduced. Each lock gate can weigh more than 1.5 million pounds (varies depending on gate height), but because the gates partially float much of the time, the effective weight on the pintle is less.

The top hinge is much more conventional, with a shaft at the top of the gate, and a bushing bearing mounted securely into the concrete at the top of the lock chamber. Because this bushing and hinge are not underwater, it is easier to maintain.

**OLD PINTLE BALL**     **NEW PINTLE BALL**

The sills of the lock Gates (the concrete bottom where the rubber seals stop leakage) and the seals around the gate sides, and where the two gates meet, were being rebuilt, and the pintle balls (bottom hinge bearing point) were being replaced. I also witnessed the overhaul of the hydraulic operating machinery and watched some of the concrete repairs in the lock chamber as well.

**THAT'S ME, LOOKING BUSY IN DEWATERED LOCK CHAMBER**

There were a total of seven trips to Panama during the 1999-2000 transfer of the Lock from United States control to Panamanian control. Some visits were one week while others lasted over two weeks long. I was working on behalf of the Panamanian Government, and my reports showed the United States-controlled Panama Canal Commission (PCC) what needed to be repaired before the Panama-controlled ACP (Authority de Canal de Panama) took over the Canal and Locks.

LOCK CHAMBER NEARLY PUMPED DRY

Many people thought the Panamanians would not be able to run the Canal without the help of the United States. In fact, Panama learned "what NOT to do" by observing the waste and lack of maintenance during the 85 years of U.S. control. At 11:59 PM on December 31, 1999, the new ACP took control and fired every PCC employee. Then, at 00:01 on 1 January 2000, they rehired approximately 60% of those employees. The remaining 40% were considered over-staffing by the United States. Those U.S. citizens who wanted to remain at the Canal, such as the Pilots, were offered dual citizenship, and most of those employees stayed. The "proof is in the pudding," because the Canal is operating at a profit with only 60% of the original employees, and the maintenance has been excellent.

GATUN LOCKS CONTROL TOWER

In 15 years, the new ACP operated at a profit (the U.S. never did) and the ACP made enough money to finance the new, larger locks, and to widen and deepen the Canal for much larger ships. This accomplishment is a huge improvement because the Canal traffic is limited by the amount of rainwater collected in Gatun Lake. To increase the ship size, the Panamanians had to develop a means to conserve water from one lock chamber, to be used in the next. If you want to see how they did that, there are excellent articles written about their ingenious design. The rumor was spread that Panama had sold the rights to the canal to China, but this is false. China bought the railroad that runs between Panama City and

Colon and owns a cargo terminal at each end of the railroad, but they do NOT control the Lock.

**FERNANDO SUCRE NEXT TO ME, ON THE LEFT**

On what would be my last visit to Panama, I decided to take my daughter, Claire, to Panama as a reward for her excellent finish to her high school career. I had told Claire she may be spending a lot of time at the hotel while I was working, but as it turned out, my Panamanian friends arranged for one of their daughters to act as a guide for Claire during her stay.

**LOCK GATE 'SILL' REPAIRS AT GATUN**

One day, after my workday, my "Panamanian boss" asked if we would like to take a tour of the tunnels beneath the lock chamber. I was not quite sure what to expect but wanted to see everything possible while at the lock. He offered to take my daughter, Claire, along on this inspection, and she still remembers the experience. We descended into the tunnels, which was a very eerie experience. While walking nearly 100 feet beneath the surface of Gatun Lake, my friend pointed to a large steel panel and asked me if I remembered inspecting it. Those panels were the bulkheads I had inspected and commented on due to their poor welding technique. My friend said that they had been repaired according to my instructions and apparently, they were doing a good job, otherwise, we might be running for our lives. It did make me see how important some of my decisions had been during my visits to Panama over those two years.

CAISSON IN USE AT GATUN LOCKS

After that inspection, I told Fernando I wanted Claire to see the ships locking through the Gatun Locks, and asked if we could take her to the observation deck which overlooked the lock. He promised me that we would get to Gatun after lunch, but he seemed to be delaying. When we arrived, I began to head towards the observation deck, but Fernando continued past the platform and continued toward the lock gates, where we crossed the chamber. We went to the control house between the two lock chambers, and then he took us up into the control tower, which was something I had never been allowed to do in the past. I then understood the delay in going to Gatun, because Fernando had been arranging this visit with Operations.

One of the lock operators explained how the locks operate to Claire and me and then told Claire that she was going to lock through the next ship. Although he stood over her shoulder and observed every move she made, Claire locked a ship through the Gatun Locks. He would tell her which lever to push and then instruct her to go outside and observe that the lock gate was

MY DAUGHTER, CLAIRE, AT AN OLD PANAMA FORTRESS

closing before coming back to the controls and performing the next

116

necessary action. I was very impressed that they allowed Claire to make this lockage, which is normally reserved for heads of state and other dignitaries. (I never got to do that, but the Latin nature was to treat a pretty girl better than an old surveyor!)

## Survey of damage due to ship striking

After my job was completed in 2000, I did not expect to return to Panama, but in 2001, an attorney from New Orleans contacted me and asked me to survey the damage to one of the lock gates at the Panama Canal, caused by a ship strike. The ship had struck one of the lock gates when the engine controls onboard the ship failed and the ship was unable to stop. The shipping company was being sued for multimillions of dollars to repair the damage to the lock gate, machinery, and seals. So, my attendance at the dewatering of the lock chamber, and removal of the gate, was needed to verify any damages that were claimed by the Panama Canal.

I explained my previous work with the Panamanians during the 1999 to 2000 changeover to the attorney and asked if this would be a conflict. He explained to me that my services had been recommended as an expert by someone at the Panama Canal Commission (PCC, now called the ACP after the transfer to Panama). I agreed to take the job and again made a trip to Panama for this dewatering of the lock chamber. Although I was technically working on the opposite side from my Panamanian friends, it was obvious that we remained friends and they cooperated during my inspections.

I returned to the United States and submitted my report to the attorney, detailing the damages that had been observed, and those alleged damages which I did not see or agree with. Some of the quoted repair costs were far above the cost of commercial repairs, and my opinion on fair and reasonable repair costs was also included in my report.

As expected, I was required to make another trip to Panama to give a deposition!

The deposition was taken at the offices of the Panama Canal, and upon entering the room, there was a large audience of engineers and other Panama Canal staff employees, who had been instructed to attend the deposition. The attorneys for the Panama Canal were trying to create an adversarial condition by having my friends in that audience, which seemed to immediately backfire. The moment I entered the room, three people stood up, hugged me, and asked me how my family was doing. It was then that the Panamanian attorneys understood that they had lost any advantage they had sought to make me nervous during the deposition.

During the deposition, I had to make several statements contradicting the statements and decisions made by my previous Panamanian work team. The opposing lawyer asked, "Are you saying that your friend is a liar?" I replied, "He's not lying, but he is definitely mistaken." I saw the smile on my friend's face and knew that he understood. He surely had been instructed to use the highest repair values possible, knowing full well that the legal system would reduce any award that might be made.

In case you are wondering what the results of the lawsuit against the ship that struck the lock gate were, it was determined that the total insured value of the ship that caused the damage was less than $2 million, and that was the maximum that could be paid to the Panama Canal. The case was settled before trial for an undisclosed sum. Such are the weird twists and turns of the maritime legal system.

## Comments on Panama

I found the Panamanian people to be very warm and friendly, and because they were used to working with Americans during the many years the United States was in charge of the Canal, they understood American culture and generally spoke excellent English.

My work in Panama was well after the days of Noriega, but many of the Noriega policies were still being used. This did not directly affect the Panama Canal operations, but the workers at the Canal were citizens of Panama, so their lives were still affected.

During the U.S. invasion of Panama to capture Noriega, my college friend, who lived in Panama for years, was involved due to the location of his house. He lived on Ancon Hill, overlooking Noriega's headquarters, so the U.S. Military took over his home as an observation post. Once Noriega's troops figured out what was happening, they started shooting at his house, and he still proudly displayed the bullet holes in his roof, shot from below!

My friend owned a Panamanian construction business and had Panamanian employees, but the laws in Panama protected the workers, to the extreme detriment of the business owner. Due to the turmoil in Panama during those times, my friend had to lay off his employees, but the unemployment laws said he was required to pay them their wages until they found another job. The employees either had a hard time finding work or figured, "Why find work when I am getting paid." My friend finally went bankrupt, so he started a new business in Belize, to avoid this problem in the future.

The Panama Canal Commission offices were located in Balboa, near Panama City, on the Pacific side of the Canal. Panama City was modern and had numerous hotels and fancy restaurants. Because of the invasion of Panama by the United States to arrest Noriega, there had been a large change in the economic structure of Panama and many of the poor citizens were suffering greatly. There were many beggars on the streets, and many of them had serious physical deformities which some people stated were caused by the Noriega secret police, while others stated their parents purposely deformed their young children so they could become "better" street beggars.

Although the President of Panama during my visits (Mireya Elisa Moscoso Rodriguez de Arias) was trying to repair the relationship with the United States, her predecessor had demanded the United States also vacate all military bases in addition to the Canal Zone properties. The military had already left Panama before my visits, but within two years of my visits to Panama, many of the fancy restaurants were closing and some of the hotels were also failing.

What the Panamanian Government had failed to realize was that the hotels and restaurants were being used by the American military and their families and that the loss of this business was creating an economic crisis. Although the new Panamanian President eventually requested the United States military to return, it was not possible because the United States had built new bases elsewhere in the Caribbean. The vacated military housing was expected to be purchased by local Panamanians for large sums of money, but due to the high unemployment rate in Panama, few people could afford it at that time. However, the economy has improved in recent years.

And although the problems in Panama City were noticeable, the condition of Colon, on the Atlantic side, was much worse. The unemployment rate often exceeded 50% in Colon, and the crime rate was terrible. Because some of my work was on the Atlantic side during several of my visits, I had offered to stay at a hotel in Colon, but my "Panamanian boss" refused to expose me to potential crime over there. We would occasionally go out for lunch while working at the Colon shipyard, but they would never let me go out on my own.

The distance between Panama City and Colon is approximately 36 miles, but Google says it is a two-hour drive, which tells you something about the trip! The highway was in excellent condition during my visits, but much of the highway does go through a dense jungle and tends to flood during the rainy season. Although I never saw any large wildlife, it is reportedly common to see a Black Panther or other jungle animals along the road. My friends told me to use my cell phone to call for assistance and never to set foot outside the car if I ever experienced car trouble.

The roadside vendors along this highway were very friendly, particularly those selling coconuts on the high bridge over the Chagres River. If they had allowed me to remain living in the Panama Canal housing areas, fresh fish from those vendors would have been great, cooked in my own kitchen. However, after my first few visits to Panama, they moved me to the El Panama Hotel. El Panama is one of the better hotels in Panama City, which has a beautiful outdoor pool where you can sit at the bar while remaining in the pool.

Across the parking lot from this hotel was a souvenir shop that sold locally made crafts, including beautiful Indian molas. Molas are the decoration on the front of the local Cuna (coon-yah) Indian ladies' blouses (mola means blouse), and they are very detailed fabric artwork, which has become popular with tourists. The lady who owned this souvenir shop encouraged the Indian women to produce their original, high-quality molas, and not to reduce their quality to sell cheap souvenirs to the tourists. Because I showed a sincere interest in the higher quality molas, this lady saved many of them for me to purchase during my visits. Because of tourist interest, molas were being used as decorations on shopping bags and other tourist items at the airports and souvenir shops around Panama City.

CATS ARE A FAVORITE SUBJECT ON MOLAS          A MAN, HANDLING TWO HORSES

TWO EXAMPLES OF CHILDREN'S MOLAS

The food in Panama was very South American and not at all spicy. In fact, it was a real treat for the Panamanians to eat Mexican food at several restaurants in Panama City because Mexican food and other spicy foods were not typical in Panamanian cuisine. They have a wonderful chicken soup, sancocho, made with yucca that is extremely tasty. They also have very good ceviche, but even they admitted the ceviche in Colombia and Peru was much better. One of the more unusual meals I ate in Panama was octopus cooked in its own ink. It tasted very good, but my mouth was blackened for the next 24 hours.

I have not been able to stay in close contact with my Panamanian friends. However, I was pleased to meet Fernando, my "Panamanian boss", at a Lock & Dam Maintenance Conference in Kentucky, while I worked for the Army Corps of Engineers several years ago. At that time, Fernando told me one of the young ACP Engineers, Jorge Quijano, whom I had worked with and liked a lot, had just been promoted to Chief Executive Officer for the Panama Canal.

The ships in the background, behind the bridge, in the following photo of the Canal, and during a bad El Nino year, the lines get very long, due to the lack of rainfall, which supplies water to Gatun Lake. Locks do NOT have pumps, as many people believe. All of the water is gravity-fed from the water at higher elevations. When the level in Gatun Lake is low, the number of lockages must be limited. This is why the new locks in Panama use a system that conserves water usage.

'BRIDGE OF THE AMERICAS' BETWEEN NORTH & SOUTH AMERICA

Panama has a lot of great natural beauty. I never had an opportunity to get far from Panama City & Colon, but I understand that the "Vulcán" region is remarkable. We saw some of the Pacific side beaches, which were quite beautiful, and of course, I did get those two fishing trips out to the Pacific Islands off of Panama City. Several Spanish forts can be visited within 30 minutes of Panama City. I sure would like to see more of Panama, with the assistance of a Private Guide, who really knows the remote areas and can do it safely.

# CHAPTER 11

## SEVEN GREAT WEEKS IN UKRAINE

In October and November 2005, I was again chosen by ABS to survey 77 Government vessels operated by the Ukraine Marine Border Guard, which is similar to our United States Coast Guard, but also has more border patrol responsibility. The United States was helping to improve their ships to detect potential terrorist activity, but they wanted an experienced Marine Surveyor to assess the structural and mechanical condition of those Ukrainian vessels.

My apprehension about the visit was to be expected because of all the bad "Press" about Ukraine since the breakup of the Soviet Union. As with many things, you cannot hand something to a person who has never had it before (in this case, Capitalism) and expect them to immediately know how to use it properly. That seems to be the case in Ukraine, as well as other ex-Soviet countries. One Ukrainian told me the only people in Ukraine who were prepared for Capitalism were those in the "Mafia." They had been using Capitalism for their benefit during Communism, and now the Mafia just become more profitable.

When Ukrainian ships visited the Great Lakes, one got the feeling that things were not going well back home. We would see shiploads of rail coming into Chicago, and we thought it was being manufactured and sold to American railroads. It was shocking to hear from the ship's Captain that it was being sold as scrap from Ukraine railroads which were going out of business. The Captain said that the next thing that might happen was to tear up the rail on the rail lines, and then you wonder what would happen to Ukraine's economy, as their railroads would be needed for growth in their new Capitalist economy. These and other ship crews from Ukraine would tell me they felt guilty eating three meals a day on the ships when they knew that their families back home were not eating even two meals some days.

## First Trip

I arrived in Odesa (Odessa is the Russian version), Ukraine, in mid-October 2005. As had become too standard on my trips to Europe, my baggage did not arrive. The European airlines could not be blamed this time (Malev, the national airline of Hungary, was wonderful on all three occasions) but United Airlines never transferred the bags during my layover in Frankfurt. Malev promised to have them delivered the next day, and they arrived on schedule, just 24 hours late. Doing some laundry in the hotel room the first night, and luckily, carrying a spare set of underwear, socks, toothbrush, deodorant, etc. in my carry-on bag, helped to reduce the stress. This was a better result than previous trips on Air France, where my bags were delayed 3 weeks **after returning home**, and on another instance after only three days, but the bags had been "inspected" and two bottles of expensive perfume were missing.

Back to telling you about Odesa; because of the lost bags, I was "trapped" inside the Customs inspection area, filling out lost baggage forms. The Ukrainians were very nice and polite, but it became obvious the language barrier would be a big problem during this trip. I was trying to explain that my client was meeting me outside, and we somehow needed to contact the people in the waiting area. I was getting nowhere. The hotel information was in an E-Mail on my computer, but even that information did not include phone numbers, or how to contact the clients. Even though my cell phone would work in Odesa, we didn't have their cell phone numbers. Without speaking Ukrainian, I was afraid the client would leave, thinking I had missed my flight.

Finally, I pulled out a letter from my client, but it only contained information on their head office in Kyiv, not Odesa. With some sign language and the help of another passenger with lost luggage, the Malev representative took my letter to the waiting area and came back with my client's representative, who turned out to be one of the company's drivers, Sasha. Sasha only spoke a few words of English, but he knew my name and was able to give Malev the information they needed, so he was able to get us past Customs.

During the departure through Customs, the first of many examples of the "old guard" way of thinking occurred. I was carrying my carry-on luggage over my shoulder, and the customs officer seemed to be upset. Sasha motioned for me to place my luggage on the table, so I thought the official wanted to inspect the contents. As I started to open the bags, Sasha again motioned for me to stop, and he helped me carry my bags out of the Customs area. It turns out that the Customs official was insulted by my assumption that he would not inspect the bags, though he had no intention of making an actual inspection. I had unknowingly shown disrespect for his position of authority.

Sasha took me outside, where another of my client's representatives was waiting. He apologized for not coming inside. He said it was because only one person could go in to help me, and he was also an American, with limited Ukrainian language skills, so he decided to let Sasha go in, which appeared to be the correct decision.

Most of the people on this project were Ukrainians who had been hired by this "major" American government contractor. About half of the Ukrainians spoke English, and most of the Americans were ex-military and ex-government employees with fluent Russian language skills. The Russian language is very close to Ukrainian, so the Russian-speaking Americans did very well, but the company used several full-time Ukrainian translators for all official business. It turned out that the Ukrainians in Western Ukraine did NOT appreciate working with Russians, and they would speak to Russians strictly in the Ukraine language to show their dislike for the Russians. In Eastern Ukraine, the opposite was true, which became apparent several years later, when Russia moved back into the Crimean Peninsula, which is in Eastern Ukraine, near the Russian border.

The drivers, like Sasha, Edik, and two others, who were part of our "team," were extremely friendly guys. Except for one who also happened to have minimal English skills. We were thankful for the drivers, as the streets in Odesa, and the roads in all of Ukraine were falling apart or had been torn up for "long-term" repairs. You would never find your way to the office from the hotel by yourself, so when I worked at the office, they sent a driver to pick me up each morning and return me to the hotel at the end of the work day. There were no direct routes, due to construction, one-way streets, and daily detours due to accidents, parades, demonstrations, etc. Until one started to learn a little about the Cyrillic Alphabet, one could not pronounce the street names. So, if a non-Ukrainian was lost and called for help, they could not tell anyone where they were located, because of the Cyrillic language street names. (I'm on a street with a long name, starting with a backward "R" or some Greek letter that I can't remember!)

We had a team of four making these inspections. The leader was a retired Naval Officer, Oleg, who was a wonderful man. He was very dedicated to the project and, although he did not speak English, it soon became apparent that he understood most of what was said. It also became obvious Oleg LOVED Ukraine and hated the Soviet Union! We had a translator who was a young Ukrainian Air Force officer who had lost his job due to the break-up with the Soviet Union. He was a nice enough man, but still a bit anti-American in his attitude. Many times, the translator would tell me something in English and Oleg would reprimand him in Ukrainian, following which, the translator then gave a much better English translation. One time, while taking a photo of a nuclear power station, the translator stopped me. Oleg reprimanded him forcefully, and the translator said it was OK to take the photos. Oleg again reprimanded him, and then the translation became, "Oleg told me the Cold War was over, and we no longer need to hide our power stations." Obviously, Oleg understood English very well!

**OLEG IN THE BACK, THE TRANSLATOR ON THE LEFT, AND OUR DRIVER, EDIK ON THE RIGHT**

From this point forward, when you hear, "Oleg said…..," it means, through our translator.

The fourth member of our team was the Ukrainian driver. They were wonderful and will be mentioned often in the following stories.

We spent about half of my first trip in Odesa, working with the office staff on logistics, reporting requirements, and learning the history behind this project. The largest portion of the fleet we were to inspect was also located in Odesa, as well as the shipyard that made repairs for the ships in Western Ukraine.

**PART OF THE ODESA FLEET OF BORDER GUARD**

Most of my free time was spent at my hotel because the client was concerned about safety after dark. The job in Odesa went very well, but other than a couple of great social events with some of the other Americans working there, it was difficult to venture out very often, except to a nearby park. The local ladies marketed locally made craft items, such as carvings and excellent quality tatted lace items, which made great souvenirs.

The other Americans had been in Ukraine for several years, and they helped me learn to appreciate the great Ukrainian food. Even the cafeteria food at lunch was fantastic, where everyone was expected to order borscht. I was trying to avoid Borscht because of previous terrible experiences with it on Russian freighters. After my first time eating Ukrainian borscht, it became a daily ritual. Ukrainian Borscht was fantastic, unlike the Russian variety, which is like red, salty water!

The hotel for my first stay in Odesa was across the street from a very impressive old building, which looked like a City Hall. Every day of the week, couples dressed up in beautiful white dresses (like in America), and men always in a tuxedo went into that building with just a few others, probably parents, judging from the ages. He would emerge a little later and would then always go to several of the same spots around that square to take photos, and then leave. Weddings are not the big social affairs there like they are in America. They seemed to want those wedding photos to be like what they had seen in some American movie, but in some cases, the dresses and tuxedos may just have been rented for that short ceremony and the photos. They might have friends and family attend a small party at their home, but I never learned those details. (In a 2019 visit, I was told the dresses were owned.)

**ODESA WEDDING PARTIES**

## Odesa Concert Hall

Many women in Ukraine, other than the poor and homeless, were dressed in clothes we would only see in high-fashion magazines. We surmised they saw those clothes in magazines and wanted to dress like American women, or at least how they thought American women dressed. Some of them went to work looking like fashion runway models. They probably did not realize that very few Americans dressed the way they saw in those magazines. None of us complained about their appearance, however. Who could even explain that most Americans seldom dress that way?

There were homeless children everywhere on the streets of Odesa in those days (it seemed much better in 2019). Most appeared unbathed for months. They recognized foreigners easily so we were constantly being hounded for handouts when we were out on the street. The Ukrainians on my team saw me having a hard time refusing them, so they suggested carrying small Ukrainian coins to give away. The children would get upset by the small coins, but they would take them and leave. One night, while alone and walking back to the hotel after dinner (against the wishes of my Ukrainian team), I ran out of small coins, so I gave one boy a $1 bill. The previous child, who had only received the Ukraine coin, came running back and despite his poor English, made it clear that he also wanted an American $1 bill. He actually returned the Ukrainian coin in exchange for the $1. I'm an easy touch!

One of our drivers spoke much better English than the others, and it turned out he had gone to college, and studied Hospitality Services. He had been in the hotel business for a while. I asked why he left that line of work and he said he never got paid. He saw the quizzical look on my face and explained that the successful hotels in Ukraine were run by Mafia or ex-government people, and they hired people to work at the front desk, or in their restaurants, but always made excuses for not being able to pay their salaries. They paid room maids because they were harder to replace. The hospitality staff was easily replaced because everyone wanted to get into the hospitality profession, thinking the money was good! Little did they know, until they had to leave and find other work. I suggested to this guy that he send his credentials to the various cruise lines because they always wanted experienced people with great personal skills. I hope he followed through on the suggestion because he had exactly what the cruise lines liked.

This hotel non-payment problem came to my attention after dinner one night at my hotel restaurant. While signing the dinner bill for my room, I added a tip to the gratuity line on the bill. The waiter spoke some English and asked me what that was. I told him it was his gratuity, and he told me the waiters did not get that money. The hotel manager took it for himself.

This was verified with Oleg the next day, and he agreed this was typical in the larger hotels. From that time forward, I always handed cash tips directly to waiters in all the restaurants I ate at during my time in Ukraine.

## **<u>WOW! Izmayil!</u>**

We did make a very interesting trip from Odesa to Izmayil (also Izmail), which is the Western-most city in the South of Ukraine. It is on the Dunay River (Danube to us Westerners). While we worked at the Border Guard base, the view directly across the river was in Romania. It was just a typical riverfront, so it was difficult to see much of Romania at the time (but I did see it on a later trip).

The drive to Izmayil required us to drive through Moldova, which at the time was known to be the poorest country in Europe! This is not the Romanian Province of Moldovia, but an independent country. Moldova is landlocked, with no access to the Black Sea. The portion of Ukraine that surrounds the southern border of Moldova is the Dunay Delta area, which is mostly wetlands, with no roads, so driving through Moldova was necessary to reach Izmayil. We stopped at an area filled with tents and open tables after crossing the border, where local farmers and merchants were selling produce and canned goods. The farmers mostly used horse or donkey-drawn carts, some of which were old, wooded style, but many of them were abandoned car chassis that they had rigged to be pulled by the horse. The prices were about half of what was charged in Ukraine, so the Ukraine members of the team stocked up on fruits and wine. I bought some wine myself to drink at the hotel, and the wine was excellent. Moldovan wine is now available in the United States. (The border crossing was still there in 2019, but cleaned up.)

While stopped at that border crossing, we all used the "restroom." The ceramic "holes in the ground" are common in many countries, like Mexico, Japan, and, even to this day, Italy. However, this time was a REAL EXPERIENCE! The facility was in what we would call an outhouse, but it had not been cleaned in YEARS! You could not even approach the hole without standing in years of waste. Visitors refused to do that, so they started to use any clean area in the building, making the entire building unsanitary.

Oleg said we should wait to clean the fruit when we reached the hotel. I did not have to ask why, because I saw the dirty hands of the vendors at the market, and also noted there was no running water near the toilet, so Oleg's comment was understood by all of us.

MAIN ORTHODOX CATHEDRAL IN IZMAYIL

Our hotel near Izmayil was a small, family-owned place that was extremely friendly. They knew Oleg, so the owner treated us to a free drink in the bar. We also ate a wonderful dinner at the hotel on that first night. Because Oleg knew the people with whom we would be working in Izmayil, we ate lunch and dinner at several fantastic restaurants, serving traditional Ukrainian food. The team was amazed when I tried everything put in front of me, even though their explanation was not understood. Other than some less appetizing egg dishes for breakfast, there were no bad meals during the entire seven weeks I spent in Ukraine. Vodka was always part of dinner meals!

We spent our work days inspecting ships, but we also had to attend one or two meetings each day to discuss my findings. Because Oleg and the Ukraine Border Guard officers needed to discuss things in private, the driver, the translator, and I were sometimes told to take time to tour Izmayil. Maybe because this area was so isolated from the rest of Ukraine, and because it had originally been a Turkish city, it had a very different "feel" to it. Izmayil is one of my favorite cities in Ukraine, because of how different it was. It was still poor, with very few streetlights in working order, and many homeless children on the streets, but the old Turkish, ethnic background was still evident. Izmayil does not have the kind of beautiful stone buildings found in Odesa, but the architecture was still striking, even on a smaller scale. (Again, conditions had improved in 2019.)

One day we visited the Russian-Turkish War Museum, which had several large spectacular murals showing the battle between Russian and Turkish troops when Russia drove the Turks out of Ukraine. The museum was simple, but spectacular in its own way.

**SEVERAL HUGE MURALS DEPICTING OTTOMAN WAR**

**THE ORIGINAL ARM PATCH**

**ENTIRE UKRAINE COLLECTION**

Another day, I commented on the very beautiful arm patch worn on the uniforms of the sailors at Izmayil and requested permission to take a photograph of the patch. On the day we left, Oleg said we had to stop at the main detachment office for one last meeting, which he attended without the rest of us. The man whose patch I had photographed, came out with Oleg and gave me an arm patch as well as a uniform hat insignia, tie clasp, and lapel pin. I was thrilled and tried to pay him. As expected, he refused to take my money. These guys all really loved it when they were complimented on anything. They're proud of their country and appreciated the sincere interest we showed during our visits.

## <u>Second Trip</u>

Traveling to Europe is always full of surprises. On my first trip, it was lost bags (United's fault) but Malev Airlines retrieved them quickly. On this trip, the Lufthansa flight left Chicago 90 minutes late due to a big wind storm in Chicago, causing a missed connection in Munich by just 10 minutes. There were 12 of us going to Trieste (I was making a quick side trip to Croatia), and the plane only holds 39 people, so you'd think they would have held the plane. But instead, they rebooked all of us. Thank God for my Croatian driver who had come to pick me up in Trieste, driving all the way to Venice so I would not waste the entire day. He knew I was leaving Croatia the same day, and he was getting paid for a round trip.

Later that evening, my driver was taking me back to Trieste, where I had booked a hotel near the airport. I was dozing in the passenger seat, realizing my good fortune. Driving a rental car through the Slovenian mountain roads, and the crazy Italian streets of Trieste, while suffering jet lag, would have been very dangerous. The Chicago joke about two seasons, Winter and Construction, also applies to Italy. Several highway detours had us on city streets which would have had me lost, but the experienced driver earned his pay that day. This Croatian driver was a sailor, who spent his time at home running a taxi service, and he is considered a "friend," not just a driver. What a great guy! When we got to my hotel, he only wanted to charge me for our original agreed price, and not the additional drive to and from Venice. I gave him 50% additional (he had spent 12 hours driving for me, round trip), and he tried not to take it. There are certainly some great, honest people left in this world!

The trip from Trieste to Munich, then Budapest, and on to Odesa, Ukraine, was very uneventful. Malev Airlines (Hungarian National Airline) is great and has the best safety record in Europe (and the world, at that time), plus one of the lowest baggage loss records in the world. They feed you on each leg of the flight, even though it may be just a sandwich. I joined their Frequent Flier Program, and try to fly with them whenever possible. They connect through Budapest, from Ljubljana, Slovenia, which is only 90 minutes from my house in Buzet, Croatia. From Budapest, Malev flies to Toronto, London, Helsinki, Beijing, Bangkok, and most major cities in Europe.

So, back to Ukraine: Ukraine is much like driving through Iowa or Indiana. Miles and miles of unbroken fields of corn stubble or winter wheat, but the weird thing is all the sunflowers, which we didn't see in the U.S. Midwest at that time. The big difference from the U.S. is the lack of fences in Ukraine. Fenced fields are used nowhere, as witnessed during a 9-hour drive of nearly 450 miles. The cows are all tended by men and/or dogs, all day long. Dairy cattle were all we saw, though they may have had beef cattle elsewhere.

The other different thing was the total lack of houses, farms, towns, or service stations along the highway, particularly in Eastern Ukraine. There are signs for cities (old Communes) along the highway, but those are located miles off the main road. The few Communes seen along the road had maybe 100-150 small houses (poor, but beautifully kept), and those people were taken to work each day. Unlike the U.S., where each farm is individually owned, the old Communist "Communes" were just workers, working on the land for the government. They were run by a Commissar, who planned their every move. The workers were not allowed to make any decisions on their own. Now, the government is selling the land, but only big corporations (many are Mafia-owned, Oleg said) have the money to buy them, so the people are still on the Communes, working for someone else.

Some Communes looked beautiful, with the crops being harvested. In other Communes, the crops were blackened in the field, even though the small houses lived in by the workers, were inhabited and well kept. Oleg explained this difference, and he said after the Commissar left, nobody bought this Commune, so the workers did not harvest the crops and they would probably not plant again unless a Mafia Company or government officials bought the farm. As he explained, "They spent almost 100 years being told what to do: when to plow, when to plant, and when to harvest. With nobody here now to tell them what to do, they're afraid to think for themselves, because they were never allowed to do that in the past." I could tell that Oleg was concerned for their future.

We drove one stretch where we saw nothing for over an hour. If you have a car problem in winter, you'd be in real danger. Although we saw 10-speed traps around the cities, we never saw a single policeman in those rural areas. The police were NOT there to "serve and protect" but to make money.

The roads are terrible in Ukraine. Our driver, Edik, was fantastic. The drive was comfortable enough to try to sleep, though you could not lay your head against the window, or even the seat, because of the constant bumps. The bad roads are both a joke and yet loved by the Ukrainians. I usually sat behind Edik, and on these long trips, I started to massage his neck and shoulders. He was tense from gripping the wheel so tightly. I asked the translator to ask Edik if he wanted me to stop the massage, and Edik said, "Please continue," and he began purring like a cat whenever he got my massages.

When our plane landed in Odesa on each trip, the runway also had the same potholes and bumps, and the passengers started to laugh as we landed and then applauded. My seatmate explained what was going on, and he said, "We've missed our bad Ukrainian roads. Now we know we are home!" The Ukrainians seem to treat problems and hardships with a joke or a smile!

We made a detour into one of only two major cities along the way, to get some lunch, and the potholes in the roads were so bad, we drove about 2 MPH for the 3-4 miles into the city. This city is near a major power plant, and all the factories in sight were closed. That was typical for Ukraine at that time. They have suffered the most after the breakup of the USSR. Mariupol has two large steel mills, but they are not doing well. The Germans had just purchased their largest steel mill, near Kyiv.

The last 90 minutes of our drive that night was in dense fog (nearing the Azov Sea, North of the Black Sea) and the temperature had fallen to 40 degrees Fahrenheit. Again, Edik was fantastic, but the fog was so bad, we had to stop at intersections to try to read the signs. Edik was purring a lot that night because he needed frequent massage therapy!

We checked into a great hotel named the European Hotel in Mariupol. We were close to the Russian border on the Northeast corner of the Azov Sea. We looked at four vessels there and then drove to Kerch, on the narrow channel that connects the Azov Sea to the Black Sea. You can see Russia across the strait. There we had eight vessels to inspect during our two-day stay. Our Guide, Oleg, had a friend living there, whose brother had a restaurant where we ate dinner. They swapped old "Ukrainian sailor stories", and it was very enjoyable, despite the language problem. It is fun to watch old friends having a good time, drinking vodka (at twice my rate), and laughing with each other. Some things do not need a translation.

In Kerch, Oleg told me to "watch their uniforms to see how we were being received!" Oleg's statement went over my head! We all sat in the opening meeting, which was conducted in Russian, and therefore, I understood nothing. The meeting abruptly ended and Oleg motioned for us to leave the room. We were not going to inspect these vessels at Kerch, and we had been asked to leave their base. Oleg made a final statement with some obvious irritation, which was not typical for him. We had been so warmly received elsewhere that I was surprised by this strange development.

After leaving, Oleg asked if I had noticed the uniforms worn by the officers in that meeting. I had not noticed and was not sure why he had told me about that before the meeting. Oleg told me the officers were still wearing the Hammer & Sickle, showing their allegiance to Russia, and the Hammer & Sickle were not allowed to be worn in Ukraine any longer. Those officers were basically "thumbing their noses" at me, and the United States. I was too naive to have noticed.

Then Oleg detailed what he had told the officers as we were leaving, and he said, "I told them, Bob is here to give American Government money to help fix your ships, but if he does not make his inspection, YOU will not get any money!" Oleg told me, we would go to lunch and see what happens. Sure enough, during lunch, Oleg received a call asking us to return and that we could inspect their ships! The return trip after lunch was much more cordial, but this time I did still notice the Hammer and Sickle on a few uniforms, but Oleg said most had been removed. When we left, one of the younger officers gave me one of the Hammer & Sickle pins as a souvenir!

Then we headed to Sebastopol, near Yalta, on the Crimean Peninsula, where that famous WWII conference took place with Stalin, Churchill, and Roosevelt. We spent three days there before we headed back to Odesa for two days.

Near Yalta, we stopped at a famous church, built high on a cliff overlooking the Black Sea. Tsar Nicholas built the church as a thank you for his family surviving a terrible railroad accident on their trip to Crimea. The rich Russians loved to come to the Black Sea for some warm weather and sandy beaches. The church is beautiful, and it was my opportunity to see my Eastern Orthodox travel partners show their religious side. It was a great experience.

**TSAR NICHOLAS CHURCH**

The food in Ukraine is wonderful and I've probably said that before in this story! You've never seen so many great fish dishes. The beef is tough but nicely prepared, their chicken is cooked in garlic sauces and fresh herbs and is wonderful, and they prepare wonderful salads, far beyond my previous experiences. Every plate has fresh green herbs on it, and not for decoration, but to be eaten. Fresh dill and parsley were somehow served at every meal, as well as tomato and cucumbers on every plate. One day near Yalta, they served fresh local fish, grilled and served with a garlic sauce with crawfish tails, plus fried rice and garnishes, all for about $6.00. The average restaurant menu has about 20 pages, and some are larger. An eater's paradise! As I explained earlier, borscht experienced on Russian ships in the past, was not worth eating, but Ukrainian borscht is rich and wonderfully spiced, with a large dollop of sour cream in the middle. You will never have a bad borscht in Ukraine.

Breakfast was always included in the hotel price, and was typically a buffet with lots of variety. The Europeans eat cheese and cold cuts, with tomatoes and cucumbers, and sometimes fresh salmon (grav-lox), but the local egg dishes were "interesting," though not very American. The Ukrainians usually have fried or grilled fish at breakfast, which is great. I always try to eat things that are different from what I eat at home, otherwise one could just stay home, right?

It was good to have experienced Crimea, because now that Russia has "taken it back," it is difficult to get there.

**YOUNG UKRAINIAN SAILORS ON ONE OF THE SHIPS WE INSPECTED**

The sailors were all extremely friendly and cooperative (except in the East, where the officers were still pro-Russian). Notice in the above photo how old and faded the uniforms appear. The enlisted men wore their best uniforms for my visits. Oleg, my guide, told me these young sailors were not paid any salary, which seemed unbelievable. Why would they stay without pay? Well, their parents did not have enough food at home to feed the entire family, so these young men stayed in the military to have two meals of cabbage, beets, bread, and potatoes each day. If they wanted meat, the ships all had fishing poles for them to fish. Some ships occasionally had pork fat to flavor their soup. Of course, they also had a warm place to sleep.

The officers were paid a salary and their uniforms looked in better condition. They also had one of the crews doing the cooking for them, so it appeared the officers had more food as well.

It was then on to Chicago for ten hours before heading to San Diego for another U.S. tanker environmental compliance inspection.


## <u>Third Trip</u>

To confirm some of my assumptions about what was happening in Ukraine, there was a serious discussion with some of my Ukrainian and American coworkers. I was trying to avoid embarrassment by asking questions about how poor things appeared (such as garbage piles on the streets, missing streetlights, etc.), but apparently, things were as bad as they appeared, at that time. Children on the streets had not bathed in months. Streetlights did not work on many streets in small cities, because people were pulling out the wires to sell the copper for money. (Things were definitely better in 2019.)

On this third trip, we made another 16-day journey along the Black Sea, with much longer road travel due to the terrible road conditions. The reason we returned to some ports was that these ships were active and on patrol. Those we had missed on our first visit were scheduled for inspections on our second trip. Ukraine has straight, rural highways, similar to I-80, I-90, and I-94 through the Plains States of Iowa, Minnesota, Nebraska, and the Dakotas. But we are used to roads that are safe in the 65-90 MPH speed range, at least in good weather. In Ukraine, these speeds would kill, and in a matter of an hour, you would have back and kidney damage from all the bumps. We were in a heavy, diesel Chevy Suburban, which got a lot of stares as we drove. We had to be either Mafia or some Government official!

Imagine the rough ride in a small LADA, the old USSR-built car, which was still the most common car seen at that time. Despite the poor road conditions, our drivers tried to keep a 120 km/hr. speed, just over 70 MPH (passing almost everything on the highway). In addition to the bumps, the roads were built with absolutely no concern for being level. You could look forward down the road and see the waviness on the roadway, both lengthwise and from side to side. This is not a matter of cold weather damage but must be that they had not laid a solid roadbed, such as compacted gravel or other leveling material. Our driver, Edik, was great. He stopped when he was tense or tired (despite my massages), and he kept two hands on the wheel constantly. He had to use both hands, just to keep control of the car over those bumps.

The poor truck drivers were driving at an estimated speed of 50 MPH, and they probably all had bad backs. These trucks all appear to be 1950 or at the latest, 1970-type designs. The truck may only be 10 years old, but the designs had not changed in all that time. The trucks are also very small, both the cab and the cargo capacity. There were no sleeper cabs on the road, other than some from Northern Europe. The few larger trucks we saw were NOT Ukraine-registered. Manpower was cheap here, so the old Soviet way was to keep people working, and big trucks did not do that. Now that fuel was more expensive, Ukraine was having a tough time. At that time, the average income was under $200/month, and a professional earned only $15-20,000/ year. Only the Mafia did well!

You could tell manpower was cheap, by looking at another phenomenon: the lack of fences around farm fields. It took me until the 4th or 5th hour of our drive to notice that there were no fences, with the fields running right out to the roadsides. All the cattle (and later the sheep) were being tended by men with herd dogs. This seems to be part of the remnants of the old Commune System, mentioned before.

**TYPICAL COMMUNE SIGN - SUNFLOWER**

There is always a sign, giving the name of the Commune, and having some symbol, showing the main purpose of the Commune. A great number of them were tall concrete wheat stalks or sunflowers (maybe 30 feet high) with the Commune name, and a dirt road leading to a small bunch of poor-looking houses, some more like huts, and most with thatched roofs. Others seemed to be more prosperous, particularly those with a symbol of a cow. By the way, there are fences around most of the houses, even around old "huts," to keep the cows out of their gardens, I surmised. The homes are very well-kept, and well-painted, even if they are poor. There is pride in ownership, just like anywhere. I think the homes of the poor in Ukraine proved they were not lazy or slovenly!

Numerous shepherds with maybe 20-50 sheep, were along the roadside. The small knolls along the road had been naturally terraced by hundreds of years of sheep walking on the hillsides while grazing. Later in the afternoon, you could see shepherds sitting next to a small fire, while the sheep grazed nearby. The amazing thing was the number of cow herders and their dogs, keeping track of the cows. There were also a lot of cows next to the roads. Some single cows were chained, just short of reaching the road. Otherwise, there were herds of 50-65 cattle with a herder, and these cows seemed to know that they could not cross the road. Maybe the dogs were taking care of that.

Along the road that crossed onto the Crimean Peninsula, we started to see roadside stands selling fish. Our Guide asked me if I liked dried fish. We all liked smoked fish, and he said they sold both dried and smoked. At one of the stands, we stopped and I started to take pictures. All the ladies at the stands started to scatter, and my interpreter said pictures were NOT ALLOWED. I was getting frustrated with the translator for constantly telling me NOT to do things. The translator was ex-military and still distrusted Americans. It turned out in this case, there was caviar for sale on the tables, and all of that caviar was "poached" by the ladies or their husbands. It was not MY PROBLEM, but THEIR PROBLEM if the pictures made it into the wrong hands. One of the men selling caviar told us to take his picture because he had the proper license for caviar.

We bought some dried fish and smoked fish. The dried fish appeared to be small "trash" fish, about 6-8 inches long, and they were hard as leather. You first try to peel off the skin, then peel the meat off the bone with your teeth. It was not as bad as expected, but pretty close. I ate three to be polite, but they were not my favorite fish in Ukraine. The smoked fish was sturgeon. It was smoke-cured, but the inside meat was still soft. It was also quite leathery and tasted funny, and was not at all like the smoked fish back home. I had some sturgeon maybe ten times in Ukraine, and it is excellent when cooked, but their idea of smoking was not pleasant to me. I tried to eat some at the hotel in Kerch, hoping it would be better with a few beers, but most of it was thrown out.

In Kerch, we had a great dinner (one of many, so my weight increased on these trips), and we watched some middle-aged Ukrainian guy dance like a crazy man on the restaurant dance floor. Ukrainians love to dance! Then a group of hairdressers tried to pick up our two drivers (had two on this trip) and the translator. After this, we went to a local army base for a Russian Sauna, called a "Bania" in Russian. It is much hotter than a Finnish Sauna, but they do use water on the hot rocks, like a Sauna. We experienced the entire treatment with the steam, branches to stimulate the skin (they use birch and oak here) and even the cold bath in a VERY chilled pool. It was a great experience, including about 60 minutes of listening to Ukraine jokes and stories (without translation). So as not to break the rhythm of their evening, I told our translator to try to remember the best ones and retell them for me during our next drive, to Sebastopol in two days. Again, it was fun to see old friends sharing stories, joking, and laughing, even though I did not understand the details of the language!

Numerous great experiences continued and unusual sights were seen, such as square water tanks (not the round ones we see in the U.S.) for these small towns and communes. The bus stop shelters were beautifully decorated with mosaic art, and piles of sand along the roadside, getting ready for winter ice on the roads (took me a long time to figure out what those sand piles were for). And an unforgettable wake-up call one morning, from the man at the front desk of our country hotel: "Stand up grandpa, time to work!" He must have known this American guy did not speak Ukrainian, and this must have been a phrase he had learned somewhere. I looked forward to hearing what he might say the next morning! Instead, it was just a grumpy woman speaking in Ukraine (which was typical), but the guy with the "Grandpa" statement was great!

By the way, the English-speaking Ukrainians in the big cities were about 1 in 1000, and most of those were found in hotels, and only occasionally in a restaurant. Even the young people only knew English song lyrics or movie quotes, much of which were swear words. Many of the English songs heard on the radio were full of swear words, and just plain vulgarity. The meaning of the lyrics seemed to go right over the heads of everyone. They didn't hear the words, but they loved Western music! Our translator said the music was getting much worse in recent years. There were no laws for broadcasting, except for politics, I assumed.

**LADY TRANSLATOR FILLED IN SOMETIMES**

My seven weeks in Ukraine finally came to an end, and I was "burned out." Between the inspection of 77 vessels in total, plus all of the driving. We drove the entire coastline of the Ukrainian Black Sea, from Odesa to Izmayil, on the Dunay (Danube) River. Then we drove from Odesa to Kerch on the far east, then down the Crimean Peninsula. With side trips, we covered nearly 3500 kilometers, or nearly 2200 miles, on roads that shook your teeth!

The word had gotten around during our travels, that I liked those arm patches, so, one came from each detachment that we visited. Even a Hammer & Sickle lapel emblem appeared, from the detachment in Kerch. In addition to those items given to me by those officers, when I was about to leave the Odesa Office for the last time, Oleg gave me a big hug and a handshake. Then he left a pin in my hand. I asked the translator what that pin might be, and was shocked by the answer; it was one of Oleg's old **KGB Lapel Pins**. Not too many Americans have one of those, and I was proud that Oleg thought enough of our relationship to give it to me. I respected Oleg and I know he understood that. I just wish we could have spoken the same language because we would have continued our friendship afterward.

I returned to Ukraine in 2019, because I had been so impressed with the country, and especially the people! My experiences during that trip are shared in my book, Autobiography of a Ship's Marine Surveyor.

# CHAPTER 12

## I REALLY LOVED GUAM!

I have been to Guam about six times, and really liked it there. These wonderful people have learned to accept and deal with the great number of American military personnel who are stationed there, as well as those who visit there, and even retire there. The weather can be a little more humid than I like, but otherwise, it is very laid back and friendly. Their only big problem is typhoons, and they don't get simple Hurricane-type typhoons at a mere 75-150 MPH winds, they get SUPER TYPHOONS which are over 150 MPH with one bad one being clocked up to 178 MPH.

My first trip to Guam was shortly after Super Typhoon Omar hit Guam in 1992. My work was at the shipyard and the first thing I saw was the flag pole, which was bent at a full 90 degrees. I later found out that the crane on top of the drydock had been blown off. Because these typhoons are a regular occurrence in Guam, all of the buildings are concrete. But even reinforced concrete power and telephone poles were broken during Omar.

My job on this trip was to inspect and certify the large floating drydock the civilian shipyard had purchased from the Navy in the Philippines. It was towed to Guam, but the shipyard could not use it on Navy vessels until it was certified by ABS.

MY FIRST DRYDOCK JOB, CERTIFIED IN GUAM

Because this job was going to take over a week to complete, it was best to rent a hotel room with a kitchen outside the Navy base. The drive from the hotel district downtown would eat up too

145

much time each morning. Fish was available from trucks along the road, and restaurant meals were only necessary a few times. However, when eating at the local "greasy spoon," they served Portuguese sausage and fried rice for breakfast, which I had come to love in Hawaii!

HOTEL DISTRICT AND BEACHES IN AGANA, GUAM

There was a lot of interesting WWII history to see while driving the entire island over the weekend. The Guamanians were very loyal during the war, and remain loyal to this day. Guam is just a Territory of the United States, similar to Puerto Rico. Guam usually votes over 80% in elections to become the 51st State, but our Congress has never acted upon their request. The Guamanians seem to understand the difficulty for the U.S. to defend Guam, if some radical government decided to "take over one of the United States!"

Guam looks like Hawaii but is less expensive and much friendlier. The hotel district is very nice, and the beaches are more accessible and not as full of tourists. There are a lot of Japanese visitors that come to Guam and go to islands such as Tinian, where many Japanese soldiers died during WWII.

CAPTURED JAPANESE MINI-SUBMARINE

One Japanese soldier, Shoichi Yokoi, was found hiding in a cave, 28 years after the end of the war. He was captured in the jungle on 24 January 1972.

There is a very moving monument on Guam to commemorate the dogs used to find the Japanese soldiers hiding on the island. Those dogs saved many soldiers' lives. The dogs that were killed were buried with honors. Each dog's name is inscribed on the monument.

After certifying the first drydock, they invited me back to certify two others. All of these were of the Floating Drydock style, which is built like a ship, with a heavily framed "pontoon" on which the ships rest, and two "wing walls" which partially remain above the water when the drydock is flooded. After blocks are set on the pontoon deck to fit the shape of the ship, the drydock is flooded and the ship comes over the top of the dock. The ship is moored to stay centered on the dock, and then the drydock is pumped to raise the ship out of the water.

FLOATING DRYDOCK: BLOCKS SET FOR A SHIP

The third of the drydocks inspected was a very large one. Big Blue could be split into three pieces, and each section could be drydocked by the other two sections. This design is a great feature because most floating docks have to be towed to a larger dry dock (usually a graving dock far from their current location) to perform hull maintenance. (Look in the Panama Chapter for examples and photos of Graving Docks.)

**'BIG BLUE WITH ONE END PAINTED BLUE DURING A PRIOR DRYDOCKING**

**FLOATING DRYDOCK WITH SHIP ON DOCK**

On one of my trips, shortly after 9/11/2001, when security was very tight at the Guam airport, the owner/manager of the Guam Shipyard, an American citizen of East Indian descent, was pulled out of line for an extra security check and strip-searched. Those of us traveling with him apologized for this treatment because we felt it was profiling. He told us, "During times like these, I understand profiling." He was a real gentleman who showed a lot of class during what was a stressful situation.

There were two more trips to Guam for those tanker audits, described in the chapter "Around the World In 8 Days". Those ships docked near the shipyard, so it was an opportunity for me to visit those guys I'd worked with during my drydock surveys in previous years. On one of these visits, one of the shipyard employees asked me if I had been going to the seafood buffet when I'd visited in the past. Not being aware of any seafood buffet, they told me it was at the Hilton every Friday night. Staying over that Friday night, I decided to try it but not expecting much!

I went to the Hilton and asked about the buffet and found out it was $35 per person, which for that time in Guam seemed a little expensive. However, I loved seafood, and it was All You Can Eat, so I decided to give it a try. Never before or after have I seen a buffet like that one. There were at least eight kinds of shrimp, several cooked fish dishes, sushi, and lobster. These were small lobster tails, probably 3-4 ounces each. I asked if they were included or extra, and the waiter said, "All You Can Eat!" I ate 14 of those lobster tails that night, plus a sample of each type of shrimp. I have not been back to Guam since, but that buffet is on my "Must-Do" list!

One sad situation in Guam, which has also spread to Hawaii, is the brown tree snake. They were originally native to the Solomon Islands and then spread to other islands by ship, as well as hiding in the wheel wells of airplanes. There were many cylindrical containers, about 6" in diameter and 18 inches long, hanging on a lot of fence posts all over Guam. They were traps for brown tree snakes. Those containers had a live mouse inside to attract the snake, and once inside, the snake could not escape. The brown snake eats rodents, but also eats small birds. They are excellent tree climbers, so the bird population in Guam and other islands, even Hawaii, has decreased drastically.

# CHAPTER 13

## HAVE SOME MADEIRA, MY DEAR?

I've always loved the racy song by the old Limelighter group, "Have Some Madeira, My Dear," although it is very un-politically correct and I've never drunk Madeira, and only knew it was the name of an island, somewhere in the Atlantic. So, when my old ABSTech mentors John Barr and Richard Goss, asked me to go to Madeira for a survey, it was an obvious yes!

I've forgotten all of the details of my flights to get to Madeira, but my last leg was from Porto, Portugal, to Madeira, which is part of Portugal. Funchal, Madeira, is known for the largest fireworks demonstrations in the world, displayed every New Year's Eve. People pay a lot of money to go there and watch, usually on cruise ships.

The ship that needed to be surveyed was a chartered, civilian-crewed, Military Sealift Command vessel, called a "preposition ship". There are quite a number of these vessels scattered around the world, with enough supplies and equipment to support 3000 U.S. Marine soldiers in case they are needed anywhere in the world. There are only a few Marines on board for security, but if the Marines are flown into a "hot spot", one of these ships will be close enough to meet them there. The ships are continually on the move, and rotating through various ports so that when one moves, the others also move. Therefore, one of these ships is never more than one day sailing from all the major hot spots in the world.

The Navy was considering purchasing this vessel from the civilian owners at the end of their current charter. The Navy did not want to assume any environmental risks that might have been present on the ship, just like a purchaser of land making tests of the ground to check for pollutants. A thorough examination of the ship was required, as well as reviewing environmental records and interviewing the ship's officers. I cannot discuss details, but if you can imagine, this entire ship was air-conditioned to 72 degrees with minimum humidity, so even the refrigeration system leakage was a big concern, in addition to the diesel fuel and gasoline carried aboard the ship.

These ships always sit at anchor, as much as a mile offshore, both for safety and security reasons. They carry enough explosives and fuel to be considered a large target, which is why they're always on the move. They would be in Madeira for about one week, during which time the crew members could go to shore, but would be called back at a moment's notice if they had to get underway.

The ship experience was enjoyable, as well as Madeira, although not much time was spent ashore. I only had one night at a local hotel in Funchal and found the people to be friendly and accommodating. The second night was spent aboard the ship, and then I flew home.

TWO PICTURES OF MADEIRA, TAKEN FROM THE SHIP. RAINY DAYS WHILE I WAS THERE

Before leaving the ship, the Captain asked if I had ever tried Madeira, and he said it was worth trying. That night at the hotel, I asked for a glass of Madeira and immediately knew it was my new, go-to after-dinner liqueur. The next day at the airport, two bottles were in my carry-on to bring home.

On a previous trip to Cadiz, Spain, I had found that I also liked good Port and Sherry, so now Madeira was added to my list of "sipping" drinks!

Madeira is one of those places where you want to stay longer, to learn more about the people and culture of the island. But because I was very busy in those years, there was no extra time or money to just stay a few extra days. For this reason, Madeira is on my list of places to see again! (We tried to get there on a cruise, in 2019, but then COVID caused us to cancel that cruise. I still need to get back there.)

# CHAPTER 14

## TANKER LEAKING OIL IN DUBAI, UAE

Not too long after my trip to Madeira, I received another one of those calls from John Barr at ABSTech. This time he asked me to go to Dubai, United Arab Emirates. An Indian-owned crude oil tanker, classed by another society (non-ABS), was experiencing oil in their ballast water, and they feared being fined for pollution. John also said that several surveyors from other companies had looked at the vessel, and were unable to locate the source of the leaking oil. Of course, I wanted to go but was concerned about being added to the long list of failed attempts. It was too long and expensive a trip to end up without a solution!

It is probably necessary at this point to give a definition of "**Classed,**" as well as the role of the American Bureau of Shipping [ABS], as follows:

*The American Bureau of Shipping, known as ABS to those in the Industry, is a Ship Classification Society. ABS name changes and subsidiary companies have been plentiful over the last 35 years (it was the American Bureau of Shipping when I started in 1974), and in the United States, it is currently known as ABS Americas. There now is also ABS Europe, ABS Asia, etc. ABSTech (ABS Technical Services) will be mentioned as well (also ABS Consulting), which is a subsidiary that performs Non-Classification marine surveys as well as other industrial inspections, unrelated to, or outside the normal scope of ABS Classification work.*

*ABS is a worldwide company similar to the English version, Lloyds Register (not to be confused with Lloyds of London), the French Bureau Veritas, the Norwegian Norske Veritas, and others. Almost every seafaring country in the world has a Classification Society (Class*

*Society) and those that do not have one, use one of the larger societies listed above.*

*In order for ship owners to obtain insurance on their vessels, they need a Class Certificate for the Hull and another for the Machinery. The owner will choose a Class Society based upon their area of operation, and it is not unusual to have a "Dual Class" with the Society from their home country, as well as one of the major societies.*

*Classification starts at the design stage when the ship design drawings are submitted to the ship owner's Class Society for approval. The ship owner informs his building shipyard of his choice for Class, and then the shipyard must order all of the materials and machinery to comply with the Class Society's requirements (e.g., ABS Rules for Building & Classing Steel Ships). The requirements change depending on ship size (e.g., vessels under 150 feet), materials (e.g., ABS Rules for Building & Classing Aluminum Ships), and the type of service (e.g., drill rigs, tankers, gas tankers, and so on).*

*When the shipyard orders steel, they might specify ABS Grade-A or Grade AH-36, for example, as required by the ship's design. The steel mill will notify ABS of this order and the local ABS office near that steel mill will sometimes visit the mill and perform testing, or if ABS has that steel mill on a Quality Control Audit Program, they just send the completed steel laboratory, chemical tests, and physical tests to the local ABS office. That office will see where that steel is to be used, and then send their approval certificate for the steel to the ABS office that is attending the shipyard where the ship is being built.*

*This same process will be done for every major component in the ship, from the propellers, propeller shafts, reduction gears, engines, generators, critical pumps, piping, most electrical equipment, and so on. The Class Surveyor in the building shipyard will be involved in the construction and must verify that the markings on the materials and equipment match the certificates, which the shipyard presents to ABS from their suppliers. These certificates can fill several large books, and copies of those certificates must be carried on board when the ship is delivered.*

## *Tanker Leaking Oil In Dubai, UAE*

*The Class Surveyor at the shipyard must witness welding procedure tests, confirm that each welder working on the ship has the proper training and certificates, and also witness X-ray and Ultrasonic testing of specific weld areas. Finally, the ship is delivered, the Class Surveyor will witness sea trials, and then issue the original Hull Class and Machinery Class Certificates.*

SIKH DOORMAN AT DUBAI HOTEL

*There is also another important function of ABS on new ships, and that is to act on behalf of the Flag State/Country where the ship is flagged. ABS will not only Class ships of the United States flag, but for most maritime countries. Those Flag State Countries entrust the issuance of the Load Line Assignments (calculation of the safe maximum, loaded draft for that particular vessel, depending on the service area, and for each major season of the year) as well as the Safety Certificates to the responsibility of the Class Society. These include the Safety of Life at Sea (SOLAS) covering lifeboats and other safety items, Safety Hull, Safety Machinery, Safety Radio, etc. Another huge responsibility is the issuance of Marine Pollution Prevention (MARPOL) Certificates, which involves another long list of equipment and material certifications.*

*Lastly, ABS and the other societies perform Annual Surveys, Intermediate Surveys (24-30 months) and Special Surveys (4, 5 or 6 years, including drydocking) on every Classed vessel, as well as smaller vessels that only have a Load Line Assignment, such as small tugs and barges.*

My travel agent was getting used to my unusual destinations, and back in those days, the travel agent's commission on such a trip was a healthy one. This itinerary was from Chicago to Frankfort and then to Dubai. The departure went smoothly, but the return trip was one to remember. You can read that part of the story at the end of this chapter!

I had not been to this part of the world before, so reading several articles about the Muslim religion and the UAE seemed like the best way to prepare myself. It would not have been a good idea to embarrass myself, but I also didn't want to get into trouble due to misunderstanding the Muslim religion. Following such guidance is the smart thing to do, if you are traveling in a different culture! For example, you will notice I took no close-up photographs of people without getting their permission, which is taboo in the Middle East. This is particularly true about taking pictures of women. Requesting permission seemed difficult in most cases, because most of the people worth photographing, were not English speakers.

This trip was long before the fantastic buildings that exist in the United Arab Emirates today, but even at this time, the hotels were better than you would find elsewhere. I stayed at the Hilton, which had a Sikh (Punjabi) doorman who was about 7 feet tall. He looked spectacular! He was also very friendly and spoke to me whenever I returned to the hotel.

Following the "911" World Trade Center incident, I had several experiences with Sikh taxi drivers around the world, particularly in the United States. Because many people thought the Sikh turban was the same as those worn by Muslims, they either refused to get into their taxis or were rude to the Sikh drivers. Knowing the difference, it was easy to start a conversation with them (a good way to learn things from any taxi driver willing to chat!) and work it into the dialogue about being aware they were Sikh. They were always impressed when I knew the difference and wanted to talk about their negative experiences after "911." Sikh people are very outgoing and friendly, and their turban is very different from those used by Bedouin Arabs and other Muslim men, so people should learn the difference!

The following is quoted from SikhNet.com, to show the feelings of the Sikh community:

"Since Sept. 11th, Sikhs, like other Americans, have been grappling with grief and fear. But their fear is not only about another assault from outside. Many Sikhs have become victims of hate crimes because of their appearance. Balbir Singh Sodhi, a Sikh American, was killed on Sept.15 as a result of mistaken identity. Across America, the only people who wear turbans are followers of the Sikh religion. Sikhs are from Northern India (Punjab) and are neither Hindus nor Muslims.

Although Sikhism encourages self-defense, it pointedly teaches not to seek revenge or retribution, and teaches observers to be free of hatred."

Most of the people working in Dubai were either from India or from other "lesser" Muslim countries, such as Egypt. Every taxi driver I encountered in Dubai was from Egypt, and they were not very complimentary of the Dubai population. The Indian workers at the shipyard and those in the hotel seemed to be happy to be working. They spoke good English and were very helpful when asked questions. Even the Bedouins in Dubai were rich enough to own a home in the city, with a car in the garage. However, the Bedouins still kept their camels out and still loved to roam the desert for months at a time.

My hotel was adjacent to a very unusual shopping center, which had an ice rink in the lobby. There was also a pizza restaurant and other fast-food-type places on the mezzanine, overlooking the ice rink. Why would I waste my time on fast food when all the unusual foods were available at the hotel, but the locals seemed to love this place, and it was a great people-watching site. Families, from grandmas to small children, were skating on the ice rink, and then eating a pizza. Everyone was dressed in the traditional Muslim garb, including burkas for the women, and many of the grandmas even wore copper eye covers, with tiny slits for them to see, as well as heavy black gloves. Pizza slices were being slipped under the front of their burkas to take a bite, but you never saw even a hint of skin. Although I was aware of these full burkas, this was my first experience seeing them firsthand.

It was interesting to see the progression of women's clothing from toddlers, to pre-teens, teens, wives, and grandmas. If you ever wondered what happened to all of those extremely gaudy, kids' outfits, with wild patterns and unusually bright colors, they're being worn by the little girls in Dubai. I guessed the mothers wanted to get the desire for bright colors out of the girls' heads before they had to wear a burka because every girl under about the age of twelve was dressed in these wild-colored outfits.

ICE RINK WITH PIZZA RESTAURANT ABOVE

The girls at about age thirteen were dressed in gray burkas, with their hair covered, but their faces still exposed. The older teen girls wore black burkas but still had their faces exposed. The wives/mothers had the black burka with the mouth and nose covered, but most still had their eyes exposed. However, some wore a light, see-through veil over their eyes. Those women did not all wear gloves. Then there were the poor grandmas, who wore much heavier clothes and full burka, as I described above. Apparently, that was the custom when they were young, and they continued. Even more amazing was to see these families out on the ice. Some obviously came here often, because they skated quite well. Very few men were skating, probably to avoid embarrassment.

Most of my meals were eaten at the hotel, which had a great buffet for breakfast. There was no bacon or pork sausage, but the selection of foods was terrific, with American, European, and Middle Eastern choices. I tried everything!

It was a great pastime to sit in the hotel lobby and observe. People arrived at the hotel with Saudi Arabian license plates. They would check in, and go up to their room, and a while later you could recognize the man, now dressed in Western clothes, and the woman with him was also dressed Western style. The woman's burka was gone, as well as the man's long white "thawb." They would get into a taxi and take off for parts unknown, apparently to party as a non-Muslim couple. I'm sure this would never be allowed in Saudi Arabia, so these couples spent a few days in the Emirates, where the same religious views existed, but were not enforced.

My contacts at the shipyard told me to go to the Gold Souk to look for jewelry for my wife and daughters. The Gold Souk only sold gold, and you would never see this much gold all in one place, even in a museum. I chose one store because the proprietor stood outside and greeted me. After looking around his shop and finding some great items, I told the Indian

**ONE OF MANY STORES IN DUBAI GOLD SOUK**

merchant I wanted to look around a little more before buying, seeing there had to be thirty more stores in the Souk. He said, "You'll be back. My prices are the best in Dubai." He was correct and when I returned, there was nobody in his store and the gold he had shown to me earlier was still laid out on the counter. After about ten minutes, the Indian merchant finally returned, having stepped out for lunch. My surprise was obvious to him for leaving the gold unattended, so he explained, "Nobody would steal from me. They don't want to lose a hand!" I didn't want to question that statement at the time but later learned that justice is swift in most Arab/Muslim countries. The police can cut off hands on the spot if they are convinced of the guilt of a thief. No court, no judge, but just the testimony of a witness is needed. The witness would not lie, because that could mean losing his tongue!

Discussing this practice with John Barr, after returning from Dubai, he gave me some personal experience on the subject. John had been stationed in Abu Dhabi for ABS, with his wife and young daughter, many years before. He told me he had driven to Saudi Arabia for a ship survey, and decided to take his wife and daughter along. He was stopped on the highway by a soldier/policeman, who instructed him to park their car and follow, without any explanation. John said he knew he was not in any trouble because the man was being very polite, though only speaking a few words of English. They were led behind a small hill, and then John realized what was happening. They were about to witness a beheading of some criminal. A public beheading apparently needed to be witnessed by a minimum number of people, and the police were two people short of the required number. They read the charges and the sentence (though not in English). The policeman directed John to cover his daughter's eyes, but John and his wife needed to watch. After the execution, John and his family were politely escorted back to their car and they drove away.

BUSY TRAFFIC IN DUBAI CREEK

During some of my free time, I walked around the inner harbor, called Dubai Creek. It is much more than a creek, being about a half-mile wide. It is very busy with large ships, many Dhows, and small water taxis dodging the larger ships. I thought better than to take a water taxi, because they all seemed to be far overloaded, and no life preservers were evident onboard. The Dhows are the old Arab sailing vessels. Many of them still had the stub of the mast in the deck, but most were now diesel-powered.

DHOWS IN DUBAI CREEK

Old men were sitting on the decks of these Dhows smoking water pipes. Having been advised to NEVER take a picture of a person, without asking permission beforehand, it was best not to record that interesting sight. Expecting a problem with the non-English speaking natives, it was just better to avoid such pictures, but wish now that I had asked, maybe using sign language.

WELL, there was a job to do in Dubai, and as mentioned earlier, there was a long line of surveyors who had looked at this vessel's oily ballast water problem before. There certainly was a reason for me to be worried! I'm not an overtly religious person, but there was still a long conversation with God during the flight to Dubai! Because John Barr trusted me, I didn't want to disappoint him, so asking God for some assistance sure seemed like a good idea. On my first day at the shipyard, the project manager told me the drydocking would be delayed because the ship that was currently in our dock needed another day to finish repairs. My ship was still outside in ballast, so he told me to return the next day.

These ship delays seem to be the story of my career, but in this case, maybe God answered my prayers

# *Tanker Leaking Oil In Dubai, UAE*

**BUSY, SMOKY, GRAVING DOCK IN DUBAI**

[NOTE: THE GATE (CAISSON) ON THIS GRAVING DOCK FAILED IN 2002, KILLING 29 WORKERS. POOR MAINTENANCE WAS BLAMED.

HTTPS://GULFNEWS.COM/TODAY-HISTORY/MARCH-27-2002-29-KILLED-IN-DUBAI-DRYDOCKS-ACCIDENT-1.2000654]

I asked the project manager if the cargo tanks had been gas-freed yet, and he responded, "Yes, but you're here to look for oil in the ballast tanks, not to inspect the cargo tanks!" Following a hunch, I asked him to get me aboard the tanker, which he did.

**TANKER WAITING AT DUBAI SHIPYARD**

The Chief Mate on the ship assisted with my inspection of the cargo tanks, and he cooperated fully. He seemed to understand my suspicions, though he said nothing. Upon entering the first tank, there was an obvious dark streak down the bulkhead at each of the four corners of the tank. Inspections in the other cargo tanks revealed the same dark streak at the same locations, except for the No.1 tank, forward. My hunch had been correct! If oil was leaking into the ballast tanks when the cargo tanks were full (ballast tanks

are empty when cargo tanks are full), then it made sense that ballast water would be leaking back into the cargo tanks when the opposite situation was true.

The Class Surveyors were already on board, so after reporting my findings to the ship's Captain, I showed the Class Surveyors what was found, and they seemed to be in disbelief, that the mystery had been solved so quickly. They

**INSPECTING WELDS AFTER THE SHEDDER PLATE IS REMOVED.
THAT'S ME, GETTING DIRTY, WHICH WAS QUITE COMMON IN MY JOB!**

may have secretly hoped "this guy from ABS would fail," as they worked for a competitor of ABS!

When the ship was drydocked the next day, we erected scaffolding and cut open the "shedder plate" areas where each of the leaks was noted, and found the welds had not been properly made. With the normal working (bending) of the ship structure, these poor welds had failed and started leaking. The No. 1 Tank did not leak because the flexure of the ship was limited at the end of the ship's structure. We did go into the ballast tanks, and the previous inspections could never have found those leaks in this manner. The oil had coated all the surfaces, not just where the bad welds were located.

**CARGO TANK ENTRY HATCHES**

*The "shedder plates" are an extra piece of steel installed at the intersection of three plates, and those plates form a pocket that would trap the cargo in a small section of the cargo tank. The shedder plate is installed at an angle, to allow the cargo to run off that area freely.*

Whether by divine guidance or just plain luck, this positive outcome was very welcome because it sure made me, and John Barr, look like experts!

I wanted to take a "Desert Safari" excursion while in Dubai, which took tourists out to a small Bedouin camp near the city, where they served a meal with local food. It was probably all set up just for tourists, and the camp may not have had any actual Bedouins at all, but it sounded interesting. However, the shipyard always seemed to find a reason for me to be there in the afternoon, and that's when these excursions occurred. Upon my arrival at the shipyard, they typically canceled their inspection until the next day. However, there was enough opportunity to see many of the local sights during my free time, so not worth complaining (too much!).

Some of the more interesting parts of this trip occurred during my return trip from Dubai Airport to Chicago. While checking in at the airport in Dubai, there was a beautifully dressed Muslim woman at the check-in counter adjacent to me. It was obvious that she was wearing Western clothes beneath her nearly transparent Burka, and her transparent veil did not cover any of her features. I quietly asked the ticket agent at my counter if the passport used by this woman had her picture with or without her Burka. At first, the ticket agent (European) did not answer me, and I thought this was an embarrassing question. However, when the Muslim lady left the ticket counter, my ticket agent immediately said, "It had her picture with the Burka." Asking the agent how she knew that she answered, "If it was without the Burka, I would have been asked to take her in the back room and compare her picture after she removed her veil." The ticket agent assisting the Muslim lady was a man, and he would not have been allowed to look at her non-veiled photograph, no less her face, if she didn't have the veil on in the picture. My next question was how the ticket agent could be sure of the identity of some of the older Muslim ladies, with the heavy cloth Burkas, if their passports only showed them in a burka. She answered, "Good question!" That answer didn't leave a secure feeling in my mind!

As I was leaving the ticket counter, there was a commotion at the security checkpoint and the security person was holding up an automatic rifle. Apparently, the weapon had been found in a piece of checked luggage, and the security agent was only admiring it. He replaced it in the checked luggage and seemed to be complimenting the owner on the gun, and it was allowed on the airplane. There is no restriction to carry such weapons as long as they're in the checked luggage, and there is no ammunition in the baggage. One would wonder if this is how weapons are brought into airports by terrorists.

I usually try to avoid flights on Air France, mostly to avoid flying through Paris. No complaints about the airline, but missed flights happen a lot in Paris, because of the very unusual layout of the security system checkpoints. It does not easily allow people to transfer between flights, without standing in long security lines between terminals.

However, following take off in Dubai, the flight attendants quickly distributed small bottles of champagne and other liquor and then announced that we needed to drink our alcohol quickly before we entered Saudi Arabian airspace. Even though we had Saudi Arabian passengers (who were also drinking "the alcohol" by the way), liquor could not be consumed while in the airspace over Saudi Arabia. We landed in Riyadh about one hour later, having drunk our champagne. We were then warned to keep any Western reading material in our carry-on luggage, and it could not be displayed while in Saudi Arabia. The in-flight airline magazine had all of the women's bodies covered by large black ink spots, which was also true from what was seen in public Dubai newsstands. However, the gift shop in my Dubai hotel, had normal magazines in the bookstore, without these black ink spots. Normal reading material, other than nudity or pornographic items, was allowed in the hotels that service Western guests. Because of this, numerous Muslim men were in the hotel bookstores, paging through magazines, such as Vogue, and even Newsweek. Hardly pornographic, but otherwise not available to the public. Our ads do get very explicit at times!

After exchanging passengers in Riyadh, the same warning was given about reading material, while in Saudi air space. The man seated next to me on the airplane, who had boarded in Riyadh, commented on the reading material statement. He was British and mentioned he had been working in Saudi Arabia for nearly 6 months. He was not able to bring any reading material with him when entering Saudi Arabia, and other than pictures of his family, he was not allowed to have any photographs showing women's bodies. One of his coworkers had entered Saudi Arabia with a copy of Time Magazine in his luggage. When his luggage was inspected at the Riyadh airport, the magazine was noted to have several advertisements that showed women's bodies, and he was detained until his employer came to the airport. The employer, a large oil company, apologized for his mistake and was able to take the man to his work residence outside Riyadh.

While waiting for my connection at the Paris airport, a Muslim gentleman was making several trips to the men's room, but quickly turned away and returned to his seat. This happened several times and then I decided to use the men's room. Upon entering, there was a woman attendant in the men's room, who was stationed there for cleaning purposes. The Muslim man would not use the restroom while the lady was there, and she did not understand the situation. I tried to explain the problem to her to help the gentleman, but my not speaking any French, she did not understand me. Who knows whether the man was able to find a restroom without a woman attendant, but that must be a serious issue for a devout Muslim traveling in Europe. Most European restrooms have women attendants, though they are not always stationed there permanently, as I experienced in Paris, and elsewhere, during my travels.

Because there was a reasonable period between flights, it was not a problem making my connection in Paris, and at least on this occasion, there were no lost souvenirs and gifts, which had occurred on other flights.

A Concord-SST was sitting at a gate in Paris. That was my only time to see one, and they were permanently taken out of service a short time later.

# CHAPTER 15

## TYPHOON HITS YAP, MICRONESIA

Another fantastic journey brought me to the island of Yap, which is one of the islands in what was previously the American protectorate, called the Federated States of Micronesia. Again, the call came from my old employer, ABS, and they asked me to spend a full 30 days on the South Pacific island. ABS had been contacted by FEMA (Federal Emergency Management Agency) because a severe typhoon had hit the island of Yap. Because of Yap's location, it seldom suffered the full impact of a typhoon, but this one devastated the island. Although there were no deaths on the island, over 80% of the coconut trees had been destroyed, their tuna fishing boats had all been sunk, and nearly every roof on every building had been blown away.

Although Yap had been given their independence from the United States, there was an agreement to continue some benefits, such as American banking protection and FEMA, in return for continued American use of their airport and port facilities. Yap has a long history of various countries trying to use the natives for monetary gain. Some European "invaders" wanted them to harvest copra (dried coconut meat) and an unusual sea slug (trepang), considered a delicacy in China, which was found in their lagoon. Yap natives were not war-like. However, they resisted these takeovers by just refusing to work. The English, Germans, Spanish, and Dutch all tried to occupy the island and finally gave up when the natives refused to cooperate. You might want to read the book called "His Majesty O'Keefe", which is a true story about a shipwrecked American sailor who befriended the natives and protected them from several of these invaders. One of the local bars is still named after O'Keefe.

It was nearly a 24-hour flight from Chicago to Yap, via Houston, Honolulu, Guam, and finally to Yap. We did overnight in Guam and picked up several FEMA personnel on our flight the next afternoon. The sleep in Guam was welcome after those flights from the States, but leaving in the afternoon meant we also arrived late in Colonia, Yap.

Those of us who arrived from the United States were jet-lagged and tired. Although it was nearly midnight when we arrived, there was a large crowd of people at the airport to welcome us. As we entered the small airport terminal, they had us go through a reception line with handshakes and a very sincere "thank you" speech. Lastly, we were given the Yap equivalent of a Hawaiian lei, which in Yap, is a crown of flowers. Young ladies dressed in the local native "costume" had us bend down so they could put the crown on our heads. When bending down to receive my crown, I was looking at two bare breasts! Although FEMA had given us a large number of documents to review before arrival, many dealing with the Yap culture, they had not mentioned the fact that women on the island typically wore no clothing above the waist. I think most of the men on the flight were a bit embarrassed, and I'm sure my face was quite red.

That night we were taken to our hotels. We found out later that there were only three hotels left undamaged on the island. My hotel resembled an old-style Holiday Inn but was very clean and modern. Some of the homeless native families were also staying at this hotel, including several children who were very polite and cute. As described above, their mothers wore no clothes above the waist, which took some adjustment on my part.

**ISLAND CHILDREN AT MY HOTEL**

These three children belonged to a man who worked for the local oil company as a professional, so these were not poor families.

However, we did find the Islander girls did wear Western clothes and a T-shirt when they were working. The next day, we were taken to the one-and-only island rental car service, where each of us rented a car. One of the young girls we had seen the evening before was working behind the rental desk, but she was wearing blue jeans and a T-shirt. The rental office was across the street from the FEMA office. Several times, as soon as she left work, I noticed that the first thing the girl from the rental car company did was take off the T-shirt and throw it in the back of her car. That's when I realized that this was not just an occasional ceremonial thing, but that we would be seeing bare breasts continually for the next 30 days.

Although the topless situation was a little unnerving for the first week, it took very little time to get used to it. REALLY! The constant 90 – 95° weather and high humidity, made things very uncomfortable. There were days when we all wished we could dress like the natives. However, the Americans were getting very sunburned, even with all the sunblock we were using. Maybe Western cultures would not be so obsessed with nudity if we did not make it such a taboo subject.

I am referring to the people on Yap as natives. However, they are in no way primitive. Most of the people on Yap have attended college in the United States and although some of them have remained in America, most of them miss the local Yap lifestyle, eventually returning to their island. Many of them own very successful businesses. The Islanders take care of one another. This was NOT a primitive culture! Nearly everyone spoke excellent English!

While working in Yap, my desk was in the rented FEMA Office. FEMA had a wonderful team of both American and Guamanian-American employees working in Yap. The agency was not only responsible for providing emergency lodging and home repairs like we see in the United States but they were also tasked with preserving the Yap culture. This meant the home repairs had to meet FEMA requirements, which involved improving the structure to prevent future damage. However, the Yap officials (both the Government and the island Chiefs) did not want their structures to look like modern buildings and lose their cultural heritage. The FEMA cultural representative told me about this dilemma and explained how she overcame the problem by mounting the bamboo corner posts of the homes being repaired in a concrete base. This improvement met the FEMA requirements and yet maintained the cultural level required by the Yap officials.

In conversations with several of the Yapese about what they experienced during the typhoon, we were told the winds had been so strong that most of the livestock on the island had been killed. It's amazing, but none of the people on the island were killed or severely injured. One lady described a situation in which her dog was trapped outside and was hiding in a small barn. The roof of that barn had already been blown away and she was afraid for her dog. She called the dog to come to the house and he responded, however, the winds caught him and she never saw him again.

Many of the Yapese described what they called "flying guillotines," which were the corrugated steel roofing panels, which were being blown off of many of the houses and other buildings. Luckily, nobody was harmed by them.

The Yapese people were very friendly and extremely honest. At first, you might worry about leaving valuables in your hotel room for 30 days, but the FEMA officials in my office explained that petty theft, robberies, and other such crimes were nonexistent on the island. There actually was a prison on the island. One day, the inmates were working outside the prison and I asked my contact at the Fisheries Department why they needed a prison on the Yap when the people were so honest. His answer was, "There are only seven inmates, all imprisoned for murder." Seeing my shock at this fact, he further explained, "They are just in prison for minor murder." There are two types of murder in the Yap laws, one requiring life imprisonment for "typical" murder, but "minor murder" was only a seven-year sentence for killing your wife's extramarital lover. Apparently, killing your wife's boyfriend is considered just a crime of passion, and only receives a seven-year sentence.

Having read several books about the Yapese culture since leaving, they not only condone premarital sexual contact but encourage it. In theory, this practice is to prevent the need for "fooling around" after marriage, but this did not seem to apply to the men as much as it did to the women.

There were 13 Chiefs on the island of Yap (plus Chiefs on the other islands that formed the Federated States of Micronesia) who at one time had complete control of everything that happened or was allowed to happen on their islands. Because Yap is now part of a four-island democratic government, they have an elected Congress proposing laws and regulations. Each State also has an elected Governor, however, none of these laws and regulations can be passed without the approval of the majority of the Chiefs on the four major islands. These islands are Yap, Pohnpei, Kosrae, and Chuuk (called TRUK during WW II), but the major, "high islands" are surrounded by numerous smaller islands, many of which are uninhabited. Yap had about 12,000 inhabitants at that time, but it appears the population is currently just over 11,000. Many of the young people who now attend college in the United States may be deciding not to return. My Fisheries Department contact had a daughter who decided to stay in San Francisco, and after I returned home, he and his wife also moved to the United States to be with her.

We occasionally talked with several of the Chiefs on the island at the FEMA office, and they would ask us many questions about our impressions of life on Yap. The first question I was asked was whether I missed having television service on the island. I told the Chief I only missed it for a few days, but the serenity that came without television was becoming quite welcome. Instead, I was reading, and occasionally renting movies, or out exploring the island (once the roads were fixed). The Chief then asked me about the lack of pornographic or extremely violent movies to be rented on the island. I had not noticed, but then he asked if they should be allowed the freedom to watch any movie or television shows the people wanted. I told the Chief their decision to keep these things off the rental shelves was a good idea. The Yapese people were wonderful, and having X-rated and violent, R-rated movies would only result in more crime and a bad cultural change.

**BARGE IN OUR PARKING LOT, PLUS ANOTHER AGROUND!**

My job in Yap was to advise the several maritime industries on how to deal with the damages to their ships, barges, and fishing boats. We had a barge and a ship that had washed up in the parking lot of the temporary FEMA office. My advice was limited to how those vessels could be removed, without them sinking in the harbor. Some required steel repairs while still in the parking lot, before refloating them. Their three tuna fishing vessels were severely damaged, fully submerged, and beyond repair. These were relatively small fiberglass tuna seiners, but those vessels supplied fish for the Islanders and the hotels. Some of the fish was exported as income for the island. They also had an island-owned, large tuna seiner that was operating far away from Yap, and that vessel survived.

**RESTAURANT BOAT, 'MNUW', AGROUND**

My biggest challenge was the historic Chinese sailing vessel, "Mnuw", a 110-year-old (at that time) South Seas schooner, which had been converted into a restaurant. It was grounded on a reef across the harbor from the hotel where it had been moored. That hotel was the home of Yap Divers, founded by Bill Acker, who had moved to Yap from the United States and married a local woman. Maybe Bill had read "His Majesty O'Keefe", and had been attracted to Yap.

Yap Divers and Bill Acker are legendary in diving circles, and they still provide diving equipment and guided tours for scuba divers, who come to Yap from all over the world. Divers come to swim in the harbor, which is known for its large White Manta Rays. While in Yap, the divers were very worried, because the mantas had left when the storm hit and had not yet returned. Later I did look on the Internet and found that the White Mantas had returned, and Bill Acker is still in Yap. The Mnuw is also back at its original position at the hotel, so I assume that my plan for refloating the Mnuw worked well.

The three remaining hotels on the island were each very different. My hotel was probably the cheapest of the three, but it was also the most "homey". As mentioned above, the hotel associated with Yap Divers was normally used by the tourists who came to the island for scuba dives, but very few of them were coming to the island after the storm (see hotel behind Mnuw, in the above photo). Their hotel suffered only minor damage. The third hotel was very upscale, yet the oldest hotel on the island. It was designed to look like a hotel from the colonial days. There was another hotel on the island which was situated in the hills above my hotel. This hotel was designed to look like the native homes, with thatched roofs and bamboo walls. Each of the rooms was a separate structure, scattered in the hills, and most of the roofs had been torn away by the typhoon. The telltale FEMA blue tarps were on all of those roofs, just like many other buildings on the island, but not on my hotel.

DAMAGED ROOFS ON THE RUSTIC HOTEL

An amazing thing occurred after about two weeks on the island. Breakfast at the hotel restaurant was always great, fried rice with chicken or pork. But this particular morning, I asked for my normal breakfast, and they said it was not available. The fried rice on the island was always wonderful and spiced differently from what we are used to eating in the United States. The waiter apologized and said that they no longer had any chicken or pork available. He then asked me if fried rice with fish would be okay instead. I did not see fish available on the breakfast menu but told them fish would be wonderful. The next morning, I asked for fried rice with fish and the waiter told me that they no longer had fish. Then, when I asked for eggs and toast, they apologized and said that they had been out of eggs all week. The staff suggested that I eat at one of the other two hotels because their supplies had been more plentiful before the typhoon. Although I hated to desert my hotel and its friendly service, it became necessary to eat at the other hotels until the ship arrived with supplies. After the ship arrived, it was back to my hotel restaurant.

How many of us in America have ever been in a situation where food was just not readily available? Because the typhoon had destroyed all of the livestock, including the pigs, chickens, and the few cows kept for milk, the island had been using all of the food they had that was either in storage or frozen. The island was becoming dependent on food being shipped in from other islands which were also now suffering shortages. A ship was coming from Guam with necessary supplies, but it had not yet arrived.

I'm not a big beer drinker, but I keep a six-pack of beer in the refrigerator in my room on long trips such as this. When we arrived, they were selling beer at six dollars for a six-pack. Gradually, the price began to rise until beer was being sold at four dollars per can. I asked how this was possible, and the shopkeeper said he was having beer flown in from Guam every few days which drove up the price. Needless to say, I went without drinking beer for a while.

Many of us were leaving after our 30-day contract and were invited to attend a party given by the 13 Chiefs on Yap. Many of the Yapese would stop us on the street and thank us for being there and for the help we were giving them. The Chiefs wanted to make this thank you official by throwing a party for us. The party was held at a beautiful beach, away from the city. There was an endless supply of both local foods and American foods, as well as hundreds of cans of beer. This was still before the ship arrived, so you must understand how expensive it was for the Chiefs to arrange this party. I had learned to enjoy the local foods, so I avoided the hot dogs and such. However, there was one item of local food that I found shocking. It was a fruit bat that had been cooked on the grill with the wings, head, and hair still attached. Despite my adventurous nature, I was afraid to try it. I, later, spoke with those who tried it and they said it was wonderful. I have since seen television accounts of people eating these fruit bats, and now wish I had tried them at the time. Apparently, they are a wonderful gastronomical experience!

**YAP CHIEFS GIVING US THANKS FOR OUR HELP BEAUTIFUL BEACH SETTING FOR OUR PARTY**

Trying to buy souvenirs for my family and friends back home before leaving was becoming a big problem. The typical souvenirs were hand-made items by local artists, but with limited tourism, the selections were also limited. Most were unusual, and not like normal tourist trinkets, but I wanted something dramatic for myself, to remember my time on Yap. I had seen a 20-foot wood carving with spectacular artwork at the airport. It depicted various scenes from island life, including Stone Money. I did find some small, nicely done wood carvings in one of the local artist shops, however, they did not accurately depict the Yapese culture.

One day, the manager at our hotel heard me talking about a wood

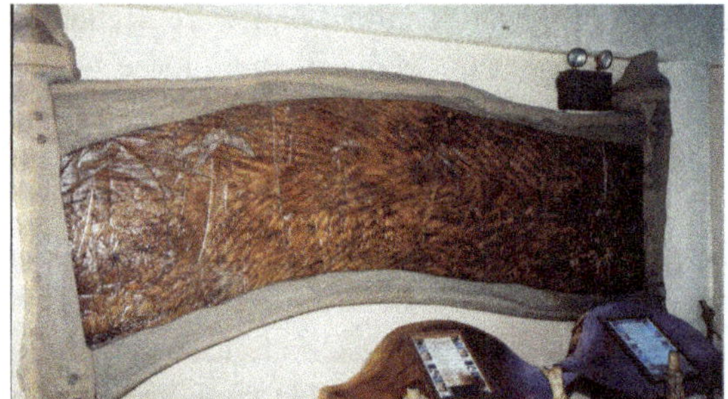

**WOOD CARVING IN THE ARRIVAL AREA OF THE AIRPORT**

**MY WOOD CARVING, A BIT SMALLER, BUT GREAT**

carving, and I told her the size and quality desired. She told me her husband was an excellent woodcarver, and she would ask him to make one for me. I asked her how much it would cost, and she said she would ask her husband. The next day, she told me she had told her husband to proceed, and she never did tell me what the cost would be. I guess it would be a surprise, including the cost. Finally, on the day before leaving, she brought the carving to the hotel - and - it was a real work of art, just barely fitting into my suitcase. From the look of it, I expected it would cost several hundred dollars, but she asked for only $40. I told her it was worth much more and I was willing to pay more. She refused to take $80 but finally accepted $50. Again, this reminded me of the fact that the Yapese are extremely honest people.

During the last few days on the island, many of us took the opportunity to tour some of the historic sites, which were now available since the roads had been repaired. Each of the Chiefs on the island had what is called a Chief's House, where they could hold meetings. It was also a place for them to get away from their responsibilities, which they took very seriously. The islanders respected the Chiefs and the Chiefs' House was off-limits without an invitation. Apparently, each Chief also invited the prettiest unmarried girl in his village to act as his housekeeper. During this period, the girl was not allowed to marry.

We had noticed soon after arriving on the island that there were large disks made of stone, with a hole in the middle. This was Stone Money! This is the only society in the world using a currency of this size. Some of this stone money was 5 feet or 6 feet in diameter and as much as 12 inches thick and therefore extremely heavy. There is no rock of this type on Yap, and you would find by reading "His Majesty O'Keefe" that the natives had sailed long distances to islands where rock quarries were located, such as Palau, 450 kilometers away, and then sailed back to Yap with these stones laid across their outrigger canoes. Such dangerous work resulted in the loss of many natives' lives, particularly on those long sea voyages. The difficulty of obtaining stone money, and the frequent loss of life, made stone money very valuable. Captain O'Keefe eventually bought a ship and helped the Yapese carry the stone money from Palau Island back to Yap. Because this reduced the difficulty and stopped the loss of life, the value of stone money was eventually lessened. However, stone money is still used as a sign of ownership in front of most buildings on the island.

STONE MONEY LINED UP ALONG THIS PATH

We also located several Japanese gun emplacements along the beach. The Japanese had invaded the island and controlled it for a short period during World War II. The Americans invaded and drove out the Japanese, which was the start of the Protectorate for the Federated States of Micronesia. It amazed me because the metal gun mounts were still in place in these pillboxes.

STONE MONEY AT CHIEF'S HOUSE

We then went to the old Japanese airfield and found the remains of a crashed Japanese fighter plane next to the runway. The gauges and controls were still in the airplane. This again pointed out to me how honest the Yapese people were. When asked about this, the locals said it was not their property, and no one would steal it. These Japanese artifacts would be worth significant money if sold to collectors, however, the Yapese would never do that.

JAPANESE AIRPLANE FROM WORLD WAR I

Remember that food was now becoming scarce on the island. My contact at the Fisheries Department invited me to go fishing with him and a basketball coach from Australia, who was on the island because of the Micronesian athletic games, which were going to occur later that year.

JAPANESE MACHINEGUN SITE

We were to have a chance to go fishing and we went out the next morning. We were fishing for small tuna that were feeding inside the reef, and we were able to catch several. The first one was hooked on my hand line, and I was pulling it in slowly. My host told me to pull quicker and then he pointed out the reason why. There was a small shark following my fishing line with the tuna, and we were about to lose it. It then got pulled a lot faster and the shark was unable to take my fish.

My "take" for the day amounted to two small tuna, which I insisted my host should keep. However, he told me he knew my hotel was short on food and he suggested I take the tuna to the hotel and share the fish with them. Doing what he suggested, I told the hotel staff that if they gave me a nice meal of tuna sashimi that evening, they could have the rest of the fish. They were thrilled and very grateful for my gift. The fresh tuna sashimi was great that evening, and the next morning there was fried fish with my fried rice, which I gladly paid for.

My host at the Fisheries Department then told me he was taking the Australian coach and his wife on a snorkeling trip the next afternoon, and he invited me to go along. Again, the invitation was accepted, and the next day we traveled along inside the reef to a small volcanic island that came out of nowhere. It was full of "rock bubbles" which had broken and were very sharp. It was the only volcanic rock seen on the island, although the island may have been part of an extinct volcano at one time. He dropped us off at the island, and then he took the boat a long way offshore to anchor it. I wondered at the time why he was doing this.

**OUR VOLCANIC ISLAND, INSIDE THE REEF AT YAP**

We had a good time snorkeling, and the conversation with the coach and his wife was very interesting. Having been to Australia several times in the past, it was interesting to talk with some familiarity about his country. He noticed the musculature of my legs and said that must have been due to playing sports. I told him that it came from playing football in high school, and also a little weightlifting during that time. He said that it still showed in my body. (He didn't mention my already bulging waistline!)

MOORING OUR BOAT, FAR OFFSHORE OUR GROUP OF SNORKELERS, HOST AT RIGHT

When it came time to leave the volcanic island, it became evident why our host had anchored his boat so far offshore. The tide had gone out, and he knew that he would've stranded the boat if moored closer to shore. We had a long walk to reach the boat, but luckily, he had told us to take sneakers along, because we were walking across the coral in the lagoon. He told us to get into the boat and he continued to pull the boat through the lagoon until we reached deep enough water for him to start the outboard motor.

SEVERAL WW II LANDING CRAFT IN LAGOON          SPEARED PUFFER FISH

On the way back to the harbor, we noticed a few old landing craft from World War II that had been stranded on the reef. The boats and engines were still visible and had not been touched since the war. We also came across another small boat in the harbor with several young men aboard who had been diving and spearing fish. The one young man was the son of our host. He came over to our boat to show us a spiny puffer fish he had just caught. This day trip made me realize why the Yapese people come back to their island, even though many of them have a college education and could stay in the United States. They loved their island and its lifestyle.

## *Typhoon Hits Yap, Micronesia*

One of the very unusual things about Yap and many of the islands in the South Pacific is the fact they nearly all chew Betel Nut! The nut is the Areca Nut, but it is rolled inside the Betel Nut leaf, which grows as a parasite on the coconut trees. Because the coconut trees on Yap had been destroyed during the typhoon, all of these plants were also destroyed. This is a major cash crop for this island, but it also meant that the Yapese did not have a supply of Betel Nut for their own use. Both men and women chewed Betel Nut, and each person carried a small pouch with the "makings" for the chew, much like people who roll their own cigarettes. The concoction leaves a telltale red stain on the mouth, gums, and lips. The nut is wrapped in the Betel Nut Leaf, and some of the people also added some tobacco, or even soaked the ready-made chews in vodka, to give it a little extra kick. Although the red stains seemed unsightly to us Americans, it was so common on the island they thought it was normal, and I read later that it was considered "sexy". They did not typically smoke cigarettes on Yap, so this chewing habit is no different than cigarettes in other cultures. I have since learned that the chews can eventually cause cancer, so despite the Yapese natural lifestyle, they found a way to hurt themselves.

Although I was glad to get home, I was quite unhappy to end my stay on Yap. The people were wonderful and friendly, and they had a natural culture that many people would love to have. I will never forget my time on Yap.

# CHAPTER 16

## CRUISE SHIPS, CRUISE SHIPS, AND MORE CRUISE SHIPS!

### First Time in Alaska

My first experience on cruise ships was in 1993 when ABSTech sent me to Alaska to survey three old, Greek-owned cruise ships. The ships were very old and of the classic design from the 1950s and 60s. I was later told that the company was in financial trouble, and my surveys were on behalf of their mortgage holder, to check if the vessels were being properly maintained.

The first flight was to Juneau, Alaska, where I was to meet the owner's representative at the hotel that had been arranged for me. This was my first trip to Alaska and it was an enjoyable flight, which luckily was on a clear day, to experience the beauty of the mountains. There was a limited amount of time available to see some of Juneau and buy a few souvenirs. Although I was aware of the Russian influence in Alaska, it was surprising to see all of the Eastern Orthodox churches and other Russian histories in Juneau.

The Greek gentleman met me in the hotel restaurant the next morning, and after breakfast, we headed for the port to meet the ship. The ships to be surveyed were named the Regent Sea, Regent Star, and Regent Sun. Each ship looked beautiful from a distance, because of its classic lines. However, my first inspection of each ship was to circle the exterior in a small boat to look at the hull condition. It soon became apparent that these ships were close to the end of their useful life.

REGENT SUN IN LAY-UP STATUS

DINNER WITH CAPTAIN & OWNER'S REP FROM GREECE LEAVING PORT IN ALASKA

The first ship was surveyed on a cruise from Juneau to Anchorage, Alaska, where my guide and I stayed overnight, then flew to Vancouver. In Vancouver, we boarded the second vessel. The second vessel also proceeded to Anchorage, and we again stayed there overnight. My Greek travel companion wanted to visit the local Greek church in Anchorage because he knew the priest at that church. We spent a delightful afternoon with the priest, talking about their home in Greece, where they had first met.

The next morning, we drove to a railway station near Anchorage where we boarded a train. This train had half normal passenger cars, and the other half of the cars were auto carriers. We drove our rental car onto one of the auto carriers, and to my surprise, we stayed in our car. We proceeded on quite a long train ride, through several long tunnels, and we ended up at the port of Whittier. I later found out that this trip is no longer done by train, and that those tunnels have been converted for bus and automobile traffic (though just a single lane, alternating one-way traffic). We had to drop our rental car at our destination because we were going to board the third cruise ship in Whittier. I never quite understood why my Greek owner's rep decided to rent a car and leave it in Whittier when we could have ridden in a passenger car.

Whittier was originally built during WW II as an American submarine base. It was a deep-water port, located far inland, thus protected from Japanese bomber attacks. The city still had a very military look to it at the time we were there. However, the Cruise Ship industry has helped to modernize the city in recent years.

This third cruise started with beautiful scenery because of the glaciers which were visible from the ship. However, as the cruise progressed, the seas became rougher as each hour passed. The vessel's Captain invited me to dinner with him that evening, and to attend the show after dinner. By the time the hour for dinner approached, my motion sickness had kicked in big time! The rest of the evening would be spent in bed, in my cabin, so I called the Captain to explain the situation. He was very gracious and said that he would see me the next morning.

CAPTAIN'S OFFICE THE MORNING AFTER THE HEAVY SEAS

The seas had calmed by morning and the Captain was on the bridge, where I expressed my regrets for having missed dinner the night before. He told me I was in good company that evening because several of his officers had also become ill during dinner, something of an unusual occurrence. He said only 25 passengers came for dinner, and maybe two or three were able to finish. Just the Captain, several Officers, and those few hardy passengers went to the show. During the show, several of the dancers also became ill, and finally, the show was canceled. The Captain said we had close to 40-foot seas that evening, which is very unusual for the Gulf of Alaska, but this was late September with winter storms approaching.

This cruise had planned to make a stop at Glacier Bay before we headed for the Inside Passage. We had to skip Glacier Bay because the ship had to alter its course during the storm. I was very disappointed, never having seen Glacier Bay before.

Another unusual event occurred as we were leaving Sitka Harbor. There was a dark spot in the ocean in front of the ship. I asked the Alaska Pilot if by chance it was a whale. The pilot told me that all of the large whales had left because it was too late in September. My camera was in my stateroom (before cell phone cameras) and I wanted to get the camera in case it was a whale but then decided not to do so after the pilot told me it could not be a whale. Ten minutes later, the whale was directly alongside the ship. With my camera, I could have taken some wonderful pictures.

## **First Time Sailing in the Caribbean**

That Winter of the same year, I was asked to survey two of those same ships while they were operating in the Caribbean, to confirm that the repairs, which were part of my recommendations, were being carried out. One of the ships became a real adventure because my disembarkation was to be in Cartagena, Columbia. I had never been to Columbia but had certainly heard about all the trouble during those years, including the kidnapping of American citizens.

This cruise was from Fort Lauderdale to Columbia, and it was unusually enjoyable because of three passengers, brothers, approximately my age, who were traveling together. They were from Boston and were real fun-loving guys. They were very interested in the reason why I was aboard the ship, without my wife, but I had to be careful how much information I gave them.

We arrived in Cartagena, Colombia, and the ship's agent came aboard to meet me and discuss the situation with the Captain. The agent was not very

ME, WITH THE THREE BROTHERS FROM BOSTON

happy about the responsibility of having an American citizen in his care for the next 24 hours. My plane was scheduled for late the following morning, and the agent needed to arrange a hotel and meals for me, without putting me in any danger. His concern was understandable, as I was quite concerned myself.

The agent led me off the ship with my luggage and explained what was going to occur. There were three inspection stations at the port facility, and each of them would question me. My baggage would be examined at all three stations. The first station was a typical port security unit which was easy. They made a cursory inspection of my bags, and the agent translated a few simple questions, such as my reason for leaving the ship before the end of the cruise, and my destination.

The next station was the Cartagena Police, and although their questions were no more difficult than the port security, they totally tore apart my bags, even opening each bottle of deodorant and shampoo, and then expected me to put them back together when they were done. The agent was watching them very closely. The third station was manned by the Colombian Army, and again my bags were disassembled and left for me to put back together.

When we were in the agent's car, he explained to me about the Cartagena Police and the Colombian Army playing games with one another and occasionally hiding contraband in the passenger's baggage, to see if the next station would be able to locate it. This is why the agent had watched the police so closely because he feared they might put contraband in my luggage. If the Colombian Army found the contraband, they may know that the police had planted it, OR, I might have been arrested.

The agent took me to a beautiful hotel overlooking a manicured beach that seemed to stretch for miles. He checked me in and escorted me to my room. He then told me not to leave my room for any reason until he came back to take me to dinner. Therefore, the afternoon was spent looking out my window and enjoying the scenery, although it would have been nice to have seen more of Cartagena. Knowing the circumstances, it would not have been wise to disobey the agent's instructions.

**ENTRANCE INTO THE PORT OF CARTAGENA**

The agent returned to take me to dinner. Although this was not my first time tasting ceviche, the ceviche in Cartagena was much better than the American version. I love all seafood, but the fish dinner in Cartagena that night was fantastic. During dinner, a young couple near our table heard us speaking English and asked where we were from. We exchanged pleasantries, after which they told us they had begun an around-the-world trip, having left Florida on their sailboat just a few weeks before. After dinner, the agent returned me to my hotel, and, again, took me to my room, and instructed me to lock the door and not venture out until he came for me the next morning. I wondered if the young couple with the sailboat had even considered how dangerous it was for Americans in Columbia during that time.

**MANICURED BEACH, DOWNTOWN CARTAGENA**

The agent met me for breakfast at the hotel and we were to head to the airport. He told me we had sufficient time before my flight, and he would give me a tour of the Old Walled City, before heading to the airport. Cartagena is very historic and quite beautiful. It was impressive to see how clean everything was, compared to most cities in South America. There were men on the beach that morning with hand rakes, which was the reason for the manicured look I had noticed the day before.

Upon arrival at the airport, the agent informed me we would be getting the same treatment with my baggage, which happened the day before. In this case, the Army inspection would be first, then the Cartagena Police, and finally the airport security personnel. This was long before the events of September 11, 2001, in New York, so this level of security was not typical in most airports around the world at that time, except for some European cities that had experienced terrorist attacks. Again, the agent watched the inspections very closely, to be sure of no trouble with contraband being planted. I thanked the agent for his hospitality and careful attention to my situation and headed to my flight. The agent was very relieved to have divested himself of this huge responsibility, namely ME!

It's good to hear that Columbia is not nearly as dangerous for tourists these days, as it was in the 1990s. I was in good hands with my ship agent on that trip, but would not have been near as confident alone. (I returned to Cartagena in 2019 on a cruise ship, and took a long tour of the city.)

## **The End of These Three Vessels**

Even though the Greek owner had done the repairs that the mortgage holder requested, these three ships were eventually sold. The newspapers later reported Regency Cruise Line went bankrupt, and left both passengers and crew stranded wherever the ships were finally "arrested." When they wanted to leave the harbor, but were unable to pay their bills, the local authorities seized the vessel. Some of the crew members were still on board one ship in Freeport, Bahamas when I made further inspections following the bankruptcy. The crew had not been paid for several months, and young sailors from the Philippines had no way to get home. Some of them were eventually hired by other cruise lines or ship owners.

One of the ships returned to Europe, and two of the ships were sold to American investors who thought they could use the vessels on short, gambling excursions to the Bahamas. I saw one of the vessels at a shipyard in Tampa, Florida, where it was being refurbished, despite its poor condition. The last of the ships, the Regent Sun, was seen in the Bahamas while I was inspecting it for American investors. This ship had partially sunk while in a shipyard in Italy many years before. Many of the lower decks were covered by carpeting and when the carpeting was removed, there were holes rusted through the deck because of the many years of saltwater being trapped in the structure. During several trips to the Bahamas on other jobs in subsequent years, that ship remained at the dock until it was finally scrapped.

**END OF LIFE FOR THE REGENT SEA, TIED UP IN FREEPORT, BAHAMAS**

## **Environmental Audits on a Large Cruise Ship Fleet**

In 1999, I was asked by my old employer, ABS, to attend a meeting in Miami with a major cruise line to discuss environmental audits, which were being required by the United States government, due to a pollution incident that had occurred on one of those cruise vessels. Others in attendance at that meeting were representatives of a well-respected environmental auditing firm, which was interested in getting the contract for these audits. Because the auditing firm did not have any marine experience, particularly in the engine room systems, they wanted ABS to assist with the audits if they were awarded the contract.

Probably ABS did not realize what a big job this would become, or they might not have entrusted the outcome of that meeting to me. However, the meeting went very well, with the auditing firm receiving the contract. ABS then contacted me and asked me to act as the marine systems expert to assist those auditors. This would involve approximately 20 audits per year, and each audit would take between four days to seven days to complete. This was a huge life changer for me because it is normally prudent to avoid long-term commitments to a particular project. You lose your regular, steady

187

clients when you're not available. At the outset, we knew the probation period was five years, but a review would be done following the third year, at which time the probation might be shortened.

We started the first audit on a ship leaving Miami, and the U.S. Coast Guard, U.S. EPA, and several Justice Department attorneys were on board. This was in addition to our original audit team of five people. Once we had our team of auditors trained, we reduced the team to three. The opening meeting for the first audit was conducted in a large shipboard conference room, with all of the ship's officers in attendance. The body language of the officers in that meeting showed their obvious disdain for what was happening. It was tense on both sides, and we all thought that this was a terrible start to a terrible situation.

There was an obvious learning curve during the first few audits, but slowly we saw the attitude of the officers changing as we went from one ship to the next. My fellow auditors earned my respect because they made it clear to the crew that we were there to help them, and not to punish them. We certainly had to report all failures to comply with U.S. and International regulations, but in many instances, we were able to prove the ship had only made incorrect entries in their logbooks.

Incorrect entries were a violation, but they could be corrected if other reliable records were available, and these resulted in just "hand slaps," instead of huge fines or prison terms. By the time we started the audits in the second year, we found the ships' crews looked forward to our visits, so we could help them with their problems. This turned into one of the most rewarding experiences of my career, because we were able to teach the crews, not humiliate them, and we kept them out of serious trouble by understanding their problems, and yet finding ways to keep them compliant.

After the third year of audits, this company was offered the opportunity to end its probation. However, the company decided to continue the audits for the full five years. This decision was based on reports from the crews, saying the auditors were helping them, and providing training for them to stay out of trouble. The ships' Environmental Officers, as well as the shore-side Environmental Managers, could see the dramatic change in the vessel crews' attitudes and morale, and they did not want to lose the gains that had been made to "change the culture" regarding the Environment.

DAVOR JURUM AT LEFT, CELEBRATING THE 1ST VESSEL WITH ZERO AUDIT FINDINGS

International law requires all records to be kept in English or French (go figure!). Although the crew members all spoke English with some level of competency, it was clear that they were limited in their English reading and writing skills. The logbook entries were often written in such poor English that a Coast Guard inspector would have to assume the worst. In addition, many of the entries in the logbooks were not in chronological order, which made them very difficult to understand. I started giving the crew handwritten examples of how certain difficult entries should be made in their logbooks. As we went from ship to ship, we started noticing my log entry examples, still in my handwriting, had somehow made their way to other vessels in the fleet. We eventually put together a full document of recommended log entries to be used in the environmental logbooks. To this

MUCH OF MY TIME WAS SPENT REVIEWING RECORDS IN THE ENGINEROOM

company's credit, they have never been in trouble with the U.S. Government again, and I believe that our method of auditing the crew was responsible for this "culture change."

After the five-year probation period was over, several of our environmental auditors joined other firms. The cruise line company requested proposals from several competing environmental auditing firms, to continue the audits. The cruise line also wanted us to provide training for safe chemical storage, swimming pool maintenance, storage ventilation systems, and other safety issues, which the auditors had raised during our environmental audits. Although a different firm was contracted for these additional audits than the firm originally holding the compliance contract, the new firm requested my services again as their marine systems expert. This additional contract ended up running for three more years.

During approximately 160 audits performed on these cruise ships, I was able to visit almost every island in the Caribbean, Panama (though I also had other work there), numerous trips to Alaska, various West Coast port cities in the U.S., Hawaii, Mexico, and Central America, and most of the cruise ports in the Mediterranean and Aegean Seas. I also made lifelong friends from the two auditing firms for whom I worked, plus numerous friends on the cruise ships, such as Per Holand, the Fleet Environmental Officer. Many of these friends remain part of my life to this day.

***Cruise Ships, Cruise Ships, Cruise Ships***

I flew to Miami to attend the wedding of Per Holand to Cindy. The wedding took place in the Wedding Chapel aboard one of the newest cruise ships, as seen in the following photo.

## **Marine Safety & Environmental Consulting**

Because of the experiences gained on these cruise ship audits, more requests came to advise other cruise ship companies and oilfield supply vessel operators, who found themselves in trouble due to environmental compliance problems. Most of those jobs were short-lived, compared to the eight years that I spent auditing that one company. However, I shared my experience to assist these other companies in making the right decisions. During this time, I also became an AWO (American Waterways Operators) auditor for the "uninspected" towing vessel fleets on the Great Lakes and Inland Rivers. Working with under-trained crews and seeing them improve their regulatory compliance, plus making their difficult life safer, has been very rewarding.

On one particular project, another large cruise line was trying to decide whether or not to "fight" the EPA and U.S. Justice Department's charges of pollution from their ships. They had heard of the work our team was doing with the other cruise company, so they hired two of us to review their log books and documents and then to make several cruises on their ships as well. We found their record keeping was also very poor, and advised them that "fighting" the charges was hopeless. They pled guilty and were eventually audited by a different audit firm. That audit company took the "punishment" approach to their audits, and after several years, this cruise line was caught polluting again. The "culture" had not changed! Our team wished we could have audited them and also helped them.

There will be descriptions of some of the more unusual and exciting experiences that occurred during these audits, but those will be in the next chapter, separated by countries and locations traveled, such as my numerous trips dodging hurricanes in the Caribbean, airport delays, and security challenges, and, of course, dealing with lost baggage. Traveling is great fun, but can certainly be challenging!

On the up-side, there was occasionally time for a quick excursion, like the following really quick trip to Monte Carlo. The ship our team was auditing was anchored off-shore in Ville France, near Nice. We were nearly done with our work and had an extra day before we had to leave the ship in Barcelona, so we decided to take the train to Monte Carlo. The Casino and adjoining hotel were beautiful, and the harbor was full of expensive, large yachts, but the rest of what we saw of Monaco was very old and showed a lack of care. Croatia is much cleaner!

**VILLE FRANCE BEACH**

**MONTE CARLO CASINO**

# CHAPTER 17

## MORE CRUISE SHIP ADVENTURES

During the eight years, which included approximately one hundred sixty environmental compliance audits on cruise ships (not counting those three old Greek ships), lasting friendships were developed with many of the other auditors. Although I traveled a lot during those years on many other projects, I was usually traveling alone. Therefore, it was enjoyable to have companions on these ship audits, with whom to socialize and share experiences during and after our workdays. The auditing firm had a central team of trained auditors, however, they would often bring in "new blood" to be sure they had enough people ready to cover this contract and their other work. This meant frequently seeing old friends and making new ones. The addition of fresh eyes and ears also ensured that we did not get complacent.

During this time, we traveled to almost every major island in the Caribbean, most of the Pacific ports from Alaska to Central America, most of the Eastern seaboard cruise destinations, including Bermuda, and every major cruise port in the Mediterranean and Aegean Seas. Although our free time was very limited in many of these cruise destinations, on some of the longer cruises we were able to fit in some sightseeing. Our audits typically required four days of work, and if we were "stuck" aboard ship for seven days, we were able to go ashore occasionally.

We particularly enjoyed some of the longer travel destinations such as Aruba, Barcelona, Venice, Rome, and Puerto Rico. The reason for this was that the cruise lines would occasionally send us to those destinations the day before we were to meet the ship, which gave us an evening in these ports to enjoy some sightseeing, and a nice local dinner before boarding the ship the next morning.

AUDITOR EXCURSION IN SANTORINI, GREECE - FREE TIME AT A SHIPBOARD PUB

Being the most regular participant in most of these audits, I was occasionally meeting new auditors who had not seen some of these ports before. I enjoyed playing tour guide and would show the new person the sights, even if I had been to these locations several times before.

After the initial tension had cleared between the ship crews and the auditors, we were also able to enjoy friendships with many of the officers we saw regularly. Although our audits were serious, the companies we were auditing had learned quickly that we were there to help them as much as possible. We would point out their mistakes and report any violations, but we also showed the crews how to avoid these mistakes in the future.

By the end of the second year, we would be eagerly welcomed aboard and asked for advice. The ship Captains would occasionally invite us to the Captain's table in the main dining room during the cruise, but this formal dinner was not always enjoyable, because the Captain was also required to invite special passengers to his table, thus limiting our open conversation. Instead, the Captains began inviting us to their staterooms for special meals, prepared by the chef at the Captain's request.

DINING IN THE CAPTAIN'S STATEROOM

These dinners were less formal, and the food was spectacular. We learned to enjoy aquavit on the Norwegian ships, and ouzo on the Greek ships. One Captain went fishing one day while we were in port in Alaska, and that evening we ate fresh halibut in his conference room.

194

**CAPTAIN PREPARING MOUSSAKA**

One particularly interesting Greek Captain had an ongoing argument with the head ship's chef about the proper way to cook moussaka. The Captain invited us to the ship's galley to witness his demonstration, and that evening, we ate dinner in the Captain's stateroom to sample his creation. I must admit it was the best moussaka I have ever eaten.

Many of the more interesting adventures occurred on trips to Europe, and you might want to read "Sue and Bob's Great Adventure" described in a previous chapter.

## Barcelona

Barcelona was one of our frequent destinations to start our cruise audits, and although I was very lucky in my flights and handling of my luggage, not all of the auditors had the same luck. Each of us flew to our starting destination from our home cities, and therefore our flights were seldom the same. On one occasion, there was a baggage handler strike in Barcelona, and one of the lady auditors did not receive her luggage before the ship left port. Several of the crew members were nice enough to lend her some clothing, and the officers purchased several T-shirts at the gift shop for her to wear. We soon found out many of the passengers had also lost their luggage, and our auditor, Judi, did not feel out of place in the dining room wearing casual clothes.

Barcelona has one of those great open-air markets, with just a roof over the top. You can buy fish, meat, produce, cheese, candy, and gifts. Some of the auditors were shocked that HORSE MEAT was very popular there. The Ramblas (boulevard) which runs in front of that market, is a popular tourist destination. It is very wide and has shops and small restaurants in the "park-like" area between the two streets used by the cars. There are even a couple of Gaudi-designed homes along the Ramblas.

Because this was Gaudi's home city, there are many areas with his designs, and of course the huge cathedral, La Sagrada Familia, which has been under construction since 1882.

LA SAGRADA FAMILIA, ONE FAÇADE INTERIOR OF THE CATHEDRAL

GAUDI PARK GUELL

Although we all loved Barcelona and REALLY loved the tapas restaurants, we had to be careful on our walks around the Ramblas and other tourist areas. Barcelona is supposedly the "pickpocket capital of the world," although St. Petersburg is trying to gain that title. At least the pickpockets in Barcelona have a sense of humor. We walked in groups, so it was hard for the pickpockets to get behind one of us. When we saw a couple of suspect pickpockets, we would keep our hands in our wallet pockets and always have one of us looking behind. A few times, the pickpockets joked about it, saying, "So, you know about us?" Then they would laugh and go to look for someone less prepared.

My luggage problems seemed to occur on return flights, and on one occasion while flying through Paris on my way to Chicago, two bottles of expensive perfume were stolen from my luggage. Otherwise, my luggage would occasionally be delayed one or two days upon arrival in Chicago, but it always eventually arrived.

## Grand Cayman

We also flew into Grand Cayman numerous times to catch our ships. There is a beautiful beach on Grand Cayman, called Seven-Mile Beach. We stayed in several different hotels along that beach, and this Sunset Photo was taken there on one of my visits. They have a contest in Grand Cayman for people to submit sunset photos, and I always thought this one could have been a winner.

### Fish For Dinner?

There was an unusual restaurant experience in Grand Cayman, that some of you may have experienced. A restaurant near Seven-Mile Beach served dinner on a boardwalk at the water's edge. After dark, one of the employees came to a small pier extending over the water, and he rang a bell. Quickly the water around that pier was full of large tarpon. Then the restaurant employee would throw out the fish skins, which had been collected in the kitchen during the day. The tarpon would put on quite a show, going after the fish skins.

Next, the man would grab a fish skin with his teeth, and then lean out over the water. The tarpon would jump out of the water to grab the fish's skin from his mouth. He tried to get a few restaurant patrons to try that last trick, but they dropped the fish skin as soon as the tarpon came close!

### Wahoo Willie

On one flight to Grand Cayman, I struck up a conversation with my seatmate. He owned a construction company in Michigan but was semi-retired in Grand Cayman. He volunteered with Doctors Without Borders and flew around the world with them to assist in their charitable work.

This man invited me to visit his home and to meet Wahoo Willie, his

Jack Russell Terrier. Wahoo Willie had his own web page and was quite popular amongst the Cayman locals. When I told the gentleman that we had three auditors coming

to Grand Cayman, he told me to invite the others as well.

That afternoon, the other two auditors and I found our host's home on the far eastern end of the island. Wahoo Willie met us at the door, and you could tell this dog had a very confident attitude. He walked around like he was in charge!

The gentleman then invited us to take a boat ride, and with no surprise, the boat was named "Wahoo Willie"! He gave us a great tour of the residential, East end of the island, which was unfamiliar to us. Because we were boarding our cruise ship the next morning, we departed early and went to our hotel. However, Wahoo Willie was a big topic of conversation on that cruise.

## **Rough Weather**

Several of our Grand Cayman cruises started or ended after Tropical Storms had passed near the island before the vessel's arrival. Grand Cayman is not a deep-water port, so the passengers are tendered ashore in the small tender boats carried on board each cruise ship for that very purpose.

On one occasion, we were getting aboard in Grand Cayman, and we went to the pier where our ship's small tender boats normally docked. However, the usual ship's crewmembers and the photographers were not at the pier. We could see our ship at anchor, so we knew something was wrong. As we got closer, we discovered the waves were crashing over the pier, where the tenders would need to discharge and load passengers. It was obviously too rough to tender safely.

We called the ship via cell phone and they informed us that their agent would be picking us up, and taking us to a small dock on the leeward side of the island. One of the tenders would meet us there and transport us to the ship. The dock was small and could not be used for the passengers, but served its purpose of getting us onboard.

After we arrived on the ship, checked in, and received our room keys, we were in the elevator heading up to see the Captain. Some of the passengers in the elevator were complaining about not getting to the island, and it must not be so rough, because they saw one of the tenders bringing some people aboard. Passengers seem to think the cruise lines are always looking for ways to skip ports, thus profiting from Port Fees and other unused expenses. After listening to them "vent", we told them we were the people in that tender, and explained just how dangerous the tender dock had been. Cruise ships want good ratings from their passengers, but safety is their first concern!

On another occasion, it was again too rough to use tenders in Grand Cayman, but this time, we were leaving the ship. Not only our three auditors were leaving, but Bowser, the singer from Sha-Na-Na, was leaving the ship, as well as the Captain. Bowser had been entertaining on board and was heading to New York for another gig. The Captain had his replacement on board and was heading home for a wedding.

Like the boarding story above, it was too rough to use the normal tender dock, and in fact, the cruise ship had to go to the leeward side of the island to get us off safely. While boarding the tender, the Captain noticed that one of our lady auditors was wearing high heels. He warned her to be careful because the tender boat was lurching in the rough seas. As she was getting into the boat, the boat did lurch, and the Captain caught her. I'm sure she told that story when she got home!

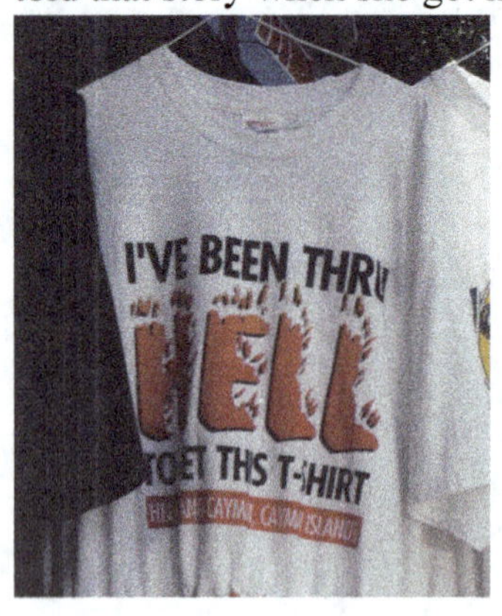


### I go to Hell for my clients………..

As mentioned in an earlier chapter, I have been to Hell twice in my career, once in Norway and once in Grand Cayman. I really should go to Hell, Michigan, to add another one to my list. Hell in Grand Cayman is not that great unless you want to buy a T-Shirt. It does look pretty rugged, with about a football field-sized area full of black limestone. Unless you want a T-shirt, maybe skip this one.

## <u>Aruba</u>

BEACH RIDING WITH MY DAUGHTER, CLAIRE

There certainly could have been a photo of Oranjestad, the Capital, which is beautiful. However, the thing that makes Aruba different from most Caribbean Islands is the rustic beauty along the coastline.

We enjoyed boarding in Aruba. It meant a flight down the day before, so we got a night in a hotel to rest, before we got on the ship the next morning. Aruba has to be the safest, friendliest island in the Caribbean. It is part of the Netherlands, but the U.S. Dollar is accepted everywhere. Their main business is tourism, with some Aloe products thrown in. Because Aruba is a desert island, the landscape is full of cacti. The aloe is probably not native to Aruba, but it grows well there. It seldom rains and has never been hit by a hurricane (though they get some winds) because of its protected position above South America, only 17 miles North of Venezuela. They have 0% unemployment, and they all speak English, which made it less stressful when we traveled there.

The Aruban food is a mixture of Dutch, American, local Aruban, Columbian, and Indonesian (another previous Dutch colony). All of these cuisines are great, so why eat American when you have those other foods available? Fresh local fish is also readily available.

## Stops in Curacao

Curacao is another Dutch island, part of the "ABC Islands" as once known (Bonaire being the third island). Aruba declared independence from Curacao, apparently due to economic differences. Curacao has an unemployment problem, and although Curacao looks VERY Dutch, as compared to Aruba, it is not as friendly as Aruba (where they say, "One Happy Island!").

The floating bridge in Curacao is the biggest tourist attraction. It is now reserved for pedestrian traffic only, with a new, high-span bridge now used for cars over the harbor. Our audit team did stay in Curacao a few times, but we preferred Aruba. We even visited the factory where Curacao liquor is manufactured.

I had visited Curacao Shipyard several years before these cruise ship audits, so I was able to play tour guide several times. On my first visit, the local restaurants were still serving iguana meat, though it was very expensive. The islanders considered iguana a delicacy, so it had been hunted nearly to extinction. They are now protected, and some are kept as pets, like those with me in the photo.

Just like in Aruba, the countryside is full of semi-wild goats and donkeys. Goat meat is served in many of their restaurants, but no donkey meat!

## Cozumel

Cozumel was another one of those ports used to meet the ships, and then ride them back to Florida. While we liked staying there, we started to feel threatened by the local hoodlums. Nothing serious happened, but we began to stay in our hotel rather than venture out to restaurants in the city, particularly after dark. We found a great restaurant near the airport, which

FLOATING BRIDGE IN CURACAO

served lobster by the ounce. The waiter would bring a large bowl of iced lobster tail, still raw, but out of the shell. You pointed to the one you wanted, and it would be weighed. The cost was reasonable and there was no shelling to be done. The last time we were in Cozumel, the restaurant had closed. We suspected its remote location made visitors feel uncomfortable, due to the problems we had experienced.

## Venice

SMALL CANAL IN VENICE

Venice is one of those places you just have to visit! Except for a few people, however, once is enough! Venice is too busy and filled with tourists. It is also very hot and humid in the summer, and everything is so expensive, including the use of toilets. Six of us sat at a table on St. Marcus Square, and it cost $100 for six cups of coffee. The waiter was very polite and did not rush us away from the table. We would normally try to find the small restaurants in the heart of the Old Town, and we looked for those where the local businessmen were eating. Those places were great!

Poor Venice has been overrun by cruise ships, and the local government is trying to limit the number of ships that can visit in one day. This problem, combined with their flooding problems, and the sinking buildings, has affected Venice. I'm just glad we could visit before things drastically change, because the cruise ships can no longer enter the Grand Canal, and passengers are now bussed into the Old City.

**ENTRANCE INTO MALTA USED AS MOVIE SET FOR 'TROY'**

## Genoa

One of the cleanest cities we saw in Italy was Genoa. It has a long maritime history, and in fact, Christopher Columbus was from Genoa, even though he worked for the Spanish Queen to discover the New World.

MARITIME THEMED PARK IN GENOA

One of the Chief Engineers on the ships was also from Genoa and considered himself to be Italian. He was blond and had blue eyes, so we joked with him about not looking very Italian and he would respond by saying, "Well, we are close to Germany and Switzerland up here. My ancestors must have traveled a little!"

Of course, Americans always identify Italians with black hair and olive skin, but the fact is that the majority of Italian-Americans came from Sicily, where that is true. On my first trip to Spain, I expected to see dark-haired and dark-skinned people only to again be surprised to see so many blonds. The thing is that Americans tend to stereotype people into categories, wrongly thinking their stereotypes are all-encompassing.

## Malta

This photo of the entrance into Malta Harbor was taken just before the movie, "Troy" was filmed. The darker structure on the white rock was part of the movie set, made to resemble Troy. I should probably see the movie myself to see what the final set looked like!

Many people like Malta, just because it is very different, both in appearance and culture. Although Great Britain controlled the island for many years, Malta has been under the control of the Romans, Moors, Knights of Saint John, the French, and finally the British. However, it is now an independent country.

Malta is a very strange island. It is one big, solid rock, in the Mediterranean with a significant maritime history, and has a large ship repair industry there. It is also apparently the center of the Knights Templar. Therefore, it is a very conservative country, and we were told divorce was illegal in Malta until 2011.

## **Civitavecchia (Port of Rome)**

When people say they are boarding a cruise ship in Rome, they are actually boarding in Civitavecchia. Although the cruise line did book a hotel for me in Rome, during a two-day stay, our team normally stayed at a crew hotel in a small village near Civitavecchia.

The ship's crew stayed at this hotel and it was very quaint and quiet. We ate with the crew, usually around 60 or more from around the world, who were replacing crewmembers already on the ship. The food was served family-style, on huge platters, all you could eat. The meal one night included a cold appetizer platter of seafood, which was a meal in itself. Then the wait staff brought out platters of hot fish, chicken, and pork, plus potatoes and vegetables. The meals at this crew hotel were better than at many big hotels in Rome.

After dinner, we took a walk along the beach and found this great castle on the water's edge. We tried to find out more about it, but all we were told was that it is privately owned.

My travels took me to Rome twice. Once was a two-day stay before meeting a cruise ship, and another visit was on my own, staying after my work was done. I wanted to visit the Vatican, which I had missed on my first, cruise-related trip. Rome is much like Venice because while you have to visit there, it is not a city to which people want to return once they've seen the sights. It is very hot, dirty, and filled with tourists. I found the people in Rome to be quite helpful, even friendly, which surprised me. You might think they would be sick of answering all those tourist questions!

ON AN OUTING IN ROME, ON A TWO-DAY LAYOVER

## Athens

TAKING AN EXCURSION TO THE ACROPOLIS

Athens is another one of those cities to visit once. Athens has so much history that it causes them problems. We were there before the 2004 Summer Olympics and were trying to get to the airport. At that time, the government was building a new subway from the airport to Athens. The subway was being built to handle the number of tourists they were expecting for the Olympic games. Unfortunately, they had to pause digging for the subway tunnel and change direction because construction had unearthed a new ancient building never discovered before.

On several occasions, we were affected by strikes in Athens. The dock workers were often on strike, causing the ships to change their order of port stops, to miss a strike day. After one of our audits, we were heading to the airport, and the taxis were on strike. Luckily, our Greek Captain called one of his personal friends, and that friend picked us up outside the cruise terminal and drove us to the airport.

It may have been on that occasion, but we witnessed a very sad event in the Athens airport on one trip. An older couple was checking in their luggage but the airline clerk noticed liquid running out of one of the bags. The man opened his suitcase and there were about ten bottles of homemade olive oil. For some reason, the bottles had either broken or the seals came open, and the oil just flowed out of his suitcase. They were probably taking the olive oil to a family member in the United States, but they really had a mess on their hands, and we really felt sorry for them.

## Greek Islands

The Greek Islands are a very different story. We loved them all, despite the tourists! Because tourism is the main income on most of the islands, they deal well with the tourists, as long as they leave lots of money!

SANTORINI; SHIPS INSIDE THE VOLCANO

Santorini is spectacular, with the buildings along the edge of the caldera, however, I don't want to be there if they have another earthquake, as pieces of the caldera have fallen into the crater several times in the past. The two most useable islands are Rhodes and Crete. They're not as spectacular as Santorini or Mykonos, but for that same reason, the number of tourists is less. We found those two islands to be very friendly and useable.

SEASIDE RESTAURANTS ON MYKONOS

On Mykonos, there are many great restaurants along the waterfront, which are flooded with tourists. However, there is a restaurant further into the village, generally used by the ship crews, which has more "family style" dishes, better for larger groups. At that

restaurant, you need to watch your plate, because they had two large pelicans, one called Petros, who would want to be fed. I heard that they have been known to steal food off the diners' plates.

## Acapulco, Porta Vallarta, and Cabo San Lucas

These Mexican ports were nice to see for the first time, and it is certainly worth seeing the Acapulco cliff divers. However, the poor kids begging and selling trinkets on the streets make it impossible to walk around freely. If you buy something from one child, there will be ten of them on the next street corner. They're cute and friendly, and it is very tough to say no to them. However, hoodlums or abusive parents take most of their money at the end of the day. Because of some very bad experiences happening to friends and acquaintances in Mexico, I personally will not return.

## Bermuda

DISEMBARKING SHIP IN BERMUDA

I am not sure of the attraction for tourists to go to Bermuda. The weather is always unsettled and it can be quite frigid except in mid-summer. The taxi drivers all have Winter homes in Miami and other warmer climates.

I was seasick on most of the cruises, so while in Bermuda, trying to work and recover from the motion sickness, I seldom went ashore. There is a great maritime museum on the opposite side of the harbor from the main city, which we did find time to visit on one trip.

**MARITIME MUSEUM IN BERMUDA**

## <u>Virgin Islands</u>

We stopped at St. Thomas often and at St. Croix twice over the years. St. Thomas has become very unsettled over the 30 years since I started going there, which is sad because it is a beautiful island. Of course, the Mongooses have overrun the place, but they don't seem to bother people.

**BUSY ST. THOMAS HARBOR**

While in St. Thomas Harbor on one cruise audit, there was a large yacht anchored in the middle of the harbor. Our team was curious about why the yacht was there, instead of at the marina. The bridge crew contacted the yacht to speak with their Captain. It turned out that the actor, Steve Martin, was on board, holding a meeting with producers about his upcoming movie, and they wanted to avoid publicity. A good place to get away from the public!

We only landed in St. Croix twice but found it to be very industrial, as compared to the other Virgin Islands. The second stop there was late evening, basically for our ship to refuel, so based on our previous experience, we did not go ashore.

### Vancouver

Vancouver is one of my favorite cities in North America. It is quaint and beautiful, and the people are sincere and friendly (once you get past the Immigration Agents)! We met ships in Vancouver many times on our way to Alaska. We always hoped one of our audit teams might get a balcony room (sometimes the ladies got one), but in Alaska, that never happened. These ships are typically booked solid on Alaska cruises. Therefore, we had to see entrances into Vancouver from the bow of the ship.

SUNRISE ENTRY INTO VANCOUVER

### Puerto Rico

We always loved meeting our ships in Puerto Rico. Good food, great hotels, and fantastic scenery. We seldom had a chance to see the sights, but

CASTILLO SAN FELIPE DEL MORRO AT THE ENTRY TO SAN JUAN HARBOR

the El Morro (Castillo San Felipe del Morro, to be correct) was near our cruise ship dock, so we got there many times.

## St. Maarten/St. Martin

Another one of our favorite Caribbean stops was St. Maarten. The island is half Dutch (St. Maarten) and half French (St. Martin), but no obvious border seems to exist. The French end of the island seems to have more hotels and fancier restaurants, plus more expensive stores, while the Dutch end of the island has more ethnic Caribbean food, and native crafts, and seemed more useable for our excursions.

We occasionally flew in or out of that island because, on longer cruises, we did not need to stay beyond 4 or 5 days. If you've not heard about that airport, watch a few videos on YouTube! The airplanes come in for landing right over Maho Beach, and people gather there to experience a plane occasionally just 40 or 50 feet over their heads on landing. When large planes take off, the jet blast literally blows people off their feet and they sometimes land in the ocean.

On one occasion, three of us auditors were leaving a cruise and headed to the airport. We were early for our flight, and since we had not seen much of the island beyond the port and the airport, we asked a lady taxi driver to give us a one-hour tour before taking us to the airport. Her price to do so seemed reasonable, and we asked her what we had time to see. She listed a drive-by the Butterfly Farm, Fort Louis, Lookout Point, and the NECCA-Bitch"! We asked her several times but the last item was always NECCA-Bitch. We figured we would just see what that was when we arrived! Finally, we pulled into a parking lot near the ocean, and we saw a sign explaining NECCA-Bitch. The sign said, "Notice – Clothing Optional beyond this point." She had been saying Naked Beach with her very Dutch/ Papiamento accent!

## United States Ports

We made it to numerous ports in the United States, from Boston to Miami, Key West to Galveston, and San Diego to Anchorage. No long and boring descriptions of those cities, because many of my readers have most likely already been there, but it is worth recounting unusual events that occurred in some of them.

## <u>Alaska</u>

HEADING DOWN INSIDE PASSGE TO VANCOUVER

My first trip to Alaska was on one of those old, Greek cruise ships, as recounted in a previous chapter. Those who have been to Alaska probably understand how difficult it is to describe and explain just how beautiful it is up there. The only other place that fits this description in my mind is New Zealand, and maybe Croatia. Every part of Alaska, particularly along the ocean, is just spectacular!

ALASKA IS BEING OVERRUN BY CRUISE SHIPS LIKE VENICE & DUBROVNIK

It is sad to see how those glaciers are receding. The cruise ships previously sounded their horns to get the ice to fall (calve) off the edge, but that practice has stopped. At least three of our cruise audits went into Glacier Bay, and on one of those cruises, a Native American narrator was on the ship's public address system, describing the glaciers, and telling us how many miles they had receded during his lifetime. Very shocking!

MY FIRST GLACIER IS SEEN IN WHITTIER GLACIER BAY FROM A CRUISE SHIP

During that first flight up to Alaska, the day was clear and bright. I had a window seat, and the views were unbelievable for a Midwest American. The mountains, glaciers, and mountain lakes were clearly visible that day, and my reaction was like that of a 10-year-old boy! I just stared in awe!

KETCHIKAN SHOPPING DISTRICT

Our cruise audits always stopped in Skagway and Ketchikan. The only times when Juneau and Anchorage were on the itinerary, we had left the ship earlier. We were billing on a per/day basis, so unless we agreed not to invoice for those extra days, we flew home. Besides, there were other clients to care for back home and a family who would probably wonder why only Dad got to take vacations! We did get to take a quick bus tour to the White Pass but could not spare the time for the long train ride. The tall poles along the roadside used to measure the amount of snow for the plow drivers, made me feel like our 12-18-inch snowfalls in Wisconsin were nothing. Ten to

SKAGWAY RAILROAD SNOW BLOWER

twelve feet of snow falling in one storm is nothing in the White Pass. That huge snow blower pictured above was used on the railroads, and it shows how serious it is to deal with the snow up there.

We asked our tour bus driver about the winters in Skagway. He had moved there about 10 years prior and said he enjoyed the solitude. In emergencies, Skagway is accessible by air and boat, but they are cut off from land access for four to five months. He told us the permanent residents make several trips to Whitehorse, Yukon Territory, before winter. They stocked up on dried and canned foods to last them through the winter, and he rented about 40 movies, which he would return the following Spring. He said the movie rental people were very understanding and always cut him a deal!

During the Gold Rush of 1896-99, many of the prospectors from the "lower 48" states, did not understand the winters in the Yukon, so before they would be allowed to proceed through the Chilkoot Pass, there was a long, prepared list of gear, which they were required to buy and carry up the pass. It took them several trips to carry it all. The shame of this situation was the good claims had all been taken before most of those men ever reached the Klondike. Over 100,000 men tried, and only 30,000 ever found any gold. However, the suppliers of goods, in towns like Skagway, became rich by selling those necessary supplies to the prospectors.

To read more about my Alaska experiences, see the Fishing Vessel Investigations Chapter, about a trip to Dutch Harbor.

## <u>Miami & Ft. Lauderdale</u>

I hope I don't offend too many people, but I learned to hate Miami. The airport is a mess, and the airport workers seem to all have short tempers. I did find the taxi drivers to be nice in Miami though, so there is hope!

Away from the airport, I was not as negative about my Miami experiences. I spent a lot of time in the Port of Miami, not only on the cruise ships but also doing a ship survey for NOAA and several cargo ship surveys.

An interesting thing occurred in Miami Harbor after the 9/11/2001, World Trade Center incident. The Coast Guard was requiring an underwater sweep by divers, and then guiding the ships out of the harbor, like they were doing in most United States Ports. When the cruise ships entered port at the end of a cruise, they wanted to moor as quickly as possible, to disembark the passengers, so they moored at their dock with the bow pointing inland. This timing is necessary to allow the crew to clean the ship, restock supplies, and load the next batch of passengers, to be ready for a late afternoon departure that same day. The vessels then turned around before they left port in the afternoon, which may have been a 15-20 minute procedure in those crowded harbors.

Due to the tense situation during that time after 9/11, the Coast Guard requested that cruise ships make their turn-around when they arrived in port, rather than before they departed. They requested this in case it became necessary for the ships to make a quick departure from the harbor (in case of an emergency). Having five or six large cruise ships all trying to make that turn at once, would take almost two hours.

All of the cruise lines complied with this request, except for one! I will not mention their name, but the rest of the cruise lines were not happy with the one company's refusal to observe this legitimate request.

Fort Lauderdale is a much easier airport and the workers are friendlier. Maybe they are less stressed! I was able to watch the Fort Lauderdale Air Show from the airport once while waiting for my flight. It was a great view of the show from a very comfortable vantage point.

## <u>Key West</u>

Key West is always a fun stop, but this usually occurred early in the cruise, and our audit process had just started. At best, we got to take in a quick lunch ashore.

SLOPPY JOE'S, HOME OF ERNEST HEMINGWAY CONTES

One time we stopped at Sloppy Joe's for lunch, and I wanted to buy one of their T-shirts, showing Ernest Hemingway, with whom I share a bit of a resemblance. While in their gift shop, the sales lady said, "Were you in the contest last year?" Not aware of any contest, my answer was no. She then said, "Well if you were in it, you would have taken at least 3$^{rd}$ Place." I'm thinking a trip to Key West for this contest might be a good excuse. Now older, it seems my face and beard look more like Hemingway each year!

My first Sloppy Joe's T-shirt came from the Chief Engineer in the above photo. He had bought it because of his resemblance to Hemingway, but after meeting me, he thought my resemblance was much closer.

So, after looking at this photo, showing me, wearing the Sloppy Joe's T-Shirt, with a picture of Ernest Hemingway, the question is: Should I go to Key West and enter the contest?

## <u>New York & Newark</u>

New York and Newark were always our departure points for Bermuda cruises. Having worked in the New York area numerous times for other jobs, usually in places like Brooklyn, Hoboken, or Staten Island, New York was not a place high on my list for entertainment.

We did enjoy the sailing time out of the harbor, and getting to see the Statue of Liberty, Ellis Island, etc. These audits occurred between 1999-2008, so we had the experience of sailing out before the World Trade Center disaster, and shortly afterwards. It was eerie to see the reactions of the passengers that first time, shortly afterwards. Normally, those sail-outs have a party atmosphere, but on that day, the ship was dead silent as we sailed past the spot where the World Trade Center towers had been.

## <u>Boston</u>

Speaking of the times right after September 11, 2001, we had a cruise starting in Boston, just ten days after the actual incident. As you may know, the hi-jacked planes took off from Boston and headed for New York and Washington. Our audit team spent a lot of time flying, and in fact, I just returned from a trip to Miami on 9/10/2001. One of our audit team members had been on a plane from London to New York that day, and he spent three days in Gander, Newfoundland, before getting home. From that day onward, we were all apprehensive about flying, particularly into Boston. Flights had been reduced or canceled into Boston, and my flight was booked into nearby Providence. I was relieved not to be flying into Boston at that time.

Because many passengers had canceled their cruise due to the fear that still gripped many citizens of the United States at that time, the entire audit team was upgraded to empty balcony staterooms. The feeling on the ship was very somber, which is unusual for a cruise. This cruise was going up to Maine and Halifax on a "Leaf Peeper" cruise, from where we would depart and fly home.

The most unusual thing happened in Boston upon departure! The Coast Guard guided us out of Boston Harbor with three small boats, which had their loaded machine guns on the front deck. There had been concern that terrorists might want to sink ships in the major harbors, so for the next year, each ship was scanned by divers for explosives and then guided out of the harbors by the Coast Guard at most American ports.

We had one Coast Guard boat at the bow and one at each bow quarter. They used their loudspeaker to tell the pleasure craft in the channel to steer clear, and in one case, a sailboat did not respond. As the sailboat came closer, one of the Coast Guard boats sped toward the sailboat, and we heard the next announcement, "Divert your course or we will open fire!" The sailboat quickly changed course. There was just no fooling around only 10 days after 9/11!

## <u>New Orleans and Galveston</u>

New Orleans was not a normal embarkation port, but several cruise lines were "trying it" as well as Galveston, to lure passengers from Texas and

Louisiana. We enjoyed those ports for departures, but the sail-out was tough for the crew because they were in a long and slow, restricted channel for most of the afternoon. There were a lot of shrimp trawlers and oilfield-related vessels in the channel, so the crew had to be on their toes.

Our audits usually started with an Opening Meeting on our departure day, which required the attendance of the Captain, Staff Captain, Safety Officer, Chief Engineer, Hotel Director, and Environmental Officer. Most of those officers could not leave their duty station during the passage through a restricted channel, so our audit could not start until the next morning.

Few of the major cruise lines have continued to use these ports except during special events, like Super Bowls, Mardi Gras, etc.

## <u>Seattle</u>

Seattle was a common stop for Alaska Departures, if not Vancouver. We never got to come into Seattle the night before, because the two- or three-hour time difference for those of us coming from the East or Midwest, allowed us to arrive the same day and make it to the ship before departure.

Although I had worked in Seattle numerous times on other projects, it was nice to play 'tourist' on a couple of these trips. None of us had ever experienced the "Flying Fish" at Pike's Place Market, so we had to see that happen. If you do not know what this is about, search for it online and watch a video. They have used the success of their friendly sales technique to help other businesses.

Because the Flying Fish has become a huge tourist attraction, large crowds stand around, waiting for them to throw a fish. Sometimes the salespersons will yell out, "Somebody needs to buy a fish if you want to see the show!" Someone usually obliges and then the show begins!

## San Francisco

This is another one of my favorite cities, but don't want to live there! My son lives in San Francisco and it is just plainly, too expensive!

We only sailed into San Francisco twice, and once was for me to depart the ship. Two days in town to spend with my son, and then flew to Los Angeles to start another cruise ship audit. It seemed silly to fly home to Chicago and two days later, leave for Los Angeles.

After two days of "pigging out" on garlic crab and clams, it was good to leave, to save my waistline!

## Los Angeles, San Pedro & Long Beach

The Port of Los Angeles is located in San Pedro, south of the actual city of Los Angeles. San Pedro is a nice town, despite the huge container terminals and oil storage tanks nearby. I had found San Pedro many years earlier while doing an insurance investigation of an oil spill in nearby Wilmington. San Pedro is a nice mix of hotels, touristy attractions, and good restaurants. However, there were also a lot of smaller restaurants and hotels, which were preferable to my tastes.

There's a great Maritime Museum in San Pedro, including a gift shop, which sells unusual items. It's a great place to spend an afternoon, plus they have a nice viewing area of the harbor. If you'd like to see what happens in a large harbor, but do not want to be exposed to the dirt and dangers, San Pedro is a good place to go and observe.

I included Long Beach in this group because it is worth going there to see the old "S.S. Queen Mary" cruise ship. It is now a permanently moored attraction vessel but is in very well-maintained condition. The hotel on board uses the original passenger staterooms for the hotel rooms, and the restaurant is in one of the original ship's dining rooms. The engineroom has been turned into a fantastic museum, with good views of the machinery. A movie tells the history of the vessel. Once you've seen the engineroom, don't miss the navigation bridge!

## Hawaii

Although Hawaii had been a frequent stop for previous work projects, I was usually alone on those trips. It was nice to be in Hawaii, including Honolulu, Kauai, Hilo, and Maui, with friends to share the sites. We tried to get as much time as possible ashore in the outer ports because all of us were familiar with Honolulu from previous working trips. We never made it up to the volcano, so that may need to stay on my bucket list a while longer! We WERE WORKING after all!

## San Diego

Our audit team always enjoyed boarding in San Diego. Not only was it more streamlined to clear and board passengers than ports like Los Angeles and Miami, but there were restaurants and parks within easy walking distance from the port facilities. It is bad enough to wait in long lines, but when you are stuck in the port building, with nothing to do, it makes it much worse. San Diego always seemed much more organized.

The following picture of the sailing ship, Star of India, is one example. This is a museum ship, within a few minutes walk of the San Diego Cruise Terminal. There are also restaurants and sidewalk food carts around, all of which make the wait enjoyable.

STAR OF INDIA

## <u>GENERAL COMMENTS ON THE CRUISE SHIP INDUSTRY</u>

We always liked those cruise itineraries that allowed us to avoid getting on the ship at the major "turn-around" ports, such as Miami, Ft. Lauderdale, New York (though Newark was OK), and Los Angeles. Doing twenty cruises a year, those long lines getting on and off the ship became very tiresome. Ports such as San Diego, San Juan, and Vancouver seemed much more organized, so we did not mind those turnarounds nearly as much and preferred getting on the ship in places like Aruba or St. Maarten and then sailing back to the United States. In the earlier years of those cruise audits, we also enjoyed getting aboard in Mexican ports, but dealing with the poor economy there, as well as the possibility of being kidnapped or mugged, eventually turned us against those ports.

While waiting in line to depart at the end of the cruise, we once heard a passenger tell a crew member, "I bet you're glad to be back, so you can rest!" If that passenger only knew, that "Turn-Around" day is the worst day of the cruise for the crew. They must wake early to start taking passengers' pieces of luggage from the hallways, down to the main deck to be offloaded. They then start cleaning staterooms as soon as the passengers vacate their rooms, and all bedding and towels need to be removed and sent to the laundry. Once the passengers have left the ship, all of the public spaces must be thoroughly cleaned and sanitized, and the passenger staterooms cleaned and made up. When the new passengers come aboard, the crew has to get their luggage to the staterooms. The breakfast for the departing passengers is barely over and then the buffet starts as soon as the new passengers come aboard. Passengers are full of questions that first day, and to top it off, the crew has to supervise the Emergency Lifeboat Drill before dinner. NO, the crew DOES NOT REST when they return to port!

The crewmembers seen on cruise ships work hard for minimal pay. The officers, at that time, had 4-month contracts and the unlicensed crew had 8-month contracts, so they were away from home most of the year. If you ever watched the Costa Concordia disaster videos, note the young men who were launching the lifeboats after the Captain and other officers deserted the ship. Most of those who stayed behind were the unlicensed crew, a majority of them from the Philippines. The unlicensed crew is the backbone of the maritime industry, particularly cruise ships. They are typically well-trained in their home countries before they ever get a sailing job, and they are extremely dedicated. When you are on a cruise and see those guys and girls painting and cleaning, realize that they are the ones who know how to save your life if an accident occurs. They fight the fires and launch the lifeboats!

I don't want to overlook the good officers on these ships. The two cruise lines we worked with over those 8 years had great officers. There are very few that would act irresponsibly, like those on the Costa Concordia. The environmental officers we worked with were extremely dedicated to their jobs – protecting the environment. However, even the officers gave a lot of credit to the unlicensed crew because there were only about 30 officers on each ship, but there were about one thousand unlicensed crew members. Those crew members are the ones that make the officers look good!

# CHAPTER 18

## FISHING VESSEL INVESTIGATIONS
## SAMOA, FIJI, & ALASKA

### <u>My First Tuna Seiner</u>

There was no reason to do many surveys of fishing vessels during my career, until John Barr at ABSTech called, asking me to attend a Pacific fleet tuna seiner in American Samoa. The seiner had experienced numerous fractures in the fish well bulkheads, which was contaminating the fish with rusty water.

My travel agent received another request, which was quite a challenge for her to fulfill. She often told me that working with my travel requests was like a course in World Geography! There were only two flights per week in and out of American Samoa, with a change of planes in Honolulu. She booked me on the next flight.

Pago Pago, American Samoa, (pronounced "Pango Pango") is in the South Pacific, East of New Zealand, and located just to the East of the International Dateline. American Samoa should not be confused with Samoa (Western Samoa), which is located just West of the International Dateline. The differences between American and Western Samoa will be explained in more detail, later in this chapter. My hotel was constructed to look like a traditional Samoan house, called a fale (fah-lay). It first looked like this was paradise, but soon I learned that life was not as perfect as it appeared, because the United States had turned this into a welfare state! The United States has mismanaged the Island with Government subsidies and hand-outs, turning an island of industrious people into one almost 100% on welfare.

Other than the Samoan natives, the few outsiders on the island were generally associated with the tuna fishing industry. StarKist and Chicken of the Sea both had packing plants on American Samoa, and all of Pago Pago harbor smelled like fish.

At any given time, there might be 20 to 30 seiners in the harbor, either waiting to unload their fish or to make repairs and replenish their supplies for the next trip.

BEAUTIFUL BEACHES, BUT ALL PRIVATE, AND "NO TRESPASSING!"

Having a lot of free time and a rental car, I drove every road on the island several times during my "off-hours." The island was beautiful, but the beaches and parks were all private. If you parked the car and went for a walk, the locals would tell you to get off their beach.

There were decorated concrete boxes on the front porches of many homes, with flowers nicely arranged on them. It was later explained to me that the Matriarch of the family was buried on the front porch and that

FRONT PORCH CRYPT OF THE FAMILY MATRIARCH

family members would return to the home to leave flowers on her grave, even if they no longer lived in the house.

I attended a Catholic Mass one Sunday while in Samoa, and it was beautiful. The music, sung in the local language, was fantastic.

Most of the houses on the island had been damaged by a typhoon a few months earlier. FEMA gave money to the Samoans to repair their homes, but many of them decided to buy a new truck with the money instead, so the telltale "blue tarps" were still on the damaged roofs months later. Almost every house I saw had a new pick-up truck parked out front.

The United States Government had used American Samoa as a strategic base during World War II, and, to pacify the natives, the United States put them on a welfare system. The residents now didn't work because there was no need. When I challenged those statements, because Samoans worked in the hotels, restaurants, and fish packing plants, the explanation was that those workers were not from this island. Those workers were all citizens of Western Samoa. So, the United States has changed this native culture, just like we did in Kwajalein!

There was some good entertainment at our hotel, with a show of local dancers. However, this dance troupe also came over from Western Samoa.

A DANCE TROUPE FROM WESTERN SAMOAN

There is a strange custom in American Samoa, where one of the boys in many families is raised as a girl. They stay at home and help their mother. The practice is called Fa'afafine, and it is very complicated to explain. You can research that term if you wish to learn more. Some of the Fa'afafine worked in our hotel, and they are not classified as gay individuals, but as a "third gender."

Back to the purpose of my trip! It was a large, Pacific Fleet tuna seiner called "Bold Fleet," which had been built in San Diego, California. The two major builders of tuna seiners at that time were a yard in Tacoma, Washington, and this one in San Diego. The "problem fractures" in the fish wells were inspected as soon as possible, and we saw all of the fractures were in the same general location in each fish well, each having a similar appearance. I asked if they had structural drawings aboard, and luckily, they did.

It was a surprise to see the steel used in the fish well bulkheads were rectangular, structural tubing. My previous ABS factory inspection experience rang an alarm bell in my head; this type of steel tubing is "cold-formed" and then welded, which makes the tubing extremely brittle. During a factory inspection in Chicago, (Welded Tube Company of America), the metallurgist at the plant had explained that this type of tubing was great for stanchions (vertical columns) in ships but was not suitable to be used in areas where they would need to flex. The fish-well bulkheads flexed continually, and these steel tubes were the root of the problem.

To confirm my suspicion, we needed to cut open a portion of several fish wells. The vessel owner was hoping for a quick fix, but he agreed to let me cut open two small areas. The two most likely damaged areas were chosen, which hopefully would confirm my suspicions. The local ship repair crew cut two 18" x 18" sections of plate between two of the suspected longitudinal frames. My suspicion was confirmed, and the vessel owner was shocked because the rectangular steel tubing in these areas had broken in half. This allowed the fish well plating, as well as the hull plate, to flex, causing the fractures. Although this now became a huge problem for the owner, my suspicions were justified, and this vessel may have been saved from sinking on a future voyage.

## *Fishing Vessel Investigations*

While in Pago Pago, the Insurance Company asked me to complete a full survey of the vessel before heading home. It was shocking to see the poor condition of the vessel's hull and machinery, but it was eventually learned from other tuna vessel surveys that the Captain and crew's job was to find and catch fish, and the Chief Engineer's job was to keep the fish frozen until they returned to the packing plant. Hull and machinery maintenance, other than the refrigeration system, were not their primary responsibility! These fishermen were wonderful, hard-working people, but they were FISHERMEN first, and not the maintenance-savvy MARINERS I was used to working with.

I called my Insurance Company client to inform them of the bad news. The Bold Fleet was taken out of service and the owner sold the boat. Several months later, an attorney for the Insurance Company called and asked me to attend a Mediation in San Diego, to decide what to do with the Bold Fleet. At this meeting, we were told the organization representing the Pacific Tuna Fleet now owned the Bold Fleet, and they wanted it repaired. They asked my opinion on what to do, and they said they intended to drydock the Bold Fleet in Whangarei, New Zealand, and make full repairs. Working with their Naval Architect to develop a repair plan, we decided to remove the damaged framing and replace it with steel that could take the flexure, and also to add more steel in those areas that had not been damaged.

After returning home to make my written report, there came another call, asking me to attend the final week of work in Whangarei, to be sure the shipyard had done the work according to our plans. This would be my first trip to New Zealand. Whangarei (pronounced Fong-ger-ray) is on the northeast corner of the North Island of New Zealand, near the Bay of Islands.

The itinerary was Chicago to Los Angeles, then to Auckland, and changing planes for Whangarei. The arrival point was at a little airport in Whangarei, where a sign for a hotel shuttle caught my attention. I approached the driver and asked if he could take me to my hotel. The driver hoped there was no hurry because he had another passenger heading in the opposite direction. This would be a good way for me to see the sights, so it was fine with me.

We dropped off the first passenger at his home and then the driver, Ian, headed back to town. He narrated the scenery and gave me some local history. When arriving at my hotel, I asked him what the charge was for the ride, and he said it was a voluntary contribution, and payment was not required. Apparently, the shuttle service is run by volunteers working for the local helicopter medical service. They accept donations but there was not a set fare. I rewarded him with a healthy donation and thanked him for the great conversation. He then asked me how long I was staying in Whangarei, and my answer of one week prompted, "Well then, you must come for dinner one night."

A dinner was arranged with Ian and his wife that week. We said we would meet again someday, but neither of us probably expected that would happen. Later in this chapter, there is a story about another meeting, several years later.

BOLD FLEET ON AN INCLINED RAILWAY DOCK AT WHANGAREI, NZ

We worked on the Bold Fleet for the rest of that week and finished the repairs. The photo below shows the Bold Fleet on drydock in Whangarei, nearing completion. The gray areas on the hull were replaced due to damages, but most of the repairs were performed from the inside of the fish wells. The Bold Fleet went back fishing and we never heard more about her. Good repairs!

VISITING THE KAURI FOREST

While in Whangarei, the Chief Engineer of the Bold Fleet had little work to do, so we rented a car for a day and drove to the Kauri forest. Kauri trees are one of the largest diameter trees in the world. They are not as tall as the Sequoia trees in California but the trees in the original forest were huge. Most of them were cut down for lumber before the people realized that it took hundreds of years to grow another one. We also stopped at the Kauri Museum, which told the history of these magnificent trees.

VISITING THE KAURI MUSEUM

New Zealand has a wonderful history, but not for the Maori people. They were poorly treated, as were most indigenous people. However, the Maori had signed treaties back when the English arrived in New Zealand, which helped their cause.

Lamb has always been one of my favorite meals, but during my trips to New Zealand, I discovered the definition of "good lamb." One time, while eating in a restaurant with the vessel owner, a "crown roast" of lamb was my choice. Having only heard of crown roast, I asked the waitress how many ribs were on the order, and she looked at me with some surprise, and said, "The whole thing!" That did not seem possible from my understanding of lamb, but when the crown roast arrived at the table, the entire rib roast was on my plate, displayed like a crown. I then remembered a statement my friend Ian, from Whangarei, had made, "When my lambs' lips touch the grass for the first time, they are sent to

LAMB USED TO BE THE MAJOR EXPORT FROM NEW ZEALAND

231

market!" That is why New Zealand lamb is so mild and tender: It is all milk-fed meat! And small!

At that same meal, my naïve nature was exposed, and the honesty of the people became clear, and certainly that of the waitress. I left a cash tip on the table for her, and as we were leaving the restaurant, the waitress ran after us and said, "Sir, you must have dropped this money!" I told her it was left for her, and she asked me, "Why?" The ship owner smiled and told me to take my money. At that time, tipping was almost unheard of in New Zealand, but they have started to learn from the tourists and they now accept tips.

## <u>Just Get Me Home!</u>

One year later, I took a second trip to Pago Pago to survey several tuna seiners for insurance renewal. I had explained to my client that I needed to be home on a certain date because my son was receiving an important scouting award. My client told me to do whatever was necessary to get home but they really needed these surveys. As previously mentioned, the flights to Pago Pago were routed through Honolulu, and there were only two flights in each direction, each week. As usual, things did not go as planned, and one of the ships was delayed. It took me an extra day to finish the job and I missed my flight back home.

I advised my travel agent in Chicago about the problem, with the following comment: "I don't care if you fly me around the world, but get me home by Saturday!" Having missed so many family events because of my career, it was important for me to keep my promise to be home for this event.

My travel agent called back later and said to me laughing, "Well, you won't be flying around the whole world, but nearly half of it, if you want to get home on time!" She had found a flight from American Samoa to Western Samoa, then another flight from there to Auckland, New Zealand. From Auckland, there was an Air New Zealand flight to Los Angeles, and then home to Chicago. The nice part of the trip was that it included an overnight stay in Western Samoa, which was of great interest to me since my first trip to Pago Pago the previous year.

The short flight got me to Apia, Western Samoa, in the early afternoon, so there was time to look around the city near my hotel. The hotel was called Aggie Gray's, and it had a lot of history associated with it. The hotel had private fales, similar to Pago Pago, but the ones at Aggie Gray's were much more elaborate.

AGGIE GRAY'S HOTEL IN WESTERN SAMOA    WESTERN SAMOA FALES, WITH ELABORATE INTERIOR

At one time, Western Samoa was a "go-to" place for celebrities, and the private Fales were named after the people who had stayed in them. There was a "Richard Nixon" Fale and numerous others named after old movie stars. At the time of my visit, fewer people were visiting Western Samoa because of the travel time needed to get there, but Apia looked like what Hawaii must have looked like 100 years ago, except with modern conveniences. There was one cruise ship per week plus the service of Polynesian Airlines, which was my flight the next day. They flew from Pago Pago to Apia, and as far as Auckland.

THE FALE USED BY PRESIDENT RICHARD NIXON AT ONE TIME

The people in Apia were very warm and talkative. My taxi driver and the hotel staff were very willing to talk, and they always had big smiles when you met them. They were much friendlier than the locals in American

Samoa, and my driver told me to come back for a longer stay. The beaches in Western Samoa were OPEN TO THE PUBLIC!

The next morning, the taxi took me to the airport and we again had a great conversation. It was noticeable that none of the houses had walls, just curtains that could be rolled up. The taxi driver told me that the Samoan people trusted one another and had nothing to hide. They did not need walls!

My flight from Pago Pago had been on a small turbo-prop, but the flight to Auckland was on a new 737 jet. I was sitting in First Class, because the Economy seats had been sold out, and was reading the Polynesian Airlines Magazine. It was full of great articles and wonderful photos. Such magazines are not normally great reading, but this one was worth reading cover to cover. I was even reading the Welcome Message from the President of Polynesian Airlines when the flight attendant came by to offer drinks. Sitting by the window, and looking over my seatmate to address the flight attendant, I recognized the man sitting next to me. It was the President of Polynesian Airlines, and his picture was above the article I was reading!

I told him that I recognized him from his picture and he was more than willing to talk to me and answer questions. He had been an executive with New Zealand Airlines and had been hired by Polynesian Airlines to "get them into the 20th Century," he told me. Polynesian Airlines' business had been good up until the expansion of the other airlines flying to Auckland and Sydney, such as United, American, New Zealand Air, and Qantas. Those airlines started in the United States, typically Los Angeles or Honolulu, and when people started their travel on one of those major airlines, they tended to stay with them on the "feeder flights" as well. His solution was to first buy the 737 we were seated in, to fly people from Auckland and Sydney, and he was on his way to Sydney to negotiate with Qantas, to buy a 747, which would make three round-trip flights per week from Los Angeles. He figured the passengers on that 747 flight would then stay with Polynesian Airlines on the shorter flights to the various Polynesian Islands.

Following up on Polynesian Airlines, his plans and proposed flights had started from Los Angeles and Honolulu, and their current website now shows that they have partnered with Samoa Airlines. It also appears that they plan to buy a new 787. It looks like he did a great job, not only to get them into the 20th Century but well into the 21st Century.

My flights from Auckland to Los Angeles, and then to Chicago went fine, and despite some terrible jet lag, I made it home the night before my son's award ceremony.

## Investigation of a Sunken Tuna Seiner

This time it was a call from an insurance adjuster in San Diego, who had received my name from one of the attorneys on the Bold Fleet incident. The adjuster asked me to review drawings of a vessel, the "Valerie," which had sunk in the South Pacific. He was also sending crew statements and photographs to help me determine how the tuna seiner had sunk. The crew saw water rushing into the hull beneath the main propulsion engines, shortly after the ship made an emergency stop. Tuna seiners encircle a school of tuna with their net, and when the ship approaches the starting end of their net, which is being held by the ship's skiff, they make a sudden stop to close the seine. However, in this case, they almost ran over their net, so they did a full reverse and called an emergency stop. The ship vibrated violently, and apparently, there was some sort of structural failure beneath the engines. The ship sank quickly, and the crew only saw water filling the engine room.

The crew was all saved, including the ship's dog. They sent me photos of two crew members swimming toward the large ship's skiff. One had the dog in his arms and the other was carrying the statues from the ship's shrine. These crews were a mixture of Portuguese and Filipino fishermen, and each ship had a shrine in the crew's hallway, just outside the galley. The crew generally made the Sign of the Cross each time they passed.

Even after reviewing everything they had sent to me, it would be impossible to do anything more than guess the cause of the sinking.

About two months after that conversation, the same adjuster called again and said a sister vessel of the "Valerie" had nearly sunk, but the Chief Engineer was able to stop the leakage. The vessel made it to Fiji safely and the British Insurance Company for that owner wanted me to attend the vessel in Fiji and determine a course of action.

Being on a machinery inspection at the Caterpillar plant in Peoria, Illinois, the best I thought I could do was to plan my trip to Fiji, after getting home to Chicago that evening. The adjuster said that he needed me in Fiji sooner than indicated. He wanted me to leave my car in Peoria and fly to Fiji from there. This seemed crazy, but it was my nature to comply. The adjuster told me my tickets would be waiting for me at the Peoria airport, and my flights would be from Peoria to Chicago, Chicago to Los Angeles, and Los Angeles to Fiji. He would have an attorney from his office meet me at LAX because one of the crew members had died during the emergency repair. The attorney would be investigating that death, and my job was to investigate the hull problems.

These were the days before 9/11/2001, so my wife met me with a suitcase at O'Hare, in Chicago. The luggage was checked to LAX, not knowing the details for the rest of the journey. In Los Angeles, the attorney met me at my arrival gate (something else we can no longer do). We claimed my bag and then we both checked in for the flight to Fiji.

After waiting at our gate for an hour, they announced that our flight had been canceled. No reason was given, but we were rebooked on a flight the next day. We asked about our luggage, and they said it would be changed to our new flight. The attorney lived in San Diego, and he invited me to come to his home for the evening, so off to San Diego we went.

The next day, we returned to LAX and boarded our plane to Fiji. Upon arrival in Suva, Fiji, we went to baggage claim and my bag was missing. They checked and found it had stayed in Los Angeles. It would arrive on the next flight, one day later.

THE 'BONNIE,' MOORED IN SUVA, FIJI

We went to the ship, the "Bonnie," and started working. The Chief Engineer described this incident, which was similar to the one which caused the "Valerie" to sink, however, the Chief was able to get the pumps started in the engine room to keep up with the ingress of water. The Chief

236

then dove under the ship, using just a pressurized hose for air, and was able to force a large bolt into the hole from the outside of the ship. With that bolt in place, the Chief then sent his "skinniest" crewmember under the engine with a rubber gasket, a steel washer, and a nut that fit the bolt. This secured the bolt and the leakage stopped.

Going into the engineroom bilges, I found numerous areas of standing water trapped behind the longitudinal frames. Feeling the steel under the standing water with my fingers, there was obvious heavy corrosion and pitting. There could easily be more leaks starting, and it was recommended to the insurance company, that this vessel must be immediately drydocked for repairs. The ship was going to head to Nelson, New Zealand, where we would meet them in a few days, seeing there was no large drydock available in Fiji.

While discussing this incident and comparing it to the one that sank the first vessel, the Captain said there was a third sister vessel, the "Jennifer", and we should probably warn them of these dangerous conditions. After speaking with the Captain of the "Jennifer" and describing the problem to the owner of these three vessels, it was decided to have the "Jennifer" go to a shipyard in Australia, where the lawyer and I would meet them and look at the condition of their hull.

While in Fiji, I fell victim to a local scam, which luckily became obvious, before I lost a lot of money. The islanders would carve some souvenirs out of very soft wood and sell them on the street for very little money. You buy a couple of items from one of these street people, and during the transaction, a well-dressed man comes along, scolds the first man, and sends him away. The second man apologizes for the unsavory actions of the first man and shows how fragile the items are, by easily breaking one in his hands. He then takes you to a reputable store, where you can buy better items. This second man appears sincere and does not ask for any money, so you assume he is OK. He brings you to the store he recommends, where you buy some nicer items. In my case, upon leaving the store, a third man approached me and said I had just fallen victim to a double scam! He did not break those items (which are still in my display case), but he now wanted to take me to another store. So late smart! This was a whole team working together, so I left that store without buying anything more. On my flight from Fiji to Australia, the airline magazine had an article explaining this scam in detail. Although I felt stupid, these scam artists were very good at their game. Luckily, suspicion arose before it cost any "real money." And, I still have those cheap souvenirs!

## My Fiji-Australia-New Zealand-Australia- Marathon!

The "Jennifer" had not yet caught any fish and was close to Cairns, Australia, so it was decided they should proceed to a shipyard at Cairns to determine if they had a similar problem. I was then sent from Fiji to Cairns before my luggage arrived.

The shipyard in Cairns was located on the Barron River. Arriving at the shipyard, the owner had arranged for a dive team to inspect the bottom of the vessel, to look for signs of the same damages found on the Bonnie. My suspicion was, the problem was an internal one, based upon my inspection of the engineroom bilges on the "Bonnie." However, it was understandable, the owner was trying to avoid an expensive drydocking.

It was surprising to see five men on the dive team who were setting up their equipment. Thinking they were "padding the bill" a little, I asked what the duties were for all these men. They said they had two divers who would be in the water, and one diver on top, in case of an emergency, also acting as their tender. The other two men were called "security". The term security needed some explanation, but then they pulled two carbine rifles out of the truck. In Australia, the need for security is serious, and one security man would be stationed on each side of the divers, looking for signs of **crocodiles**! Diving in Australia is quite different than diving in Lake Michigan! I should have asked if one of them was named Dundee!

As suspected, the divers found nothing suspicious under the water, so the ship was scheduled to be drydocked the next morning. I also needed to see the "Bonnie" when it was drydocked in New Zealand, and that ship had just arrived in Nelson, NZ, that morning.

We had the crew cleaning the bilges once the "Jennifer" arrived in Cairns, so as soon as the ship was drydocked, we started with a full inspection of the engineroom bilges. It was tough, but we were able to get close to the suspect area under the engines, and one of the "skinnier" crewmembers was able to get into that small, suspect area, while I directed his actions from nearby. Although there were no actual holes in the hull, we could see that the steel was severely pitted and very thin. Ultrasonic gauging from the outside of the hull later determined the hull was less than 1/8" thick in that area. Although this hull was built with mostly 5/16" thick steel, it is typical to reinforce the "bilge well" areas with ½" or thicker steel because the water sits in those areas and causes accelerated corrosion. That had not been done on these vessels, which were all built in Italy.

We next began to examine those areas where water had collected behind the framing in the engineroom bilges. I looked for "mouse holes" at the ends of the frames, thinking they had been plugged by dirt, trapping that water. We found no mouse holes at all, on any of the frames.

*Mouse holes are small, ¾" to 1" holes, typically formed by cutting off the corner of a hull stiffener frame, before the frame is welded to the hull plating and bulkheads. These holes allow water to drain away from the longitudinal frames on the side of the vessel, so the water will instead collect in those "reinforced" bilge well areas at the bottom of the vessel. The bilge pumps then suck the water from those bilge wells, keeping the framing areas dry and reducing corrosion.*

There was serious corrosion behind those frames on this ship as well, and in one area, my tapping lightly with my inspection hammer, the rust fell away and my hammer went through the side shell of the ship.

THE 'JENNIFER' ON DRYDOCK AT CAIRNS, AUSTRALIA

We now understood the extent of the problem, and a quick report was written to my insurance adjuster in San Diego, which he forwarded to the Insurance Company in London. My recommendation was to fully sandblast the exterior of the "Jennifer" and the "Bonnie" and then to cut mouse holes at the ends of all the longitudinal frames. In those areas where corrosion was found severe, the shell plate needed to be cut away and new steel inserted. It was also recommended that all accessible areas of the bilge be cleaned and coated with rust inhibitor and then repainted. The "Valerie" had already sunk from these conditions, and we were finding severe problems with the "Bonnie" and "Jennifer," so there was no argument, and the work was started immediately.

Then it was off to Nelson, New Zealand, to verify if the same conditions existed on the "Bonnie." There were no direct flights, so they flew my lawyer companion and me from Cairns to Sydney, with an overnight stay there, and then to Auckland, and finally to Nelson.

Our overnight stop in Sydney was interesting. We checked into a hotel near the airport and went to the hotel lobby looking for a beer and a good dinner where we were informed of an unusual law in that part of Australia. The law required that people join a club to drink alcohol, and the hotel did not qualify for such a club arrangement. The hotel recommended we go to a local Rowing Club within walking distance of the hotel. We thought this was just too unusual of an experience to pass by, and we walked to the Rowing Club.

Club Membership was inexpensive, and the club also served meals, so we joined the club to get a nice meal and a few beers. We began talking with others at the club, some of whom were truckers. They drove those long, "Trailer Train" trucks across the Australian desert. It made for a very interesting evening.

On our flight from Auckland to Nelson, we met some of the most interesting people! We learned that Australians liked to joke about the Kiwis (New Zealanders), and the New Zealanders like to poke fun at the Aussies, but they do not appreciate an outsider making such jokes. They may "rib" each other, but they respect one another and almost seem to be protective of one another, which was my observation. There was also a group of Americans flying to Nelson, on their way to a fly-fishing camp in the mountains south of Nelson. The fishing is excellent in those mountain streams.

We arrived at the shipyard in Nelson, and the "Bonnie" was already on drydock. We already knew the "Bonnie" had a hole in the hull under the main engines, so my concern was to see if the lack of "mouse holes" had caused the same conditions on the sides of the ship. The insurance company asked me to complete a full survey of the vessel's hull, and this uncovered numerous other corrosion issues that also needed to be addressed. It was obvious the "Bonnie" would be on drydock for an extended period. The insurance company then asked me to return to Cairns, Australia, to determine if these same corrosion problems (over and above the corrosion that caused the sinking) also existed on the "Jennifer."

So, back to Cairns, but this time, alone! My attorney companion had enough information for his investigation of the death that had occurred on the "Bonnie," so he was returning to San Diego. This flight to Cairns included a change of planes in Melbourne, but I never saw anything outside of the airport there.

While gone, the shipyard had completed the sandblasting and had blasted holes fully through the hull plating of the "Jennifer" in several locations. These holes were found to be in those areas which we found had no "mouse holes" at the ends of the frames. This further confirmed the conditions reported to the insurance underwriters in London.

We also found those other corrosion problems on the Jennifer, but the small shipyard there did not have enough time and resources to get all of this work done promptly. After all, the owner was in the middle of the prime tuna fishing season, and he had two vessels sitting in shipyards, in addition to losing a third. A decision was made to make temporary repairs in Cairns and send the "Jennifer" to Nelson, with the "Bonnie", because they were a larger shipyard, capable of working on both ships, and the owner could attend to both projects at one location.

At this point, my 3-4-day trip to Fiji had turned into over three weeks on the road, and by the way, my lost luggage never caught up with me. When it finally arrived in Fiji, the airline contacted me to claim the bag, but I explained that I was in Australia, and probably on my way to New Zealand.

Rather than have the bag sent to Australia, it was suggested they just send it back to my home in Chicago, which they did.

## <u>Food, Take-Aways, and Side Trips in Australia</u>

While at the shipyard in Cairns, my lunches were eaten at the local "Take-Aways." Takeaways were small, family-owned, fast-food shops that served local specialties. They also had Takeaways in New Zealand, and the different foods available were most enjoyable. One of the shops outside the shipyard served deep-fried fish in a very light batter. The owner said his fish was always caught the day he served it, and based on the taste and quality, he was not lying. In some ways, the Take-Aways reminded me of Tapas in Spain. They occasionally had small dishes or even one-bite food items, and you could say, "I'll take one of those, two of those, one of those, and a piece of fish." Great tasting treat!

On my first trip to Cairns, the ship owner treated us to dinner at a nice restaurant. Something on the menu caught my eye called "mud crab." It said "market price" so it was probably expensive, and we found the price was $75, which was very expensive back then. With the rest of the menu at $12 or $15, that was far out of line, even if it was the ship owner who was paying the bill. The ship owner told me to order it, but it was just too expensive. However, when returning to Cairns on my second trip, and being alone, I returned to that restaurant. I asked about the mud crab and the waiter told me it was still $75 at dinnertime, but if I came to eat before 5:00 PM and finished before 6:00, the price was $50. So, the next day at 4:30 the mud crab was ordered, and when it was served, it was obvious why they wanted me out before the busy, dinner hour. The crab was served whole, and it was huge! It took me a long time to eat it, and it was messy. Yes, it had a slightly muddy taste, being taken from the local rivers, but it was delightful.

During the time spent in Cairns, one free weekend was spent driving up the Coast. The Great Barrier Reef is just offshore from Cairns, so there were a lot of excursion and dive boat businesses related to the Great Barrier Reef. The area along the coast is very lush and green.

However, as soon as you drive up the hills onto the central plains, the color turns brown and it is just desert. There were numerous termite

mounds, but no kangaroos, which was my goal to see. Stopping for lunch at a roadside restaurant (too big for a takeaway) there was my first kangaroo. The shop owner had found a dead mother kangaroo on the side of the highway, and he noticed that she had a baby in her pouch. He rescued the baby and took it home.

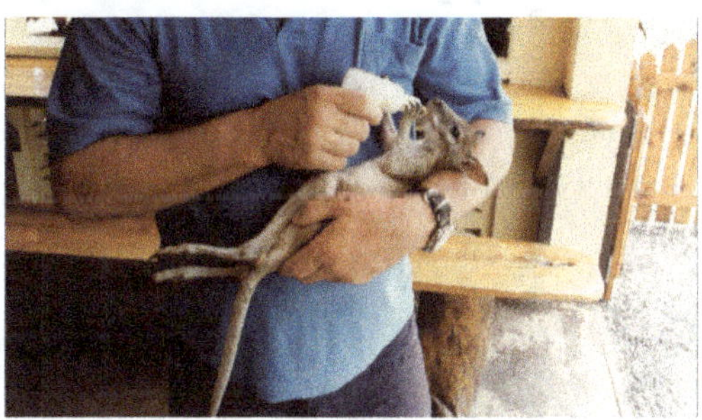

After the temporary repairs were completed on the "Jennifer," the underwriters considered her safe for one fishing trip on her way to the shipyard in Nelson, New Zealand.

Chicago, here I come, FINALLY! This quick, 3-4-day job became nearly one month, and living only with clothes and toiletries purchased along the way. My insurance company client was very grateful for my services and they paid well, including my unusual expenses, but my family back in Chicago wondered if I was ever coming home.

The shipyard in Australia was a real experience, starting with the divers, needing two security men to keep the Crocks away from the divers. It amazed me how much the average working man drank in Australia. The shipyard kept a large wooden cooler full of beer, which the workers paid for, by putting money into a "swear jar"! The payment for swearing appeared to be on the honor system, and the money collected was used to keep the beer cooler full. After their work day was done, many of the workers sat and drank beer, until the shipyard had to call their wives to come and pick them up! They showed up the next day for work and started over again. I have more stories, but if those appeared, my book might be X-rated!

One last anecdote about food in Australia. When you have great food available, avoid those ever-present American chain restaurants, particularly fast food! However, the special burger at McDonald's in Australia is a Beet-Burger! Australians like a thick slice of red beet on their hamburgers, and McDonald's added that to the menu. Never tried it, but it does sound good. I still hate McDonald's!

## <u>Return to New Zealand For Final Repairs</u>

After returning home, there were many phone calls between the insurance adjuster in San Diego, the Insurance Company in London, another in France, the owner's rep in New Zealand, and myself. All were concerned and wanted the repairs done properly, so these problems would not reoccur. They asked me to return to Nelson, New Zealand, to oversee and approve the repairs. When asked how long they wanted me to stay, they said, "Until both ships leave in good condition," and they estimated that it could take about three more weeks. I was granted permission to invite my wife, Carol, on this trip.

In my previous story about my first visit to Whangarei, New Zealand, I met a volunteer driver, Ian, who worked with the local Helicopter Emergency Medical team. Ian had kept in touch with me in several emails over the years and I contacted him to tell him about this extended stay in Nelson, New Zealand. We planned to travel up to Whangarei on my first weekend so that my wife could meet him and his wife.

We checked into a very rustic, but nice hotel in Nelson. I had used the hotel restaurant during my first trip to Nelson, so I knew the food would be good. I checked in at the shipyard each morning to monitor progress on various repairs, but unless they needed me for something in the afternoon, we were free to drive around and see the sights. We drove as far as we dared because the roads became quite hilly and curvy when driving very far from Nelson. Although my left-side driving was quite good, sitting on the right and using a stick shift with my left hand to downshift on hills, curves, and round-a-bouts was stressful.

The "Jennifer" had done some fishing on her trip from Cairns to Nelson, and witnessing the unloading of the fish was an interesting experience. The unloading operations in American Samoa were only visible from a distance. This time I was on the "Jennifer" and looking down at the operation.

## Fishing Vessel Investigations

*The fish wells were mentioned in the chapter about the NOAA vessel damage in Kwajalein, but further explanation may be necessary at this point. The fish wells are large tanks, which are part of the ship's hull. They are filled with clean salt water when the vessel leaves the port. As tuna are caught, different types of tuna are separated and placed into different fish wells, through large hatches in the deck. The water in the fish wells is displaced by the fish, and the water runs out the top of those hatches as the fish well is filled with fish. The water runs out of the fish well, onto the deck, and drains over the side, back into the ocean. (Those who have watched "Deadliest Catch," on TV, have seen those crabbing vessels operate the same way.)*

*Once they have fish in a fish well, the engineers start the refrigeration in that fish well, and add rock salt to the water in the fish well, to keep the water from turning to ice. However, the fish still freeze solid. The refrigeration systems on older ships like these, circulate ammonia through tubing in those fish wells to produce the cooling. Ammonia refrigeration is much cheaper than freon, however, ammonia is also very dangerous. Inspecting those center tunnels between the fish wells, there was always an ammonia smell in the air, which made me nervous. Fishermen have died due to ammonia leaks on those types of vessels.*

When a ship reaches port to unload, there will normally be a large number of refrigerated cargo containers ready to transport the fish, unless the unloading is done at the packing plant (like in American Samoa). In this case, the "Jennifer" was going to have the fish sent from New Zealand to market by containers. Because the fish have been "sloshing" back and forth against each other in the salty water, much of the skin has been worn off and the fish look pretty terrible, to be honest.

The larger tuna seiners normally carry a small, two-man helicopter. They are used to "scout" for schools of tuna and lead the ship to the school. Some owners have two or three seiners fishing together, and they may conserve and use just one helicopter in their group of vessels if they stay together. In my experience, almost every vessel had its own helicopter.

Another interesting use for the helicopter was to transport any large tuna to shore, usually bluefins. These large tunas are sold and transported directly to Tokyo by jet. Here is a Wikipedia quote about the current, record fish: "…..the restaurateur Kiyoshi Kimura forked over $1.76 million for a 489-pound Pacific bluefin tuna just last year. That tuna—at a jaw-dropping $3,603 per pound, or roughly $178 per piece of sushi—stands as the most expensive fish ever sold. Jan 6, 2014"

'JENNIFER' AT FISH UNLOADING DOCK, NELSON, NZ

LARGER TUNA, PROBABLY YELLOWFIN

Large Bluefins are more common in the Atlantic Ocean (up to 1000 pounds), but large schools of tuna are more plentiful in the Pacific, therefore more tuna seiners operate in the Pacific.

SMALLER TUNA, PROBABLY ALBACORE

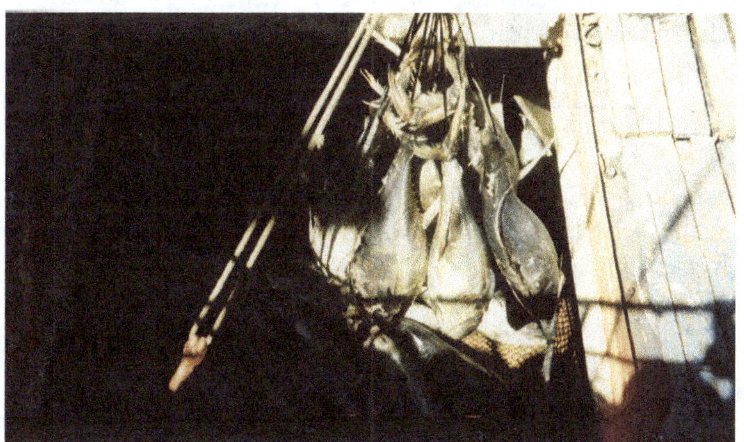

OPEN FISH WELL WITH YELLOWFIN TUNA BEING REMOVED

After the fish was unloaded, the "Jennifer" was drydocked for repairs. The "Bonnie was already on dock and repairs nearing completion.

247

The cause of all these problems was poor vessel design details and poor shipyard construction. These Italian-built tuna seiners were purchased from the lowest bidder, without giving any thought to the design details. The 5/16" steel hull was minimal for this size vessel, and the failure to include reinforced (thicker) steel in the areas where water was meant to collect (the bilge wells), was against all good marine practice standards. Then the failure to have "mouse holes" at the ends of the frames, allowing water to collect, was not a cost item, but a purely careless construction technique.

## Side Trips and Experiences in New Zealand

I wanted Carol to experience New Zealand. Our first trip was to Whangarei to visit my friend, Ian. The area around Whangarei, which is far north on the North Island, is proud of its warm weather, which they refer to as "Never-ending Summer."

ME, MY WIFE, CAROL, WITH IAN AND HIS WIFE AT THEIR HOME.
NOTE THE WARM JACKETS, DUE TO THE MISSING, "ENDLESS SUMMER" THAT WEEK

We arrived to 40-degree weather in Whangarei. We had just left a cold, Chicago Winter, so we still thought it was warm, but Ian and his wife were in total shock! Their home had minimal heating, but they did have a nice fireplace. The bedrooms had no heat, but we got to experience a heated mattress cover (not a blanket), which we had not yet seen in the United States.

Ian gave me and Carol a grand tour of the Bay of Islands and other great sights around Whangarei. We didn't go back to the Kauri forest, which I had visited on my first trip, but we did visit the Kauri Museum. Note the dimensions written in this sign, showing 23 feet in diameter and over 160 feet high.

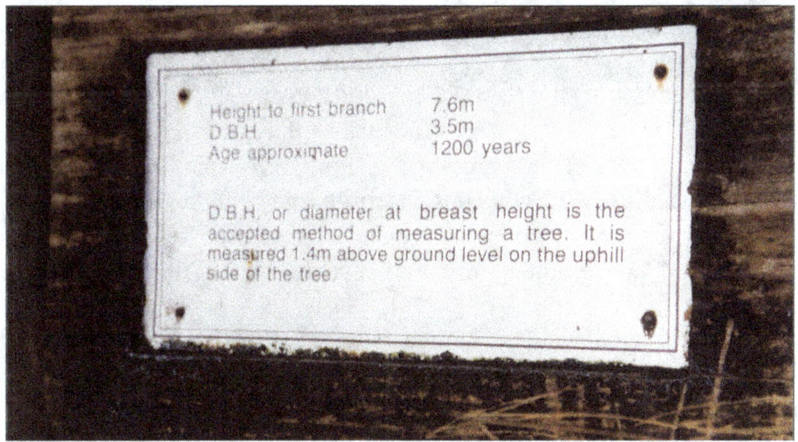


On our return to Nelson, which is on the South Island, we stopped in Auckland and toured Rotorua, an area of geysers and bubbling mud pools, similar to Yellowstone Park in the United States, but much smaller. We also visited the Glow Worm Cave at Waitomo, near Auckland. My saying about New Zealand is, that *there does not seem to be one square inch that is not either beautiful or spectacular*. There is something amazing for everyone - Alpine Skiing on the South Island, Rain Forests on the North Island, as well as the Volcano, Glow Worms, and other wonders near Auckland. New Zealand is truly amazing!

**ROTORUA, GEYSERS AND MUD POOLS**

After this trip to Whangarei, Carol only stayed a few more days and then decided to return to our children and the cold winter in Chicago. She departed Nelson's airport to Auckland. I told her to spend all her New Zealand dollars before she got on the plane, to avoid having to get rid of them when we returned home. With a little bit of New Zealand money, Carol followed instructions and boarded the airplane in Auckland, which ended up sitting at the end of the runway for a long time. The Captain said the delay was due to ash from a recent eruption of one of the volcanos near Auckland, he could not take off for fear of damaging the engines. I'm not sure of the name of the 'guilty' volcano, but a search on Google produced over 70 volcanos listed on and around (undersea) New Zealand. Most are now inactive, but nine of them erupted between 1972 and 2017, and a few have erupted more than once during that time.

Carol was treated well by United Airlines and booked into a Hotel/ Casino with free meals. The casino even gave her a voucher for some free gambling! However, these were the days before ATM cards, so Carol was unable to do much else.

The next weekend in Nelson, the fishermen of both the Bonnie and the Jennifer planned to make an excursion to a remote beach up the coast where they wanted to dig clams. New Zealanders are not fond of clams because they have those wonderful, green-lipped mussels. The crew had heard clams were plentiful in this area because the locals didn't dig them. We all climbed into two large vans supplied by the shipyard and headed west from Nelson along the coast until we found the beach.

We had all been warned to use sunscreen because the sun in New Zealand could be very bad, made worse by the "hole in the ozone layer" which happened to be over New Zealand. I thought the crew seemed a bit optimistic because they took two large, 30-gallon plastic trash bins onto the

DIGGING CLAMS NEAR NELSON, NZ

beach and also had a bucket for each of us. In less than 90 minutes, we filled the two trash bins, plus our buckets as well. Never having dug clams before, I thought this was amazing! You watched for the bubbles emerging from the sand and just used your two hands to dig into the sand. Even though you could only dig 6-8 inches by hand, each attempt came up with 4-6 nice clams. Those using shovels were getting 8-12 clams per shovel of sand. The plan was to freeze most of the clams on the two ships, but first, we would eat our fill that afternoon.

We planned to have clams for lunch, but having been out in the hot sun all morning, the shipyard driver suggested that we stop for a beer along the way. He knew of a good bar at a beach outside of Nelson. We pulled into a large park with a guard at the gate, and the driver told the guard we were going to the bar, so we were admitted. The bar seemed normal enough, but when we looked out at the beach, we noticed that the driver had purposely taken us to a Nudist Camp, which explained having the guard at the gate. We learned one thing about nude beaches that day! All of the "pretty people" stay at the far end of the beach, well away from the public areas. All of the people we saw around the bar should have kept their clothes on. It appeared to me that most of those we saw were just exhibitionists who had nothing worth exhibiting! Clothing was required INSIDE the bar, by the way.

The Captain and Chief Engineer had rented an apartment near Nelson, high up on a hill, overlooking the harbor. It was a nice place with a beautiful view. We spent the afternoon steaming and eating clams, with beer of course, until none of us could eat another one. Everyone loves the green-lipped, New Zealand mussels, but those fresh clams were spectacular as well, and much cheaper!

**VIEW FROM CAPTAIN'S RENTAL APARTMENT**

The crew dropped me back at my hotel for some well-deserved sleep and took the rest of those clams to the ships to be frozen. The next morning, I awoke and hopped out of bed to find my ankles were burning and sore. The back of my legs had been sun-screened, but somehow the back of my ankles had been missed. They were fire red! By that afternoon, they turned almost purple. Being on that beach, down on my knees, the sun did its nasty work on that small area of unprotected skin above my heels. I called home to get some sympathy from Carol about my sore ankles, only to be told that Chicago had just experienced a terrible minus-20 degree-F cold snap, freezing the water supply to our home. She was not in any mood to hear my sad story, because she had to hire a welding contractor to thaw out our pipes.

One last unusual thing happened in Nelson before I left to go home. The shipyard was very safety conscious, and I normally complied with their safety rules, but wearing a hard hat while inspecting deep ballast tanks is "a real pain!" My hard hat was usually placed outside the tank upon entering. On one of my last days, while in the Fore Peak tank, looking at repairs, I bumped my head. It hurt, but I didn't think much about it (hard head, and all!). Walking into the shipyard office, one of the foremen asked me about the blood on my back. I had ignored the wet feeling on my back, thinking it was just sweat. I took off my hard hat and there was a fairly large gash in my scalp where my head had hit something inside the tank.

We figured the bleeding would stop on its own, but an hour later, it was still bleeding, so the shipyard personnel drove me to the hospital, dropped me off, and said they would come back when this "new damage" was repaired.

The hospital staff was great, they cleaned the wound and shaved the area around the cut. I only needed three stitches. When they were done, I asked how much the bill would be, and they told me medical services were free in New Zealand. Even though I was not a New Zealand citizen, medical care is free for everyone, even non-citizens. However, they did say it would be

## *Fishing Vessel Investigations*

OK if I could pay for the actual stitches, which they would need to replace. My total cost was under 5 New Zealand dollars! Amazing!

## <u>Trip to Dutch Harbor, Alaska</u>

Those who have watched the Reality TV show, "Deadliest Catch," are familiar with the Alaskan port of Dutch Harbor. The City itself is named Unalaska, Alaska, but the port is called Dutch Harbor.

VETERANS' MEMORIAL PARK, UNALASKA, ALASKA

The Attorney/Adjuster, Pete, from my trip to Fiji, Australia, and New Zealand, had remained a friend over the years. Pete had investigated the death that occurred on the "Bonnie," when one of the crew members dove over the side to assist the Chief Engineer. Pete had since moved to Alaska to partner in a similar insurance adjuster business up there, and we had done some co-consulting projects on several insurance claims. The previous claims had all been handled by telephone and E-Mails.

This time, Pete wanted me to survey the damage to a propeller shaft, which had fractured on a small fishing vessel. This was not one of the larger "crab boats" from the TV Series, but there were several of those moored in Dutch Harbor.

The internet said the weather for Dutch Harbor had average August temperatures of 58 degrees F, so the plan was to dress warm and pack a bag for cold weather. We then flew to Anchorage, Alaska, where Pete met us at the airport. We first went to his office, reviewed reports and photos, and then went out to have a few drinks and dinner.

After a short tour of this part of Anchorage, we pulled up in front of Chilkoot Charlie's, which has to be one of the most amazing places you can imagine! Their slogan is, "We Cheat the Other Guy and Pass the Savings on to You!" They also have a bar, called the "Bird Cage," which they say was saved from its original location following the earthquake back in the 1970s. We also heard it is a replica of the old bar, which burned, but whether the original bar or not, it is weird! The new bar was built with all the surfaces slanted, similar to the damage done during that earthquake. Whether the bar was saved or recreated, it doesn't matter, because it is really fun! The signs say, "Adults Only" and they should include "Only if you have a thick skin and a sense of humor!" There is no nudity in the bar, but the walls and ceiling are covered with women's undergarments, just to make you wonder! The bartender, on most nights, was Wicked Wanda, a 65-plus-year-old lady, who never swore but made you blush every few minutes with her antics. She is a great person, and a great entertainer, who is tipped very well!

They have a great trick to play on newcomers, but we saw that some of the newcomers knew ahead of time what would happen and played along anyway. The bartender tells the new patron there is a flock of ptarmigans, the Alaska State birds, that roost on the roof of the bar. If you use their bird call, several of the ptarmigan will come into the bar and want to be fed. They give the patron the brass bird call and when he blows in the tube, his face is covered with flour! He then gets to sign a book behind the bar and is expected to buy a round of drinks. He then has "bragging rights" about the event. We experienced this twice, getting one of those free drinks each time, but Pete, our host, warned us not to fall for the trick. Those drinks were straight booze, mixed from several different bottles of "rot gut," but the entire experience was great. Just be warned, the language can be pretty foul! And by the way, their food was great!

The next morning, we boarded an Alaska Airlines flight for Dutch Harbor.

DUTCH HARBOR CRAB FISHING FLEET

VIEWS OF DUTCH HARBOR FROM HILLTOP ARMY FORT

WORLD WAR II MUSEUM & VISITOR CENTER ONE
OF THE RUSSIAN ORTHODOX CHURCHES

THIS STORE HAS EVERYTHING! FISH OR CRAB IN REFRIGERATED CONTAINERS

**TRAFFIC STOP SIGNAL AT
THE END OF RUNWAY**

An interesting thing on the island is the airport. The runway ends at the public roadway, which surrounds the airport. The planes are just overhead of the cars during take-off and landing, so as a safety measure, this signal is installed to stop traffic whenever a plane lands or takes off.

The actual vessel inspection was uneventful. The propeller shaft had fractured while the vessel was out fishing, and we eventually traced the cause to a defective piece of steel, as well as a misaligned shaft, causing the shaft to flex. The flexing finally fractured the shaft at the exact location where the defect was located in the steel. No surprise!

There is only one hotel on the island, which is owned by the Island's major fish-packing plant. They also have large barracks buildings for their employees. Most of these employees are hired from various countries to work part-time, depending on what fish or crabs are being fished at various times of the year. Our hotel was great and the restaurant was good. We were surprised the crab dinner was just as expensive there as it is in Chicago though. Seeing that it was caught right there, you'd think it might be cheaper! We only found three restaurants on the island, so we could not be fussy, but the food was quite good, despite the high prices.

Dutch Harbor has a lot of World War II history, because the Japanese were invading islands in the Aleutian chain, and the United States finally stopped them at Dutch Harbor. There is a wonderful visitor Center for WW II history, plus a fantastic Inuit Indian Museum on the island. Many of the Inuits were captured by the Japanese downrange of Dutch Harbor, so the United States evacuated many of the Inuit, hoping to protect them. However, they were displaced from their homes for many years and it seriously affected their culture.

We also found the people on the island wanted to talk to us because we were "outsiders." They seemed to be hungry for conversations about where we were from, what we did, etc. We were even stopped by a couple of teenage boys, not afraid to talk to some old-timer visitors.

We visited a WW II fort, in the hills overlooking the harbor. Many of the gun placements and tunnels are still intact. The views were dramatic!

## <u>Vessel Corrosion Investigations</u>

Strange things cause corrosion in vessels, and the previous story about the tuna fishing boats Valerie, Bonnie, and Jennifer, showed how serious one minor design flaw can cause one vessel to sink, and its two sister vessels to have serious consequences.

Another odd combination of events brought me to inspect a large charter fishing boat in San Diego. It had been drydocked for minor repairs, but the shipyard noted it had the start of minor rust pitting on the submerged portion of the hull. The shipyard recommended a total sand-blasting and then repainting the hull.

The owner had charter commitments to fulfill, so they told the shipyard to just paint the bottom and they would return later for a full blast & paint job. The boat was busy and two years went by before they returned to drydock. During this time, many of those rust pits corroded nearly through the hull.

From my previous experience, the quick paint job on a saltwater vessel was the wrong thing to do. Pitting develops small bubbles beneath the paint and rust, containing salt water. When they are exposed to seawater, the zinc anodes installed on the vessel will reduce the rate of corrosion. However, once the quick paint job was applied, the bubbles of rust and water were isolated from the zinc anodes, and the rusting process under those rust bubbles was accelerated. The shipyard had denied the warranty because of the incomplete preparation, which the shipyard had correctly recommended, so the owner's claim for coverage was denied.

# CHAPTER 19

## VISITS TO PERU FOR TANKERS & FISHING VESSELS (WITH SIDE TRIPS TO VENEZUELA, JAMAICA & CURA-CAO)

Over the years, I made several working trips to Peru. Several friends in my life had been Peace Corps Volunteers in Peru, with one who married a lady from Peru, so when the chance first came to take a job in Lima, Peru, it was very welcome. This was another one off my Bucket List!

My first visit to Peru was at the shipyard in Callao, a section of Lima. One of the major worldwide tanker companies was chartering a small gas tanker, carrying LPG (liquified petroleum gas). The tanker company had hired a local marine surveyor to inspect the tanker, but they didn't believe his "good" report on the condition, based on the advanced age of the vessel. They needed the vessel examined on drydock, and for me to report on the conditions found. This visit was quite short, with no time to do any sightseeing, other than a few good meals near the shipyard.

This tanker was quite old and had areas of the hull plating that were so heavily rusted that the hull could be dented just by hitting it with a hammer. By the time the inspection was complete, I had written thirteen handwritten pages of defects I'd found, ranging from minor to serious. Because of the major discrepancies between my report and those of the local surveyor, this made a good impression on my client. They asked me to attend numerous ship inspections in South America over my years in business because they needed someone honest. Not having met the Marine Surveyor who provided the erroneous report, it is impossible to say whether it was a lack of training and experience or fear of the owners for reporting how bad their ship was. However, this situation provided me with a lot of work over the years, including another tanker inspection in Curacao, which will be detailed at the end of this chapter.

## <u>Extended Visit in Lima, Peru</u>

My second visit to Peru was several months later when the first client recommended my services to a Chilean oil company. This time, the Chilean oil company representative met me in Lima. We stayed at a very nice hotel near the Lima city center, and each morning we would take a taxi to the shipyard.

On the first morning, the oil company representative and I arrived at the shipyard where things had changed drastically since my last visit. When the taxi approached the front gate of the shipyard, the cannon barrel of a military tank was pointed at the car as we drove a zigzag pattern through concrete barricades. We were also greeted by several young men in Navy uniforms, who were carrying machine guns. We showed our passports, and when they saw mine was from the United States, they greeted me in a friendly fashion. However, my friend from the Chilean oil company was taken to a separate office and interviewed by an officer for over an hour.

While my friend was being interviewed, it turned out the young Navy men spoke good English. Because things had changed so drastically since my first visit, I tried to find out why. Several of the young men stated "Shining Path" but the term wasn't familiar to me. While speaking with the young men, it was obvious they did not feel threatened by my presence. They leaned their machine guns against the side of the building to talk to me. Several times, one of the guns would fall and hit the ground. There was no reason to feel threatened by these men, however, there certainly was concern about being accidentally shot.

My Chilean friend finally finished his interview and said we would need to call a taxi and return to the hotel. Because he was from a neighboring country, he needed additional clearances before he would be allowed to enter the shipyard. It was not obvious during my first visit to Callao, but it just so happened that the civilian shipyard was surrounded by the Peruvian Naval Base. During our taxi ride back to the hotel, I mentioned the Shining Path statement that was made by the young Navy men and asked what it meant. My Chilean client explained that Shining Path was the Communist

Party in Peru, and they had been very disruptive in recent times. At the time we were there, one of the leaders of Shining Path had been arrested and was being held in the federal prison, which was inside the Callao Naval Base. Because of all of the security due to this captive, my Chilean client was being looked at very carefully by the Naval Security Forces.

When we arrived at the hotel, my Chilean friend made several phone calls to his Chilean company about the situation. He told me that it could be several days before he was allowed access to the shipyard, and in the meantime, he told me to enjoy myself and see the sights of Lima, at full pay.

The following morning, the oil company representative told me he had to visit several Peruvian government offices, and asked me to tour the city on my own. So, I asked the hotel staff to plan a tour for me after breakfast. At breakfast, I received a menu with no English translations. Fortunately for me, by this time, I had learned enough Spanish to read most portions of a menu. My spoken Spanish, however, remained nearly nonexistent.

The waiter came to my table and began speaking Spanish, so it was clear that he spoke no English. He appeared very frustrated and walked away from my table. I was trying to point to items on the menu, but he did not seem willing to assist me. A young busboy was cleaning tables nearby and saw what was happening, so he went to the kitchen and returned to my table with a large tray. He then pointed to a bowl of eggs and very politely said, "huevos." Next, he pointed to the ham and said, "jamon." This kind boy continued to give me a lesson in Spanish food names. When he was done, he pointed to the eggs again and said "huevos con jamon Y queso?" and then "Usted quiere omlet?" I didn't realize that omelet was a Spanish word as well!

The next morning, I had a much better experience in the restaurant even though I was afraid to ask for anything other than an omelet. I happened to be sitting across from an older American couple who was having problems with the same waiter. When they spoke to the waiter in English, and he walked away, the man yelled at him, "What's the matter with you? Don't you speak English?" Although I was also having problems with this waiter, his "Ugly American" attitude upset me, and I told the American, "This is Peru, and the waiter is not required to speak English." The American did not say anything back to me, so hopefully, it finally occurred to him that English was not a "required" language in Peru! And, hopefully, he was embarrassed enough to be a little more polite next time.

My lack of language skills was a constant struggle, but it was MY problem. Being polite and apologizing to my acquaintances in other countries, for being unable to speak their language, normally produced a smile. In most countries, the native speakers didn't expect me to speak their language. However, in many Latin American countries, my hosts were surprised by my lack of Spanish.

After breakfast, I went back to the hotel clerk who spoke excellent English, and he offered to help me with a tour of Lima. He said a personally guided tour by taxi was not expensive, and he would find a taxi driver who spoke good English. He asked me to return in 30 minutes, at which time he had a taxi waiting for me. He introduced me to the taxi driver and told him to take me anywhere I wished to go. The driver asked me where we should go and I told him his recommendations would suit me just fine. He had visited the United States several times and spoke excellent English, so we were able to communicate.

The cab driver's first recommendation was to visit the National Museum of Art. When he dropped me in front of the building, he told me to be sure to go into the "special room." The museum is filled with very interesting, pre-Columbian art. Upon leaving, one of the ladies working in the museum asked me in English, "Don't you want to see the special room?" That was a surprise, to hear the same term used by the taxi driver, but she just pointed me in the direction of a closed door, which had been closed the entire time of my visit. When she opened the door, I was confronted with a large penis, at least eight feet in height. The artwork in this room was beyond erotic, showing group sex, sex with animals, etc. I am not at all prudish, however, this was quite shocking. It appeared to me the Indians during those ancient times had become obsessed with sex. When I returned to my waiting taxi, the driver asked me if I had

MUSEUM DISPLAYS, NOT IN THE SPECIAL ROOM

enjoyed the museum. Then he added, "Did you get to the special room?" Answering yes, he just smiled.

I then told the driver that we should find a good place to eat, my treat. I told him to be sure to take us to a restaurant serving good local food. I can't remember much about the meal but there was never a bad meal during my stay in Peru. Peruvian food is excellent! However, INCA COLA is not my favorite drink. I'll take a Pisco Sour instead!

After lunch, the driver said the Museo Oro del Peru, or The Gold Museum, should not be missed. This museum was quite a distance outside of the city center, and the drive to the museum was most interesting. No stoplights were working and the driver told me that the poor people had pulled out the wire to sell the copper. However, the cars were stopping at the intersections and observing normal traffic rules, which greatly surprised me. The driver also warned me not to open the car windows because of the many children on the streets who were selling packages of gum and trinkets. The driver said once they see someone buy something at one intersection, the children at the next intersection would see what happened, and they would surround the car, begging for money. It was very sad to see, but I complied with my driver's request.

Many of these children were living in cardboard boxes in the boulevards between the streets. They were in terrible physical condition. Many of them were carrying bags for sniffing glue, which I recognized from my previous experience in Ecuador.

When we arrived at the Museum of Gold, the driver told me there would be several young children at the museum selling trinkets. He said if I wanted to buy any of the trinkets for souvenirs, first look into the eyes of the child to see if they were already on drugs or sniffing glue. He explained to me that seeing a sparkle in the eyes meant the child was not yet a drug user. That's because drugs or glue affect the look of one's eyes, making them cloudy. When I got out of the car, several of the children came to sell me souvenirs, and there was one child who still had that

**MUSEUM OF GOLD, OUTSIDE OF LIMA, PERU**

sparkle. I bought a number of the trinkets from him, and could tell the kids who were on drugs were quite upset that they did not sell any to me.

The Museum of Gold is spectacular! It not only contains numerous pieces of gold jewelry but also entire gowns, dresses, and costumes which were made from gold fabric. These must be the treasures that the Spaniards tried to find centuries ago!

The next morning, my oil company representative told me that he was now approved to enter the shipyard, and we made our way to inspect the ship, which his company intended to buy. The survey went very well. The ship was in good condition. The shipyard manager invited us to accompany him for lunch at a ceviche house, which served over 30 varieties of ceviche. Ceviche had become a favorite from my experiences in Ecuador and Columbia, so the invitation for lunch was welcome. The number of choices on the menu was amazing, and we allowed the shipyard manager to make the selections. He ordered at least ten varieties of ceviche for us to share, including sea snail, conch, and other varieties most of which I had never tried before. Years later, when working in Panama, my Panamanian friends were jealous of my experience with Peruvian ceviche. The Panamanians told me that the best ceviche in the world is made in Peru, and I would not argue with them over their opinion.

## Broken Crankshafts in Fishing Vessels

My third trip to Peru was another request from ABS Worldwide Technical Services (ABSTech). ABSTech had been hired by a major diesel engine manufacturer to determine the cause of numerous crankshaft fractures in their larger engines, all taking place in Peru. Because of my prior diesel engine experience, ABSTech requested my services in Peru for this investigation. This time, a representative of the engine dealer met me at

the airport, and he became my guide during this entire visit. He was a fantastic gentleman!

The following little fishing boats were not the size we were working on, but it amazed me that these fishermen would brave the seas in these little boats.

The next morning, we began visiting several fishing vessels that had the subject engines installed. However, all of the damaged crankshafts had already been replaced. My request for dial indicators was met by the engine dealership, and we set up that equipment on the engines to determine any movement while the engines were operating. I had a suspicion that the failures were heat-related. Engines must be installed so that the drive shaft end is solidly mounted, but the remainder of the mounting must allow the engines to move forward when the steel expands, due to the normal heating they experience while running.

We had one of the fishing vessels make a short run around the harbor at Callao, and within several minutes the dial indicators showed the center of the engine was rising, which would cause the crankshaft to bend, and eventually fracture. This proved to me the engines were installed improperly. However, the engine dealer told me they had followed the manufacturer's installation specifications exactly.

**TRUJILLO HARBOR FISHING BOATS**

The following day, we took a road trip to Trujillo, Peru, to visit another fishing vessel that had experienced the same problems. We took the same measurements on that vessel and also found the same engine expansion, causing the center of the engine to rise, thus bending the crankshaft.

SCHOOL GIRLS IN TRUJILLO, PERU, PRACTICING THEIR ENGLISH WITH US

The visit to Trujillo was extremely interesting in more ways than just the engines we were inspecting. Trujillo is a major fishing village with a fish packing plant, mainly for sardines and anchovies. The entire village smelled of fish. However, on the positive side, we met a group of young schoolgirls who were thrilled to meet an American. They said they had few chances to practice their English. We sat around the docks and spoke with them, and before they left, they posed for the picture below.

On our return drive from Trujillo to Lima, we drove through the village of Huanchaco, Peru. There were long reed boats, lined up along the beach, and they were familiar to me from reading the book, "The RA Expeditions", written by Thor Hyerdahl.

Thor wrote this book about his theory of how people had first traveled from Egypt to the Caribbean on reed boats. He then theorized that they sailed from Peru to Easter Island on balsa rafts ("Kon-Tiki", also by Thor Hyerdahl). He believed that these reed boats had been

REED BOATS ON THE BEACH, HUANCHACO. PERU

PERUVIAN HORSEMEN, GIVING ME A DEMONSTRATION

lashed together, either for long fishing excursions, or possibly actual attempts to explore the Pacific Ocean by those ancient natives of Peru. Thor Hyerdahl made such a journey with a vessel constructed from similar reed boats, and he employed Peruvian natives to build the boats he used. These photos were taken by me at Huanchaco.

During our return drive, we stopped at a horse show to observe the horsemanship of some Peruvian cowboys. They are very accomplished horsemen and they were very friendly to me, although we needed a translator. We watched them display their skills for quite a while but finally had to head back to Lima.

There were other shocking and interesting sights along the highway, such as the truck pictured below, piled dangerously high with hay.

Another interesting thing was the walls, and guard towers at many corners of the homes and businesses, seen along the Highway. My hosts

HIGH CENTER OF GRAVITY?

GUARD TOWERS ON HOMES & BUSINESSES

explained the purpose of these towers was to stop thefts. They said home invasions were very common in these outlying districts. Because there was minimal police protection, the residents "occasionally" had guards in these towers. Although the guard towers were not always manned by an armed guard, the homeowners did sometimes employ a guard, and the "potential" presence of a guard, discouraged local criminals. Apparently, South American thieves believe that unprotected property is an open invitation to be robbed. This same thing was seen in Ecuador, where old men with unloaded guns were hired to stand in front of businesses as a means of protection. In Peru, these guard towers were a signal to the thieves that the property may be guarded, so beware! To avoid any chance of injury, the thieves left that property alone.

Upon returning to Lima, I obtained a copy of the installation manual, which had been given to the Peruvian engine dealer. After reading the manual, the problem that had caused the crankshaft failures in Peru became obvious. The broken crankshafts only occurred in 16-cylinder engines, and the installation instructions for the 16-cylinder engine were different from the instructions for a 12-cylinder engine. The 16-cylinder engine instructions had been supplied as an addendum to the manual after the manual was originally provided. Unless that addendum was noticed, and provided to the mechanics who installed these engines, they were not drilling the forward mounting holes large enough to allow for the added expansion of the longer, 16-cylinder engine. Surely, the limited understanding of the written, technical English language also contributed to these failures, and although the engine dealer was held responsible, the mechanics had tried to do a proper installation. Language problems played a big part in these crankshaft failures!

## Venezuela and Jamaica

BEACH AND HOTELS IN CARACAS, VENEZUELA

My client from the second trip to Peru, the Chilean oil company, called to arrange another inspection of a different tanker in Venezuela. They said they would send the same representative who had accompanied me in Lima, Peru. In Caracas, Venezuela, my Chilean friend met me at the airport. We arrived late in the evening and then arrived at our hotel after dark.

The next morning, a beautiful sunrise greeted me and there was a pristine beach extending for a long distance outside my hotel room. At breakfast, my Chilean friend gave me bad news. The ship which we were to inspect near Turiamo, Venezuela, had been diverted to Jamaica. He had already made airplane reservations for us to fly to Kingston, Jamaica, where the ship would be servicing a bauxite plant west of Kingston. There was time for a quick walk along the beach, but we saw very little of Venezuela.

During this trip, it was my turn to act as the translator for my Chilean friend. He was having a lot of trouble with the Jamaican accent, so I would explain things to him. This made me feel much better about my lack of Spanish skills. Jamaica has never been on my list of favorite countries, because there are many pushy and/or dishonest natives there.

At the airport in Kingston, we were waiting for a taxi, and a young boy constantly bothered us about carrying our bags. He continued his pushy attitude, even though we told him that we were waiting for a car and did not need our bags carried. Finally, he told us, "If you would just pay me, I would leave you alone." Since we had just left Venezuela, there was still some Venezuelan money in my pocket. He wanted American dollars, but the foreign currency was what he got, a large denomination note from Venezuela. He asked me if it was worth anything, and I said, of course! He took the note inside the airport and soon came back to us. He crumpled the Venezuelan note in his hands and threw it at my feet, swearing at me. Swear words sound just as bad in any language! The note he tried to exchange was probably only worth $0.25.

When our taxi arrived, we headed for the bauxite facility where our tanker was refueling its fuel storage tanks. Not having experienced the beautiful forests and hills of the inland portion of Jamaica previously, it made for a most enjoyable drive. When the taxi stopped to refuel, my Chilean friend decided to go into the service station to buy some snacks and drinks. It was taking him a long time to return, and the taxi driver and I went inside to assist him. As suspected, the store manager was taking advantage of my friend's poor English skills and was arguing about how much money should be paid. The taxi driver rescued him and probably saved the Chilean a lot of money.

Upon our return to Kingston, we had to stay overnight and catch our planes the next morning. The hotel near the airport seemed decent, but it had metal bars on all of the guest room windows. We decided to eat in the hotel bar, and when the Chilean arrived, he was carrying his briefcase. There had been trouble getting me paid for the job in Peru because the Chilean government had some complicated rules about sending payments to foreign corporations. The Oil Company had told me they would send payment along on this job. Thinking they would just hand me a check, I was shocked when my Chilean friend opened his briefcase and took out a wad of U.S. money. Sitting there in the bar, he counted out my payment in crisp $100 bills! It was hard to sleep that night. I was afraid the locals who saw that money might want it for themselves. But they didn't. Maybe they figured this was some kind of drug deal, and they were afraid that the Chilean guy was a Columbian drug lord, and I was the American buyer. Maybe they didn't want to mess with us!

That was my only trip to Jamaica other than the cruise ports, and it is the most beautiful island in the Caribbean, filled with natural beauty. However, one feels very uncomfortable there (even before that money transfer in the bar), and after another dozen or more business trips to Jamaica, that opinion has not changed. There are now Jamaicans in all of the Caribbean tourist islands, and those islands are not happy to have them. Too bad! Jamaica is beautiful, but you feel constantly threatened. Even cruise ships warn passengers about the pushy salespeople, and restrict their crew members from buying things ashore, so the problem is becoming well known.

I eventually lost touch with this Chilean Oil Company. I don't know if they ever bought a tanker. While I was communicating with them, the subject of hunting and fishing came up. As it turns out, Chile is overrun by rabbits, and hunting them is not popular. The Chileans told me to visit Chile, and they would provide the gun and ammunition for me to hunt rabbits. (Sorry, animal lovers, but these rabbits were not native to Chile. They are an invasive species!) They said it was possible to shoot 100 or more rabbits each day and by the next morning, the property would be full of rabbits again. I never made it to Chile, however!

## **First trip to Curacao**

Long before my cruise ship environmental audits, which frequently stopped in Curacao, the tanker company that hired me for the small tanker in Lima, at the beginning of this chapter, requested a damage survey of a chartered tanker, at the shipyard in Curacao. They sent one of their Fleet Superintendents to accompany me on the survey. This man was born in Yugoslavia, now living in New York, and was a very knowledgeable and gregarious person.

He told me a story about a pollution incident in Alaska, caused when the vessel grounded. He knew the Captain and several of the crew members on board, and although this story cannot be verified by me, the facts seem to ring true, as well as the interpersonal relationships that might affect such historical events.

Apparently, the voyage from Valdez to the open sea was quite a lengthy trip, and after leaving the harbor, the Captain gave the responsibility for the voyage to a junior Mate, which was an acceptable practice at that time. During the departure, the Coast Guard contacted the ship about a large ice flow in the channel and granted the ship permission to divert their course outside of the channel to avoid the ice. The Captain reminded the junior Mate and told him to get back into the channel after the ice flow was behind them.

There was also a wheelsman on the bridge, in addition to the mate. The wheelsman was a woman. What the Captain did not know was that the Mate and the wheelsman were smitten with each other, but just then, they were having a spat! The wheelsman reminded the Mate about re-entering the channel as the Captain had directed, but each time she reminded him, he decided to wait until it was his decision, not hers. One thing led to another, he waited too long to correct his course, and finally, the tanker went aground. The Captain was held responsible!

# CHAPTER 20

## TRINIDAD TANKER EXPLOSION

A shipyard in Trinidad, Port of Chaguaramus, contacted me and said an explosion had occurred during repairs to a tanker while in their shipyard. They wanted me to travel to Trinidad and assist them with the investigation into what had caused the explosion. I would be working together with two local gentlemen, independent of the official investigation, and reporting our findings directly to the president of the shipyard.

At least one man had died in the explosion and several were injured, so the atmosphere at the shipyard was very solemn. The official investigation was conducted by a panel of attorneys and the Trinidad government. Our team was given access to interview the known witnesses, but only after their official interviews were completed. However, we used the knowledge of the two local team members to visit and interview people in the surrounding area, as well as ships' crew members on neighboring ships, whom we assumed had witnessed the accident.

## *Trinidad Tanker Explosion*

We were told that preceding the accident, the shipping company had contacted several shipyards in the Caribbean to make minor structural repairs in one of their cargo tanks. The scheduling and prices at the Trinidad shipyard met their needs, so they came to Trinidad for repairs. The shipyard used a local gas-free chemist to supply a certificate for hot work on the vessel. The cargo tank in which the repairs were to take place had been cleaned before arriving in Trinidad and then tested by the chemist. The chemist reported the tank was within safe limits for hot work. The chemist reportedly asked the ship's crew what was in the adjoining tanks, and the crew told him that it did not matter because they were only going to weld in the tank that he had inspected.

*Definition of **Gas-Free Chemist**: A Certified Marine Chemist is a difficult title to achieve. First, you need to have a Bachelor's Degree in Chemistry, and then you need to serve a lengthy apprenticeship with an already Certified Marine Chemist. Before anyone can enter a confined space on a vessel, the Chemist must certify the tank(s) is "Safe for men". Before any hot work (welding, grinding, or cutting) can take place on a vessel, the Chemist must certify that the ship is "Safe for fire". Before any flammable cargoes are loaded onto ships or barges, the Chemist certifies that the cargo tanks have been properly inerted (usually by placing dry ice in the tanks, to form a blanket of CO2).*
*Definition of **Hot Work**: This is any work on a ship using welding, torch cutting, grinding, or any equipment causing heat or sparks.*

Repairs began that first evening with no problem. However, the following morning, when the sun began to heat the deck of the tanker, gases began to leak out onto the ship's deck from the adjoining tanks which had not been cleaned. One of the shipyard workers on deck noted a blue flame at one of the small bolted deck openings, which may have had a leaking gasket. The firehose that had been placed on the deck for this purpose would not reach the area where the flame was noted, so the man filled his coffee cup with water from the hose and ran towards the flame. Just as he reached that area, the explosion occurred, and it blew the man's body into the harbor. An enormous portion of the tanker's deck plate was also blown approximately 300 yards into the harbor, over 150 feet of the tanker's side shell plating was flattened against the dock, and numerous pieces of small debris were blown into the adjoining street and everywhere in the shipyard.

Our team sat in on many of the interviews, one of which was very disturbing. It was the foreman for the shipyard crew who had been working that day. He had been inspecting the welding repairs inside the tank which had been cleaned and was just exiting the tank when the explosion occurred. The poor man was sobbing when he described seeing the man running down the deck with a cup in his hand. The Foreman did not understand what was happening, but then he witnessed the actual explosion and saw his friend blown overboard. The foreman was only slightly injured by the blast but he felt responsible for the death of his co-worker and friend!

Although it was becoming obvious that the tanker had not cleaned the adjoining tanks, we recommended that a diver, with a hose to supply his breathing air, be used to enter the remaining cargo tanks to obtain samples of the contents to determine whether the tanker had cleaned all the flammable contents from their tanks before they entered the harbor. If they had not done so, this was a violation of International Maritime Law. We needed the diver because it would not have been safe for a person to enter the tanks without their own air-breathing supply. However, the ship owners were delaying this by claiming that it was even dangerous for a diver to enter the tanks.

While we were waiting for the Trinidad government to decide on how to proceed, our team decided to visit several local ships that had been in the shipyard during the explosion. One of the Captains on a local tugboat invited us aboard and showed us some of the small debris from the explosion which had settled on his upper decks. While we were speaking with him, he also informed us of a rumor, saying that several of the crew members from the tanker had made travel plans and were departing Trinidad that evening. The crew of the tanker had been instructed that they were not to leave Trinidad until the investigation was over, so their early departure appeared to be an attempt to avoid prosecution.

Our team visited the Trinidad officials and informed them of what we had heard. That evening the tanker crew members were arrested at the airport before they could board their plane. This changed the entire scope of the government's investigation because the attempt to leave Trinidad was viewed as an admission of guilt.

We had been waiting for a very prestigious fire investigator from Great Britain. When he arrived, our team accompanied him to learn the cause of the explosion from a technical point of view. The fire investigator agreed with our assumption: the surrounding tanks had not been cleaned. We asked the fire investigator what might have happened if the man had reached the flame with his small cup of water and had dumped it on the flame. The investigator stated the small amount of water would certainly have cooled the area sufficiently, extinguishing the flame, and the tragedy very well may have been averted.

The focus of the investigation began to turn toward the gas-free chemist. I called my friend in Chicago, Gerry Bernardo, who was a Certified Marine Chemist (gas-free chemist) to ask for advice. He told me that under no circumstances should hot work take place when the adjacent tanks had not been cleaned and certified as gas-free. He also asked about the qualifications of the gas-free chemist in Trinidad. In major maritime countries, a gas-free chemist must have a Bachelor's Degree in Chemistry and have served as an apprentice with an established Marine gas-free chemist for two years before becoming Certified.

Our team, as well as the fire investigator, attended the interview with the Trinidad gas-free chemist who had inspected the ship before repairs started and found that the Trinidad government had no specific requirements for gas-free chemists, other than they had to have purchased the proper equipment needed to perform the inspections. The chemist in Trinidad had no degree and no specific chemistry background, AND his full-time job was as an elevator inspector at the local hotels. He had bought his equipment to perform gas-free inspections with no training or experience. When he was informed of the fact that he should have required the ship to present the other cargo tanks for inspection, he seemed bewildered, because he could not accept the fact that he had caused the explosion and death.

The result of this incident was that the ship owner was found responsible for the death and the damages to the port. The ship was towed away and scrapped, as the damages were too severe to be repaired. The ship was owned by a large group of Scandinavian doctors. Being a Corporation meant that the owners were limited by the extent of their insurance, which was the value of the ship. We were told the ship's crew knew they were skirting International Law, and they were reprimanded but did not face any charges. The shipyard was reprimanded for not providing a proper fire watch (longer hose), and the gas-free chemist only lost his license to perform such services in the future. All of them had to live with the knowledge that their negligence had caused the death of that shipyard worker.

Before leaving Trinidad, I told the attorney leading the investigation that he owed it to the shipyard foreman to tell him he had done nothing wrong. That foreman was the one person who felt responsible and they needed to clear his conscience by explaining what had happened.

Because of the circumstances surrounding this project, it was difficult to enjoy my time in Trinidad, and I never really had the opportunity to see much of the island. The one unusual experience was at the hotel where I stayed. The hotel was built on the side of a hill, and the entrance was on the top floor. My room was on the third floor which was actually two floors **beneath** the main or lobby floor. It was quite confusing the first few days before getting used to the unusual elevator numbering system, which was the opposite of normal.

# CHAPTER 21

## DOMINICAN REPUBLIC JACK-UP RIG & STOWAWAYS

A Great Lakes marine constructor had taken a contract to build a portion of an offshore loading facility for natural gas tankers in the Dominican Republic. My contact from one of my largest insurance company clients reached out to find out if I could work on a major damage claim involving this facility.

This sounded familiar because another one of my clients had previously asked me to research this site for a different contractor in Virginia, just the year before. At that time, I had contacted several of my Captain friends to find operators familiar with that area, and every one of them had told me, "Beware of the seas from the southeast. They hit that harbor 300 days per year, and the contractor will find very few days in which they can work." It seemed the Great Lakes client had not heard about this problem, so their completion date did not allow for lost days due to bad weather.

The contractor chartered a six-legged jack-up rig to use as their work platform. Jack-up rigs are large floating barges, some are generally square but always wider than a normal rectangular barge. Most rigs usually have three or four heavy, structural legs, either square or round, which are lowered beneath the floating barge until the legs touch the floor of the ocean. When the legs continue to be lowered, the barge portion of the rig is raised out of the water. These legs can be as much as 200 feet long, but 100-120 feet are more common. The longer the legs, the heavier the leg structure must be to keep the rig properly supported and stable, without bending the legs.

## *Dominican Republic Jack-up Rig*

**JACK-UP BARGE AT BOCA CHICA, DOMINICAN REPUBLIC**

The problem with this means of jacking up a huge structure is before the legs are firmly jacked down into the ocean floor, the rig is floating, and therefore it is rolling and pitching in the waves. Until the legs firmly reach the bottom, the legs bounce on the bottom, and do so at various angles. In this particular case, the rig had to be moved numerous times in the harbor for the work that was being performed. Because of the heavy seas, for which this contractor was not prepared, they were jacking up the rig numerous times in weather that exceeded the safe limits specified for this rig.

Arriving in Boca Chica, near Santo Domingo, I met the Marine Surveyor representing the construction contractor. The owner of the jack-up rig was a well-known marine salvage contractor and the rig that had been damaged was an important part of their salvage equipment. The owner had chartered this rig to the contractor. We quickly determined all six of the legs had been bent in various amounts. We also knew that repairs could not be made in the Dominican Republic. The rig would need to be towed back to Florida for repairs. In addition to the damaged legs, there was additional structural damage because the tugboats were hitting the sides of the rig due to the heavy weather. The original on-charter survey had not been well documented, and we found it necessary to make a full survey of the rig to determine which damages were new, and which damages were pre-existing.

We started looking for towing contractors to transport the rig to Florida, as well as prepare the rig for ocean transit. We determined the repairs could be made at a shipyard in Tampa, Florida, and the towing company was contracted to make the tow. The legs were raised as far as possible, but because they were bent, some portions of the legs stuck below the barge, slowing down the towing operation.

Once the arrangements were made for the tow, the intention was for me to meet the rig when it arrived in Tampa, about one week later. While at home in Chicago, a phone call was received from the construction contractor, who told an incredible story. Stowaways had been detected on board the rig, and the US Coast Guard refused to let the rig enter the United States. Apparently, the crew aboard the towing vessel saw people on board the rig waving to them. The rig had a large accommodation space on one end of the deck, which had a full galley and sleeping quarters for the crew. The accommodations were not intended to be used while at sea; only while the rig was working near shore. The stowaways did not realize how long it would take the vessel to reach Tampa, and they had run out of food and water. They had men, women, and children aboard and they feared for their lives, so they started waving to the tug crew for help.

The tug and rig were diverted to the Bahamas, where the stowaways were arrested and returned to the Dominican Republic. This delay, additional towing time, and the cost of returning the stowaways were also charged to the construction contractor, and then to his insurance company.

The rig finally arrived in Tampa Florida. I gathered with the rig owner, the construction contractor, and the shipyard to discuss repairs. It happened that the legs were bent to such a degree that they could not be removed from the rig without cutting them into pieces. Because of this, none of the legs were reusable and six new legs had to be built.

We had numerous meetings in the Chicago offices of the insurance company with the construction contractor, underwriter, and claims specialist from the insurance company. The expenses on this claim just never seemed to stop. Even though insurance covered the damage repairs to the rig, the failure to meet the contract in Boca Chica caused this contractor to file for bankruptcy.

The bankrupt contractor was lucky to find another large contractor who was trying to enter the Marine Construction business on the Great Lakes. That new contractor bought almost all of the assets at the bankruptcy auction, outbidding all of the other potential buyers. The other bidders thought this new contractor was crazy, but they were not aware of what was happening. The buyer had won a huge contract to rebuild a large Great Lakes harbor but did not have enough equipment to complete the job. Outbidding the other potential buyers at the auction ended up being cheaper than trying to buy out a complete business. The new contractor also continued to employ most of the marine construction personnel from the bankrupt company, so the only loser was the insurance company.

# CHAPTER 22

## A FEW CRAZY YACHT JOBS:
## AND SOME SAD ONES

I tried to avoid working with yachts for most of my career. Naval Architects must decide, while in college, to finish the later portion of their studies either in commercial ship design, or yacht design. Never interested in yachts, my selected path was for commercial vessel design. Early in my A3Pi career, just for the income, I occasionally took on yacht survey work when owners would call me for a pre-insurance survey, and sometimes, a pre-purchase survey. Surveyors that typically do a lot of yacht surveys are "affectionately" called "yacht groupies"! They have no real training in surveying, and their reporting skills are terrible. One Chicago Yacht Surveyor's reports were just a series of checkmarks........HULL-✔, ENGINE-✔, Radio-✔, and so on. No details were given nor comments on the condition. Certainly, not all yacht surveyors are that bad, but there are too many like this. I had two excellent yacht surveyors that I met in Wisconsin, and I tried to refer yacht work to them.

The other problem with yacht surveyors is that the larger survey companies hire college kids for the busy summer season. They have minimal training and no experience, and their employer may give them a manual, which supposedly gives them all the information they need. That manual includes recommended repair costs for different damages but shows no range of costs between marinas in Chicago vs. a marina in Dubuque, Iowa, for example. Repair costs vary with the cost of living in each area, and the size of the boat involved, but these young surveyors do not have the experience to see this, and they embarrass themselves because they are following their boss's outdated and incomplete manual.

Yacht survey costs are typically determined by boat length, which I never understood. If I got a call and the person asked, "How much do you charge per foot for a survey?" I knew they owned a yacht. My question to the yacht owners who asked me that question was, "Does an engine inspection take less time on a 25-foot boat than on a 50-foot boat? What about the time to inspect and record details on your radar, radios, and other electronics?" Therefore, there was no good reason for me to charge half the price for a survey on a 25-foot yacht than for a 50-foot yacht. Certainly, the hull inspection may take longer on the larger yacht, but my surveys were always quoted in \$/hour, including travel time, plus expenses. This got me less work, but it only attracted knowledgeable, serious boat owners. Even then, would they pay?

Although some yacht owners were honest, my running joke was about how the yacht owners are able to purchase their expensive vessels, by not paying their surveyors. In my 35 years of experience as a Marine surveyor and consultant, nonpayment occurred only six times, and five of those were by yacht owners. An Attorney was the other non-payment.

During the "hungry" period in my early career, I performed numerous small yacht surveys for BoatUS, which was a subsidiary of CNA Insurance at the time. These were typical small damage claims, such as groundings, collisions (two boats hitting one another), dock or bridge strikings (also known as allisions), and engine damages, which usually occurred from sucking a plastic bag into their cooling system or hitting a rock while trying to get into a shallow beach. As soon as my commercial survey business grew, I avoided those yacht assignments. I will occasionally take a yacht job from insurance companies if they are unable to find a surveyor over a weekend (I work 7 days a week when asked), or when the yacht is located in a remote area where no surveyors are available (or willing to go).

Luckily, some of my commercial insurance clients would send me yacht-related insurance claims. Most of these claims involved an investigation into the cause of accidents, fires, sinkings, vandalism, and other such incidents, which were very interesting.

Two incidents in particular involved large pontoon houseboats on Lake Powell, which is on the border between Utah and Arizona. Because the state of Utah has no boating regulations, most of these houseboats are based on the Utah side of the lake. Not only are the houseboat designs somewhat lacking, but with no Coast Guard or State regulations, it creates occasional serious accidents.

The first time I received one of those calls to Lake Powell was for a sinking. An insurance claim adjusting firm located in San Diego, which specializes in ship and airplane-related insurance claims, referred me to their client. One of the adjuster's representatives met me at Lake Powell, where we inspected the vessel after it had been pulled out of the water. It was interesting to note the passenger list supplied to meet the boat rental company requirements, including names such as Daffy Duck, Gypsy Rose Lee, and other fictitious names. We found out all of the passengers were in a Hollywood-based production company, and this was supposed to be a party to impress potential clients. The witnesses at the rental company told us they saw at least twenty cases of liquor and twenty or more cases of beer loaded into the aft pontoon compartments. There was a ramp on the stern of the houseboat to carry one Ski-Doo, yet the houseboat left the dock with two Ski-Doos loaded on that ramp.

The only requirement made by the rental company was the person paying the bill had to sign a form, which said they were familiar with boat operation, and they took full responsibility for the operation and any damages that occurred. Our investigation determined the boat had left the dock with the stern of the pontoons at the waterline. The engine compartment was located in the stern of the houseboat, and the propeller wash caused water to begin entering the engine compartment when the vessel was underway. Water then progressed forward through small holes in the bulkheads. After several days, the houseboat returned to the dock to take on more fuel (and possibly liquor). After filling the fuel tanks, the vessel left the dock and it began to capsize, eventually sinking. Because several of the pontoon compartments now contained large amounts of water, the filling of the fuel tanks caused the stern of the houseboat to go underwater.

The operators of the houseboat were very lucky

TYPICAL LAKE POWELL PONTOON HOUSEBOAT

that the sinking occurred near the fuel dock because other boaters in the area came to their assistance almost immediately. If the sinking had occurred in some of the remote areas of Lake Powell, Daffy & Gypsy Rose could have drowned.

## <u>Second Visit – Carbon Monoxide Death</u>

Two years after my first visit to Lake Powell, the same insurance adjuster called asking me to attend to another serious incident on Lake Powell. A family had rented a large houseboat, similar to the model that had sunk in the previous incident. A father, grandfather, young grandson, as well as other family members, were on board the houseboat which was moored in a small remote cove on the lake. There were several sleeping compartments on these houseboats which were located below the main deck, actually in the large pontoons. The young grandson was sleeping in one of the pontoon compartments while the grandfather was sleeping on a sofa in the after-salon on the main deck. The rest of the family was sleeping forward in bedrooms on the main deck.

The grandfather, who was sleeping on the sofa, had opened the rear door of the salon to allow fresh air into the houseboat. The generator, located in the engine compartment below that aft deck, was running to operate the lights and air-conditioning. The generator exhaust system had been changed from an exhaust pipe leading to the upper deck, and the exhaust was now discharged between the two pontoons. There was a small drain hole in a gutter on that aft deck, which collected water and also drained out between the two pontoons. Carbon monoxide from the generator exhaust collected between the two pontoon hulls then came through the drain hole in the gutter and crept into the aft salon on the main deck.

The father of the young boy heard his son coughing and went into the hull compartment to investigate. That's when he smelled the generator exhaust and took his son out of the compartment and up onto the main deck. He was able to revive his son, after which he went to investigate the source of the exhaust smell. And that's when he saw his father lying on the sofa in the aft salon. The generator was running outside the open door. He tried to wake his father but his father had stopped breathing. The man performed CPR for a long time but was unable to revive his father.

Our investigation discovered that the family had called the boat rental company on the radio that morning, complaining about an alarm buzzer that had been sounding, and they were not sure what was wrong. They located the source of the alarm and disconnected it, intending to return to the dock the next morning so the boat rental company could make repairs. It turns out that the alarm buzzer they were hearing was the carbon monoxide alarm. Because the houseboat was moored in a secluded and sheltered area, with no appreciable wind to dissipate the exhaust, carbon monoxide had been entering the vessel all day, whenever the rear salon door was left open. The shocking part of this scenario was that both the grandfather and father were firemen, who should have known not to disable any alarms.

Our investigation at the boat rental company showed the generator exhaust had always been piped above the second deck for discharge, but had been changed by the houseboat manufacturer for undisclosed reasons. We suspected the exhaust pipe was considered unsightly, or the heat from the exhaust was considered to be a problem on that open second deck. The manufacturer had not informed the boat rental company of this change.

Part of our investigation team included two members of the National Park Service. Lake Powell is a National Park which came under their jurisdiction. The Park Service personnel told us, for many years the incidence of drownings related to pontoon houseboats in National Parks was much higher than drownings on other types of vessels. The reason for this was a mystery until the Park Service began demanding autopsies on the drowning victims. They found a large majority of the drowning victims on pontoon houseboats were found to have carbon monoxide in their system. Their investigations further disclosed most of the drowning victims had been swimming between the two pontoons. Just as in our case, carbon monoxide tends to fill the void between the two pontoons, when the vessel is moored in a secluded area, protected from the wind.

Although the family tried to hold the houseboat manufacturer responsible for this poor design, there were no laws in Utah that could be used to file charges. The manufacturer was a Canadian company, which also complicated matters.

*A Few Crazy Yacht Jobs*

## Broken Mast on Sailboat

One of my commercial insurance company clients asked me to inspect a sailboat near Chicago. The sailboat had reportedly survived a serious windstorm, damaging the mast, while sailing on Lake Michigan. First, I warned my client that sailboats were outside my area of expertise, but went to the marina north of Chicago and inspected the sailboat anyway. There was no obvious sign of damage and the sailboat was moored adjacent to an identical sailboat which had a mast of identical design. My call to the insurance company described my findings and again emphasized my lack of expertise on yachts, particularly on sailboats. However, I was aware of a well-respected yacht surveyor located in Wisconsin, whom I recommended that we call for advice. The insurance company agreed, and they made the call to this surveyor, whom I had once met on a passenger boat survey.

The following day, after returning to Chicago, the Wisconsin surveyor called me and explained what he had found. The sailboat adjacent to the one in question had also sailed in the same storm, and both boats had identical damages (a weak spot in the mast design?). He asked the marina if they were aware of the damage to the second boat. This damage had gone undiscovered before our two inspections. Although I did feel a little stupid, at least my observation that both boats were identical was certainly correct. They both had identical damages! The insurance company was not upset with me; in fact, they were happy to find this experienced sailboat surveyor for future reference. We have maintained a friendship to this day, and we occasionally worked together until he retired. He was always recommended by me for yacht surveys when those calls were received.

## So, When Did This Damage Occur?

One of my insurance company clients asked me to investigate a Vandalism Claim on a large yacht located near Indiana Dunes, outside of Gary, Indiana. The boat reportedly was on a trailer at the insured's home over the winter, where some person(s) had allegedly broken into the boat and "trashed it". The boat owner was a young man who looked very "rough around the edges" as I like to describe such people. He did not appear like a typical yacht owner. However, he was quite pleasant and showed me the boat and the damages. He did have a pistol tucked into his belt, so needless to say, it seemed best to also treat him with respect!

This was in April, and the owner was alleging the damage had occurred over the recent winter. He even gave me a set of photographs allegedly showing the boat and the damages when he first found them. The vandal(s) had broken into the boat through a glass hatch on the front deck, over the lower cabin, the interior of which was wet and covered with dead leaves. The vandal(s) also tore open the isinglass enclosure around the flybridge on the boat, and the area was full of wet leaves and debris as well.

There were evident problems with the man's story; because his photos showed the leaves on the trees fully leafed out, yet during my survey, the trees were just showing buds and not fully leafed out. There was also a small maple tree growing out of the vinyl seats on the rear deck, where the torn isinglass had exposed the seating to the weather. The tree was large enough, and I realized it couldn't have grown that large since the recent past winter. There was also moss growing in the wetted, lower cabin, which seemed too advanced for that time of the year.

My job is to gather information and report to my insurance client. It is not my job to make accusations or to tell the boat/ship owner that his/her claim is suspect. However, this claim had too many discrepancies, so I asked the owner if he had repair estimates, which he supplied. The estimates were recent and fairly priced for the damage, so I thanked him and left for home. The insurance company client was notified about my suspicions, stating this damage was old, at least one, maybe even two years old.

Yacht insurers have a "bad habit" of providing/binding insurance without getting a pre-insurance survey unless the yacht is a high-value yacht. I suspected that this damage had occurred one or more years earlier, and the owner collected on a claim from his insurance company. When he saw how easy it was, he changed insurance companies and collected again. My insurance client may even have been the third attempt at this claim. If the boat owner had not shown me those pictures with the fully leafed-out trees, which, obviously seemed to have been taken in a previous year, and if he had cleaned out the larger trees and moss growing in the boat, he might have collected on his claim again.

If you get upset about the increasing cost of insurance, this may be one of the reasons why. To save money, the insurers tend not to always have boats inspected before they are insured, so they insure previously damaged property, and sometimes pay fraudulent claims. This does not occur very often in the commercial insurance business, because most ships, tugs, barges, and construction equipment must be surveyed before they are insured, and then surveyed regularly (every 3-5 years) thereafter.

## When Did They Put That Breakwall There?

One of my insurance company clients called, asking me to refer someone who could perform a salvage job in the South Chicago/Hammond area. A yacht surveyor was working for them on a claim of a grounded vessel, and their surveyor had hired a small marina to perform the salvage. The marina had a small, self-propelled barge with a crane mounted on the barge. They were attempting to lift the grounded boat off the top of the Calumet Harbor Breakwall, when they nearly capsized their small barge, almost causing another claim.

With a couple of phone calls, I found one of my local marine contractors working at the casino in Hammond within an hour's tow from where the yacht was located. They said they were changing locations the following morning and could pull the boat off the breakwater. I didn't go out to the breakwater to see the boat, but my contractor called me from the site to describe the scene, and he sent me the photo below. He told me the boat had not just run into the breakwater, but must have been going fast enough to nearly go over the top of the breakwater, and end up perched on the harbor side. The boat was fully perched on top of the breakwater, with none of it in the water. My contractor easily plucked the boat with his crane, set the boat on the deck of the barge, and brought the boat to the marina adjacent to the Hammond Casino. My

WHERE DID THAT BREAKWALL COME FROM?

survey and damage assessments were completed ashore. The boat did not look too bad, other than the bottom being nearly torn away. The other noticeable thing was the blood over the console and steering wheel.

In incidents like this, any Coast Guard and Police reports are submitted to the Insurance Company with my report. I filed a Freedom of Information request with the Coast Guard, but for Marine Police Reports in Chicago, they knew about my work (I surveyed the Chicago Police Marine Unit boats many times) and with a phone call, and explanation about the Insurance Company claim, the Police would cooperate and share their reports. In this case, I also asked to speak with the investigating officer, who then called me.

I explained to the investigating officer why details were needed for inclusion in my report to the insurance company, he shared all the details he could. He stated the officers at the scene were surprised nobody had been killed.

The boat owner used a marina on the Calumet River, and he and his girlfriend, plus another couple, had gone to Navy Pier for a concert. All of them had been drinking heavily, and after the concert, they decided to head home around midnight. The boat owner and the other couple were very drunk, so the girlfriend drove the boat home. The boat had good electronic equipment, even a good GPS, but the lady did not know how to use them. She knew where the mouth of the Calumet River was located and headed in that direction.

It was a very calm night with no clouds or fog, so when she approached the Calumet Harbor lighthouse, the backdrop showed all of the city lights and streetlights, and she could not find the harbor entry. When she finally saw the mouth of the river, she was going at full speed, still outside of the breakwater, and she hit the breakwater at full speed. Those who were asleep in the cabin were jostled around some, but the poor girlfriend steering the boat was thrown into the console with her face, breaking the only radio on board.

When the other three emerged from the cabin, the boat was perched on top of the breakwater, and the girlfriend was unconscious and bleeding on top of the console. They tried to use the radio for help, but it had been destroyed when the girl's head hit the console. They started yelling for help, but no other boats came close enough to hear them, because the actual channel was quite a distance from their location. They sat there until daylight when they were able to flag down a passing boat. People in the passing boat are the ones who called the Chicago Marine Police.

I never get to hear the results of most of my jobs, but the Police said the girlfriend was recovering from a badly broken nose and broken ribs, while the three passengers only had hangovers! The boat was a total loss.

# CHAPTER 23

## GAMING VESSEL WORK

One of my more unusual types of work performed in the United States was on casino gaming vessels. The following are just a few of my experiences with these vessels.

### Design & Conversion of New Illinois Casino Boat

Because the laws in several states had been changed to allow for gambling on floating casinos, a group of Illinois-based investors contacted me. They had been awarded a Gaming License and were looking to place a gaming vessel on the Mississippi River. Because I was a Naval Architect and had designed several Coast Guard-approved passenger vessels in the past, they asked me to design a large casino boat to be located near East Dubuque, Illinois.

This was early on in my independent surveying career when business was still very slow, so I agreed to take on the design of this vessel. The vessel was designed and Coast Guard-approved, and a shipyard on the Ohio River was chosen as the builder. However, the Illinois Gaming Commission threatened to revoke the gaming license for this group if they did not have the vessel in operation within six months. We knew it would not be possible to have the vessel constructed in six months, so the design/build project was shelved.

The investment group then commissioned me to find an existing vessel, which could be converted into a working casino boat in a short period. There was a new dinner boat being constructed in Oregon, to be used in San Francisco, which would be suitable for this purpose. After a full examination of the vessel, the investors purchased it.

After the purchase, they found a shipyard in Mobile, Alabama, that could meet our construction schedule. We also found a delivery service in

**SILVER EAGLE, FORMERLY LOCATED IN EAST DUBUQUE, ILLINOIS**

Florida that agreed to prepare the vessel for an ocean transit through the Panama Canal, delivering it to the shipyard in Mobile.

Luckily, this vessel had been built with aluminum covers for the large main deck windows, because the weather in the Caribbean was terrible during that time of year. Although the vessel was not originally intended for ocean service, we obtained Coast Guard approval for the one-way delivery voyage. We also needed to obtain International Tonnage Certificates for the Panama Canal passage.

The vessel was delivered to Mobile with minimal damage and with adequate time to complete the modifications for delivery to the operation site, and meeting the gaming commission's requirements.

It later became clear that although the investors were well-connected with contractors in the casino business, they were not aware of Coast Guard requirements and all the problems involved in marine operations. For instance, because most casino boats are built with very high ceilings, we had problems with the dinner boat meeting the surveillance camera needs in the casino areas. Although we were able to maintain many of the beautiful features in the vessel's interior, much of the vessel had to be torn apart to add the cables for surveillance equipment and the additional air conditioning needed to handle the heavy heating load of the slot machines.

For the three to five days a week spent in Mobile, it made more sense for me to rent an apartment to avoid the trouble and expense of hotels during my frequent stays. Crawfish, fresh flounder, and the wonderful Mobile Bay shrimp were readily available and inexpensive, so I cooked my own dinners and loved the food.

One thing I noticed while in Alabama was that even though the Civil War might be over, many of the hard feelings remain. While in Mobile over the Memorial Day Holiday, I asked the shipyard if they would be closed for the three-day holiday. The reply surprised me, "What holiday are you talking about?" When I said, "Memorial Day of course!" He replied, "That's a Yankee Holiday, and we don't celebrate that here!"

After some research, it so happens that Memorial Day had originally been declared to commemorate those who died in the Union Army during the Civil War. Although it was eventually expanded to include those in the American military who died during wars fought by all Americans, many parts of the South still consider it a Yankee Holiday. The formal holiday given in place of Memorial Day was Mardi Gras Tuesday.

It was worth experiencing Mardi Gras in Mobile. It was the first city in the United States to celebrate Mardi Gras, and it is much more serious than the party atmosphere associated with New Orleans. They hold numerous formal balls, parties, and other celebrations which did not seem to have the "wild and crazy" feeling that occurs in New Orleans.

BATTLESHIP 'ALABAMA', IN MOBILE, AL

MORE THAN JUST THE 'ALABAMA' AT THIS PARK

Mobile is a great place to visit, with numerous activities and historical sites. The Battleship Alabama, several historical forts, and the nearby Naval Air Museum in Pensacola, Florida, are all extremely interesting. Mobile was a great place to spend most of those three months, but now back to the casino vessel.

During the modifications that converted a beautiful dinner boat into a glitzy casino boat, I accepted all of the responsibility for the structural and mechanical changes. It was made clear to my employers that the elevators, air-conditioning, and any of the casino-related wiring and electronics would NOT be my responsibility. Looking back at that project, that was a smart decision, because all of the problems we encountered were in those three areas. During the delivery trip up the Mississippi River, the vessel developed numerous leaks in the new air-conditioning piping because of the flexure of the ship. After the ship was delivered to Illinois, the elevator got stuck in the shaft several times, and we finally determined the cause was due to refueling the vessel. The fuel tanks were located in the center of the vessel and when filled, the hull flexure caused enough distortion in the elevator shaft to cause the elevator to jam between floors. As long as the fuel tanks were not filled to the top, the elevator worked fine. The elevator was not only important for transporting disabled passengers but also for moving money and chips between the casino and the vault, located in the hull.

Many of the investors in this casino had doubted my ability to make the conversion and deliver the vessel on time, but when the boat arrived in Illinois, ready for operations, they all congratulated me on the success of the project. Glad to be done with that project, and vowed NEVER AGAIN!

## Largest Floating Casino in the World

ABSTech contacted me again to be an inspector for a large casino vessel that was being built in Hammond. Indiana, where the Milwaukee Clipper had previously been moored (see the "Closer to Home" Chapter). The casino was being constructed on several large barges, which had been built on the Ohio River, and then delivered up the Rivers to the Great Lakes for this project. The state of Indiana was using ABSTech as their maritime inspection service below the main deck and was using their normal Fire Marshal inspection for the above deck construction. Although the barge would never be moved, it had engines and four propulsion systems, including a small pilothouse (which the gamblers would never see), to comply with the regulations for floating casinos. The casino was certified to hold approximately 12,000 people, including a large showroom, which is two decks high. When built, this was the largest floating casino in the world.

The barge had a very complicated ballasting system which enabled the casino to automatically maintain a perfectly level boarding ramp from the shore, so the patrons never realized that they were afloat. In addition to typical structural inspections, each of the ballast tanks and pumping systems had to be tested as well as a very complicated fire detection and sprinkler system. Although living near the Hammond/Chicago area, it was more convenient to stay at the local hotels, because of the busy inspection schedule and long days. They had announced an opening day, and casinos only care about making money. The owners expected the contractors to handle the problems, and open on time!

The project was finished on time and was very successful. However, I have never visited that casino since it's been opened.

My largest job on the project was to assist in the testing of the ballast system, which led me to work on two other casino boats in the Chicago suburbs, performing tests on similar equipment. In all, my services were used in the construction and testing of eleven casino boats in Illinois, Iowa, Indiana, and Missouri, plus pre-purchase inspections on numerous others. Working with people in the gaming industry was educational, but very frustrating!

## Slip & Fall Lawsuits

Large lawsuits happen to be a very common thing in floating casinos because the patrons claim the motion of the vessel or uneven decks causes them to slip and injure themselves. When this occurred during the Coast Guard-approved years, the casino would contact a maritime Admiralty Attorney to serve as their defense. These attorneys frequently contacted me to act as an expert witness and to investigate the conditions aboard the vessels on which the patrons claimed to have been injured.

Ships that are open to the public, particularly those leaving the dock, are covered by Coast Guard Regulations. Because the Coast Guard has the responsibility to protect people from fires and sinking when the vessel cannot quickly reach shore, the ship designs require areas of safe refuge, where passengers can safely gather while awaiting rescue. On land, the objective is to get everyone out of a building, but this does not work on a ship or moving casino boat. This leads to open deck areas on the top decks, which become slippery when wet or frozen, and passengers who are looking for a lawsuit easily find these areas. Luckily, the casino boats have many well-placed surveillance cameras, both on the casino floor and on those open decks. Even with those surveillance tapes, the casino must be prepared to defend itself against any accusations in court.

Most alleged injured persons can find a "shady" lawyer (ambulance chaser) to take their case, but luckily, these attorneys know little or nothing about ships or maritime regulations, making the best defense against them, using their incorrect statements about ship safety. It always felt good to show them why they were wrong! In all of the "slip & fall" cases I worked on, a well-written report citing Coast Guard Regulations usually won out. In my depositions, the opposing attorneys would cite OSHA and we would delightfully tell them why OSHA did not apply on ships. Those "ambulance chaser" types of attorneys seem to do very little research before filing lawsuits!

Once the casinos went completely shore-side due to state regulation changes, this all changed. Floating casinos now have to meet BOCA (Building Officials Code Administrators) and Fire Marshall regulations, and the Coast Guard regulations no longer apply. Because of this, those calls no longer come for me to defend the casinos, and I'm happy to no longer be involved.

## **Gaming Vessel Site Visits**

Another interesting part of my Gaming Vessel involvement was to visit proposed site locations with the people who had already obtained licenses for floating casinos. The State Rules for Gaming Vessels normally require the vessel to be located on a Navigable Waterway of the United States. In some cases, this would be "a real stretch!" If you see the Casino just outside O'Hare Airport in Chicago, you may not even notice that it is floating. The Casino owners excavated a small lake, connected to a tributary river of Lake Michigan. This qualified them under the Illinois gaming regulations.

Several sites were visited on the Mississippi River, one on the Missouri River, and one in Eastern Illinois, on a river that was eventually denied by the Illinois Gaming Commission because it did not qualify as Navigable. I had told them it would not meet the requirements because there was a dam on the river, with no lock to make it navigable. They thought they could talk their way around this, but failed!

I made two separate trips to Norfolk, Virginia, with one license holder, to help him look at various sites on the James River. The bad weather, dangerous river currents, and other problems made them reconsider that location.

Developing a reputation for seeing too many problems (I thought that should be part of my job), this type of work eventually stopped coming my way. Casinos do not want to hear about problems!

Somewhere between twelve to fifteen vessels were inspected, both modern and paddlewheel type, which various casino owners wanted to buy if the vessels met their requirements. It became second nature to look for ceiling heights, air conditioning, and other requirements that casinos needed. These vessel surveys ranged from West Virginia to Louisiana.

Then came the time when my involvement was needed for the modifications required to convert the "operating" vessels into shoreside casinos, once the laws were changed to eliminate the need for the casino boats to cruise. Although "land Architects" were making these changes, they occasionally asked for a Naval Architect to be involved, to advise them on the vessel structure and ballast tank arrangements, which had to be properly maintained.

**'RETIRED' GAMING VESSEL**

# CHAPTER 24

## CLOSER TO HOME

Although my world travels were very exciting and interesting, probably half of my projects were in the United States. Because of my location in Chicago, the majority of the domestic work was located on the Great Lakes, but there were also numerous jobs on the East and West Coasts, with many around New York, and a few on the Gulf Coast as well. Not only were these projects important to my income, but many of these projects were just as interesting as the ones I did overseas.

### <u>Sale of Two Articulated Catamaran-Tug/Barge Units</u>

In the chapter entitled, "Long Term Projects Requiring World Travel", I discussed the Environmental Audit inspections of that fleet of seven tankers. Two of these tankers were chartered by the tanker company, and the owner decided not to renew the charter, but to sell both vessels.

These tankers were an unusual articulated tug/barge combination. Most barges of these combinations have a large notch in the stern of the barge, into which the bow of the tug is designed to fit. Many of these combinations are called articulated tugs/barges because the tug is secured in the notch by a combination of mechanical and hydraulic equipment.

**ONE OF THE TWO TUG/BARGES, WAITING AT SPARROWS POINT FOR DRYDOCKING**

What made these two tug barge units unusual was that the tug was designed with a catamaran, dual hull design, and the barge had a "tongue" structure that fit between the two hulls of the tug, just the opposite of how most articulated tug/barges are built. Most articulated tug/barge units are designed for the single-hulled tug to fit into a notch in the barge. Although this catamaran created a very secure attachment between the tug and barge, this design presented numerous problems, such as:

- The tug had two separate engine rooms, which required the engineers to leave one engine room, go up to the main deck, and then back down to the other engine room. As a result, one engine room was always unattended.
- The storage space for spare parts and other supplies was very limited. Both engine rooms were very cramped for general maintenance purposes.
- The size of the auxiliary tanks on the tug, such as slop oil tanks, was very limited. This is what caused the original pollution incident, forcing the chartering company to be audited.

**UNUSUAL, CATAMARAN TUG HULL DESIGN**

**BARGE 'TONGUE' FITS BETWEEN TUG HULLS**

Above the main deck, this tug had very large and comfortable accommodation spaces, because this portion of the tug was much larger than normal.

Because of the intended sale of these vessels by the owner, the apparent purchaser was requiring both the tug and barge to be thoroughly inspected by an independent third party. The purchaser chose ABSTech to be that third party, and because of my experience on these vessels during the environmental audits, ABSTech chose me to perform these surveys.

## <u>Sparrows Point, Maryland</u>

The first of these two tankers was drydocked at the old Bethlehem Steel, Sparrows Point Shipyard, near Baltimore Maryland. Sparrows Point is located southeast of Baltimore, on the east side of the narrow channel leading to Baltimore, in Chesapeake Bay. Rather than find a hotel in Baltimore, it was easier to stay in a small town called Glen Burnie and take the toll road bridge between the hotel and the shipyard. There were several fantastic restaurants near the hotel serving Chesapeake Bay crab and other seafood, again experiencing a gastronomical "7th Heaven." There was also a crab takeout establishment near the hotel, where you could purchase fresh crab, or cooked crab by the dozen. Buying a dozen cooked crabs and a crab hammer, along with some beer, I must have left the hotel staff wondering. There were shattered crab shells everywhere in my hotel room each time this occurred.

When the tanker was drydocked, the tug was separated from the barge to make a full inspection of the tug hull and the barge hull. Every cargo tank, ballast tank, and other miscellaneous tankage was required to have a full internal inspection. Luckily, the cargo tanks were stainless steel because these tankers were originally designed to carry chemicals. Other than some minor corrosion, and scattered piping problems, the cargo tank inspections were relatively easy. However, the ballast tanks had not been well maintained and were heavily corroded. The ballast tank structure was carbon steel, and although the paint coatings were of good quality when first applied, the saltwater ballast had severely affected some areas within those tanks.

It took nearly one week to inspect the tug and barge while on drydock, and then to produce a very detailed report. In addition to the normal condition of machinery and accommodations, the report was required to rate each cargo and ballast tank on a 1 to 5 scale. No. 1 meant all of the paint coatings had failed and severe steel wastage had occurred, and No. 5 meant all of the paint coatings remained in good condition and no wastage was noted. What made this job very difficult, most of the ballast tanks were in the No. 3 condition, which would require a painting contractor to sandblast the interior of those tanks, everywhere in which the paint coatings were loose, and then repaint those areas. The argument between the owner and the purchaser revolved around the possibility of some tanks being in the No. 2 condition, requiring some steel replacement, or maybe in the No. 4 condition, which may only have required local hand preparation and hand painting.

The charterer was also involved in these inspections because they would be blamed for any perceived lack of maintenance, which led to these poor conditions. It was becoming increasingly difficult to mediate these arguments. There was a major difference in repair costs between the No. 2, No. 3, and No. 4 levels of condition, thus the ship's owner and charterer were trying to have more No. 4 conditions, and the purchaser was trying to have more No. 2 conditions. The cost of sandblasting and painting for even a No. 3 condition in just one tank was approximately $1 million, and the purchaser wanted as much repair done as possible, to reduce his future maintenance cost. They wanted No. 2's!

Because of these continual arguments, ABSTech became worried about my inspection technique and ratings. Therefore, an Engineer was sent from the ABS technical office in Houston, to reinspect several of the tanks. He was accompanied by me, the owner's representative, and the charterer. After a full day of these re-inspections, everyone agreed with my original assessments, and the survey was completed. I was VERY relieved!

## **Mobile, Alabama**

The second of these tankers was drydocked in Mobile, Alabama. Again, the tug was separated from the barge to make a full inspection of the tug hull and the barge hull. The same rating system was also used to grade the condition of the tanks. Because of the agreement made at the end of the

Sparrows Point drydocking, there were fewer arguments over the conditions found in the tanks. However, there were many discussions about mechanical conditions found in the cargo handling systems and the tug's propulsion machinery. This time, I requested assistance from the ABS Houston office, because my first-hand experience with machinery such as "inert gas generators" and cargo tank washing systems was very limited, and there were conditions that differed greatly from those of the first vessel. It turned out there was an experienced surveyor in the local ABS Office in Mobile and we spent a couple of days together looking at the equipment. One should not make decisions, which might cost a lot of money, if unsure of how to judge the actual condition of the equipment. Better to ask for help! And, I learned a lot from this engineer as well.

As discussed in the chapter about Gaming Vessels, a lot of time was spent in Mobile previously, and it was worth rediscovering the good food, boiled crawfish, Mobile Bay shrimp, and whole-cooked flounder, which are the local delicacies.

The tankers were eventually sold and returned to the chemical trade, for which they were originally designed.

### **Insurance Work - Condition & Valuation Surveys**

The majority of my domestic projects were related to insurance clients, both pre-insurance surveys, known as Condition and Valuation Surveys (C&Vs), and Damage Surveys following accidents and other such incidents. However, some projects were also to perform Condition and Valuation Surveys for banks and financial companies. A smaller portion of my projects came from shipowners and were generally on-charter and off-charter surveys. Occasionally, vessel owners would ask me to perform Pre-purchase surveys, but this was my most dreaded type of survey. Although most of my domestic work included valuations, in a Pre-purchase survey you were asked to provide a reasonable Fair Market Value (FMV) to the buyer, pointing out any poor conditions that might cost them money after buying the vessel.

*Fair Market Value is defined as, "The money (US Dollars) at which the property would sell, as agreed between a willing seller and a willing buyer when neither is under any compulsion to buy or sell, and both are aware of the equipment condition and other relevant facts, as of a specific date."*

However, the Fair Market Value provided to insurance companies and banks is typically under the best conditions, whereas the Fair Market Value supplied to a potential buyer is to save him money (looking for potential problems or non-suitability for the buyer's intended usage), without insulting the current owner. For this reason, when Fair Market Value is discussed with someone new to the maritime industry, and they are questioning a value found in a survey report, the first question is: On whose behalf was the survey carried out? Insurance valuations tend to be high, bank valuations are somewhat lower, and pre-purchase valuations will be lower still. Although this may seem contradictory, insurance companies can justify somewhat higher valuations because the insurance premium is based on the valuation, and the owner of the insured equipment wants to be adequately covered for a potential loss. A bank wants to be sure that they are making loans at a reasonable Fair Market Value. However, banks also require an Orderly Liquidation Value and a Forced or Distressed Liquidation Value to be provided, in case the equipment owner should file bankruptcy unexpectedly during the life of the loan. Then the bank would need to sell the equipment to recover their money. Therefore, the bank will normally make loans at or near the orderly liquidation figure.

However, the pressure is toughest on the surveyor when he is recommending a value to be offered during a purchase negotiation. If your value is not questioned by either the purchaser or the current owner, you have done a great job!

Upon occasion, clients asked me to provide a valuation for a potential buy-out between partners owning marine equipment. In some cases, they wanted me to provide a very low figure, well below Fair Market Value, and those projects were refused. The reason for those requests was understood. However, in my mind, it was not ethical for me to provide a lower valuation than in a pre-purchase. Luckily, these requests did not come very often.

## <u>Insurance Surveys</u>

The most frequent survey requests are received from insurance companies, and those were more enjoyable than any other. It was very difficult to be recognized by insurance companies at the beginning of my career. However, I received a call from The Great Lakes Towing Company on a Sunday evening early in my career. The President of the company at the time, Ron Rasmus, described a problem involving a dredge that had capsized during a tow across Lake Erie. They had towed the capsized dredge into the nearest harbor and had hired an established Great Lakes marine surveyor to represent them and their insurance company during the salvage operation. That surveyor was expected to develop a plan to return the dredge to its upright floating position, and also to recommend repairs. After several days of work, Mr. Rasmus did not see reasonable progress and wanted to find a different marine surveyor.

Luckily, two of his company's employees knew me from their previous employment, and they recommended me to replace the current surveyor. Ron Rasmus, Joe White (their shipyard manager), and I discussed the situation over the phone and, apparently, my verbal recommendations sounded reasonable, and Mr. Rasmus told me to be on-site the next morning.

The salvage plan was modified slightly and we were able to turn over the dredge within two days and make repairs in a timely fashion. Because of the success of this operation, The Great Lakes Towing Company has used me for nearly all their survey work to this day. Then other insurance companies started to call me. It turned out that there is a great amount of networking between insurance underwriters and insurance claims managers and my success on that first project opened the floodgates for other such work. Most of my original work was claims-related, but eventually, they called for pre-insurance surveys, which are the Condition and Valuation Surveys described above. I owe much of my continued success to Mr. Rasmus for trusting me on that first big insurance job!

Insurance companies require vessel owners to follow the requirements of their Classification Society (ABS, Lloyds Register, etc.) and the U.S. Coast Guard, and this includes drydock surveys. In many cases, the insurance company would request my attendance for updated Condition and Valuation Surveys being performed while the vessel was on drydock.

LARGE GREAT LAKES GRAVING DOCK

LARGE TUG AND BARGE IN GRAVING DOCK

The larger vessels would typically be drydocked at Sturgeon Bay, Wisconsin, Toledo, Ohio, or Erie, Pennsylvania. However, there were some drydock surveys in Canada and occasionally at the shipyard in Superior, Wisconsin. In addition to the larger vessels, many tugs, barges, and small passenger vessels were drydocked in Escanaba, Michigan, Chicago, Cleveland, and Sault Ste. Marie, and other small shipyards with floating drydocks.

TUG ON A FLOATING DRYDOCK

SMALL FERRY ON A FLOATING DRYDOCK

MODERN TRACTOR TUG WITH AZIMUTH PROPULSION

ROPE ON THE PROP SHAFT

Although the Condition and Valuation Surveys are the "bread and butter" surveys performed during most surveyors' careers, the damage surveys, such as the capsized dredge described above, were much more interesting. Many damage surveys were merely groundings, bridge strikings (also called allisions), or collisions between two vessels. Many of them included an investigation, which would be reported to the insurance company. Sometimes, my findings resulted in recommendations to prevent such occurrences in the future. When necessary, I would be deposed by opposing attorneys, if these insurance claims resulted in a lawsuit. This part of my responsibility will be discussed in a separate chapter (Expert Witness Work), describing my frequent testimony in such cases.

**CRANE HIT RAILROAD BRIDGE**

One of the more interesting damage claims experienced in my career was due to a construction crane being towed from one harbor to another on the deck of a barge. The crane had to pass under a railroad bridge which was of the type that could be raised vertically above the waterway. The man in charge of this towing operation had towed another crane under this same bridge previously, with no problem. However, he did not check the height of the crane and this second crane's boom was 20 feet higher than the first. The crane boom struck the underside of the bridge, bent the boom backwards, and when the boom fell, it struck the pilot house of the tug which was pushing the barge. The tug Captain narrowly escaped injury by exiting the pilot house when he saw the boom was going to fall. In the above photo, the crane boom should be pointing in the opposite direction!

Numerous times, clients called me to represent their insurance companies during the salvage of sunken tugs or barges. These were always very interesting projects, which typically required a 24-hour per day attendance (with call-outs from a nearby hotel) until the tug or barge was raised. This normally took 3-5 days, and my duties included assistance for the owner of the sunken vessel, to find and hire divers and salvage contractors, as well as planning repairs and estimating repair costs.

In addition to re-floating the tug, there was most often a pollution containment and cleanup element involved in these projects. Marine equipment owners must carry insurance for pollution in addition to their Hull and Machinery damage insurance policy. My job was not only to raise the vessel and to estimate repairs but also to minimize the repair costs and other related expenses, as the insurance company representative. In many cases, the pollution prevention and cleanup crews would expend unnecessary time and supply unneeded equipment, for which they would charge large sums of money. In one case, the pollution cleanup equipment included two small aluminum boats with outboard motors, yet the entire harbor where the tug had sunk was frozen, and the small boats could not be used. The excuse given by the pollution cleanup crew was the boats were always part of their on-site equipment. They were then told to return the boats to their storage and to stop all charges for such equipment, which was not received well by their manager.

Earlier in this chapter was a description of the first salvage performed on a capsized dredge. A similar involvement in a capsized cargo barge occurred on Lake Michigan early in my career. The barge had been chartered and was carrying a cargo of expensive, specialty scrap steel, which had shifted during a storm. The barge capsized, lost its cargo, and the barge was towed, bottom side up, into Chicago's Calumet Harbor to be righted. My role was not acting on behalf of the actual salvage on this occasion, but to witness the operation as the representative of the barge owner's insurance company. The barge had been chartered by the towing company, and it was the surveyor from that towing company who was in charge of the salvage.

A local salvage company had been hired to provide a barge with a small crane, and a large, powerful deck winch mounted on the barge. The towing company's surveyor had obtained the services of a Naval Architect to recommend a ballasting procedure, which would allow the barge to be turned over by the deck winch on the contractor's barge. Looking at the preparation of the ballasted barge, it did not appear the barge had been ballasted sufficiently for the winch to turn it over. Being relatively new as an independent surveyor in the Chicago marine industry, my statement of this fact to the other surveyor was not well received. He told me the Naval Architect whom he had employed, knew the situation better than me. It appeared to me and I stated, that the cables being used on the salvage winch would probably break before the barge turned over, and fifteen minutes later, after saying this, the cables broke as suspected.

The following day, everyone returned to the site to find that the broken cables had been replaced and rigged in a way that put the majority of the tension on two large bollards, installed on the dock. At this point, showing my frustration, I told the other surveyor that all this would do was damage the bollards. Again, the salvage operation commenced and within fifteen minutes, one of those large bollards was physically pulled out from the dock.

**CAPSIZED BARGE DURING SALVAGE OPERATIONS**

At this point, the towing company representative who employed the other surveyor, as well as the barge owner, who had employed me, asked me what we should do differently. Being familiar with this barge from my previous ABS surveys, I asked if the center ballast tanks of the barge had been recommended for flooding by the Naval Architect, who had developed the salvage plan. The towing company's surveyor appeared surprised and admitted he was not aware of the center ballast tanks on the barge, and therefore, he had not reported this to his Naval Architect. I recommended those center tanks be flooded, and then believed the deck winch would be able to turn the barge as planned.

The salvage company diver was able to find the deck hatches (now underwater) to access those center ballast tanks and was able to remove the hatches. While the center ballast tanks began to flood, the salvage master began rigging his cables again. Before he could begin to pull on his cables, the barge began to turn over on its own. Within an hour, the barge was being pumped, the barge was fully righted, and it was pumped dry by the end of that day.

Using my theory of "being properly prepared" and understanding the situation before starting a large project such as this, avoids embarrassment and mistakes. Luckily, being familiar with this particular barge and the arrangement of the ballast tanks helped me to impress the people involved. Also using some common sense to look at the preparation and the angle of the cables helped me in this case. A little common sense and some basic engineering knowledge told me that it would not work as originally rigged.

I gained some respect from the other surveyor that day. Later, he would occasionally ask me to assist him on other projects. The towing company responsible for the capsizing also started giving me work after this incident. This barge owner had given me some work in the past. However, they gave me all of their survey work from that point forward. Success tends to lead to more opportunities!

It was never planned to purposely make my competitors look bad. However, it was necessary to point out mistakes when noticed and comment about my feelings on how a project was being planned. This has always worked to my benefit. In more than one instance, it resulted in a good relationship with the other surveyor, but not always.

## <u>Differences of Opinion!</u>

In one such case, a client asked me to survey the damage to several hopper barges that had allegedly occurred during unloading operations at their Chicago bulk terminal. My client was the bulk terminal manager, and damage surveys had already been submitted to the barge owner's insurance company, by the surveyor representing the barge owner. The barge owner's insurance was now requesting the bulk terminal pay for repairs, based on their surveyor's estimates. Those surveys had laid all of the blame for damages on the bulk terminal, and the terminal owner did not believe that his unloader could have caused so much damage. The total repair estimate was over $350,000 for the six barges that were affected.

First, watching the unloading operation at the bulk terminal, I noted they were using a back-hoe type of unloader, an excavator, to scoop the bulk cargo out of the hopper. Excavator buckets typically have heavy, sharp teeth on the digging edge of the bucket, but in this case, the teeth had been covered by a flat steel plate, welded over the teeth, to avoid damage. The bulk terminal's equipment operator would scoop the bulk cargo out of the hopper, and he would occasionally scrape up the side of the hopper, causing minor vertical scrapes, but no serious damages like those being alleged.

Joint surveys were then attended with the surveyor appointed by the barge owner, and together we looked at several of the barges, plus looked at photographs of the damage on those barges that had already left the Chicago area. The major damages seen on the barges, and in the photos, appeared to have been caused by heavy indentations from equipment operating horizontally in the barge hopper, not vertically, as witnessed in the Chicago bulk facility. The small vertical scrapes occurring at the bulk terminal could not have caused the serious damages being alleged. There were some localized indentations, which looked like the excavator bucket had struck the hopper in some areas, but in my opinion, the damage caused by the local bulk terminal was less than 20% of the damage alleged by the barge owner's surveyor. In many areas, the light vertical scraping, attributable to the excavator, could be seen over the top of those major horizontal damages, which had to have been caused by other equipment. When these findings were pointed out to the other surveyor, he shockingly said, "The last damage always has to pay for any previous damages." I told him that the theory certainly did not apply in this case, and no insurance company would agree with him.

Because of the disagreement, this case had been turned over to attorneys in a lawsuit. I asked the bulk terminal to make a request for a loading and unloading history for the damaged barges. We received the requested documents and there was a consistent pattern, showing each of the damaged barges being unloaded at the same terminal on the southern Mississippi River over the previous few months. Calling that southern terminal and asking about their unloading equipment, we found they used an unloader inside the barge hopper, running horizontally. Because of this information, my report stated the probability of the southern terminal causing the major damages, and the Chicago terminal causing superficial vertical scraping on top of the old damage. I also reported some scattered "striking" damages had been caused by the Chicago terminal.

While briefing the attorney representing my client, the Chicago bulk terminal, he read my report and saw my assessment: that our client was responsible for less than 20% of the alleged damage. He also saw in my report, the other surveyor's statement about the last damage paying for all previous damages. The attorney said he was meeting with the opposing attorney, representing the barge owner, the next day.

After the attorneys met, our attorney told me the barge company was settling the claim for 20% of the original claim, which was the amount of damage we had recommended. It turned out the attorney for the barge owner was someone who had worked with me on several damage claims in the past, both for him and against him. When he saw my letterhead on the report, given to him by "our" attorney, he said (paraphrasing) "If this is Bob's report, I know he doesn't lie. Let me review his findings and figures." By the end of their meeting, the barge owner agreed on my figures, and the lawsuit was dropped.

This was very satisfying, knowing my reputation was such that an opposing attorney would believe my "differing" report over the report given to him by his client's surveyor. It was never necessary for me to "decide when" to be honest in my findings because it was something instilled in me by my parents, teachers, and good bosses/mentors. I have occasionally joked with my clients about not lying for anyone, and that included not lying for my clients. That philosophy has worked in my favor throughout my career.

## **<u>Bridge Damage Surveys</u>**

On a few occasions, my insurance claims involved bridge strikings (allisions). Ships sometimes rely on tugs to assist them while navigating rivers and other congested waterways, while others depend on the use of bow and stern thrusters to avoid hitting structures in the channel. Strong currents, winds, and sharp turns in the channel can adversely affect a vessel's control at slow speeds, and river navigation is one of a ship captain's toughest challenges. Stopping a 100,000-ton vessel is tough!

The photo on the left shows relatively minor ship damage caused when the ship struck a bridge during an assist tow (being guided by tug boats). However, the bridge damage was more substantial. In such cases, the ship's damage must be surveyed for the insurance company, as well as the damage to the bridge. My job is not to decide which party was at fault, but to gather the facts, both visually and by interviewing the ship's crew, tugboat crew, and the bridge tender, when possible. All of this information is given to the insurance company in my report, and the lawyers decide the outcome!

The Calumet River in Chicago and the rivers in Toledo and Cleveland are very vulnerable to bridge damage. While still working for ABS, a Greek-flagged ship hit a railroad bridge in Chicago's Calumet River, and it was stuck under the bridge for several days. The bridge operator was blamed for the accident, and the bridge was never repaired. The ship's pilothouse was destroyed and a "temporary" pilothouse was installed, using a cargo container, so the ship could continue its voyage back to Europe.

On three separate incidents, the insurance company for various towing companies asked me to represent them, after damages occurred to bridges owned and operated by the City of Chicago. The City has its own repair crew and is the City expected to make the necessary repairs themselves and then submit their invoices for payment. When working on these damage claims, my requirement to the City was to obtain additional competitive repair estimates and to submit those with their estimate, to justify the repair cost to the insurance company. The City was not used to this procedure, but in one case, the City agreed to use my recommended contractor for the repairs, and they were very happy with the results. The City crew was busy elsewhere, so this worked to everyone's benefit.

Railroad bridges tend to be old and in poor repair. The railroads try to claim a lot of unrelated damages as part of an allision claim. It was necessary to point out the heavy rust scale on old damages as compared with the shiny scrapes and fractures on the current damage, proving that the old damages were unrelated to the current incident. Rust on the Great Lakes takes months to develop a rust film, and many years to develop a heavy rust scale, and it was usually very easy to prove my case.

## **Cargo Lashing & Towing Approvals**

A very common survey for a Commercial Marine Surveyor is to witness the loading of cargo, either in a ship, into a hopper barge, or onto a deck barge.

Insurance companies want these surveys for several reasons:

- Confirm that the barge Stability is sufficient for the weight and center of gravity of the cargo being carried. Being a Naval Architect, the Stability Calculations were many times my responsibility as well, at least for barge loadings.
- Confirm the structural condition of the ship or barge is good, usually requiring a full On-Charter Survey, including internal inspections of all the void tanks.
- Confirm the loading does not exceed that shown on the Load Line Certificate, for the season of the year (Tropical, Summer, Winter, Winter North Atlantic).
- Confirm the lashings, holding the cargo to the deck, or inside the ship's cargo hold, are sufficient to prevent the cargo from tipping over or shifting in the weather conditions allowed for the tow. Again, being a Naval Architect, the design calculations for the lashings were usually my responsibility.
- Finally, setting instructions for the Captain, relative to weather and seas under which the tow can proceed. The wind force against the deck-mounted cargo (sail area) and the allowable amount of "slamming" the barge will experience in heavy seas must be taken into account.

On the Great Lakes, most of the cargo was large diesel engines, boilers, or structural welded components for machinery, or subassemblies for ships, being built at several locations. Large kiln tubes for a cement factory were once moved from one facility to another, as well as new and used manufacturing equipment, being relocated, were some of the frequent projects attended.

UNLOADING LARGE ENGINES ONTO BARGE

My first large cargo towing project, shown above, was in Buffalo, New York, where two large boilers were transported to Chicago on a barge. This was my first experience with multi-axle trucks transporting large loads like this.

UNLOADING LARGE ENGINES ONTO BARGE

However, cargo loadings and discharges became a common project. The engines shown in the accompanying photo were delivered from Germany and unloaded in Marinette, Wisconsin. The engines were headed to Michigan. You might ask why the ship did not unload the engines in Michigan, and the reason was the port was not deep enough for this ocean vessel. It was necessary to unload in a deep-water port onto a barge, and then the barge could enter the shallow harbor safely, to deliver the load.

**ANOTHER BIG-ENGINE-MOVE FROM SHIP TO BARGE ON THE GREAT LAKES**

Another unusual move took place moving a kiln from Sault Ste. Marie, Ontario, Canada, to Georgia. The kiln was moved by train, then heavy-load truck equipment, in order to arrive at the waterfront. There, my supervision began, getting the kilns loaded onto several barges. In Chicago, the kilns needed to be trans-loaded onto River barges for the rest of the journey. My involvement was not requested when reaching the off-loading site.

**TRUCKING EQUIPMENT TO THE BARGE DOCK**

A second similar move was to transport several large pieces of equipment from a chemical plant in Sarnia, Ontario. It also involved transloading in Chicago, to avoid the bridge clearance problems on the Illinois Waterway.

**SUPERVISING THE BARGE LOADING IN SARNIA, ONTARIO**

**LOADED BARGE WAITING FOR A TOW ON ILLINOIS WATERWAY**

Another unusual move was to transport a large, fiberglass yacht from Savannah, Georgia to the Great Lakes, where the yacht was to be completed by Palmer Johnson, in Sturgeon Bay, Wisconsin. The yacht was not heavy, but the wind load was a concern for the portion of the trip on the ocean, occurring outside the Intracoastal Waterway, so lashings were important.

**LARGE YACHT TOWED FROM SAVANNAH TO CHICAGO ON A DECK BARGE**

The shipyard did not want any damage from lashings, so it was tricky to find ways to lash the vessel securely to the barge. When the barge reached Lemont, Illinois, on the Illinois Waterway, the fiberglass top had to be cut off, and the barge ballasted down, for the vessel to pass under the 19-foot clearance railroad bridge, which was welded shut after World War II. Although my recommendation was to trans-load into a hopper barge before getting to Lemont, the client thought they would save time by trucking around the low bridge. They found out too late, there was no way to truck around, which I had warned them about. Then in Chicago, the barge and cargo were again inspected and approved for the Great Lakes portion of the tow, with the removed section of the yacht also lashed on deck as well.

A few of the more unusual items loaded on barges for such tows, and approved using my services, included the following:

**A RESTAURANT IN AN OLD RAILROAD DINING CAR**

**DAMAGED/SUNKEN RESEARCH VESSEL**

Maybe one of the most unusual barge cargoes was this old bridge structure in Cleveland, which was lowered onto a barge and moved away for scrapping.

This process has been done several times in Chicago, to remove old bridge spans, then place the new span in position. Although A3Pi Services was not involved in those, the City orchestrated the switch very well, and the L-Train traffic was only out of service for a few days. Vehicular traffic was restored shortly thereafter.

## **Export Packing Inspections**

Not all cargo work is on ships and barges. Calls frequently come from insurance companies to load containers of equipment being shipped overseas, called an Export Packing Inspection. These inspections involve verification of the actual cargo loaded, against the list and description shown on the Proforma Invoice. It also involves the markings on the containers and boxes within the container.

In one instance, the Proforma showed a drawing of the markings, having the address of the purchaser and the part number of the contents, enclosed in a Diamond Shape, on the outside of each carton and container. The manufacturer was upset with my rejection of his shipment because they had used a rectangular shape to surround the words, instead of a diamond. My explanation was that these parts were going to Cambodia, and the workers probably did not read English. Their instructions would be to send all the

Diamond Shapes to one site location, and all of the Rectangle Shapes to a different site location. The parts from this manufacturer would have ended up lost, or sent to the wrong location! They made the change as directed, and the shipment was approved. Sometimes you just need to think in very basic terms.

A couple of the more unusual Export Packing jobs were:

This equipment was inspected for compliance with the construction terms in the contract, and also for operation. This was a floating "aquatic weed harvester" manufactured in Wisconsin, for shipment to India. The shipment included a lot of spare parts and packaging for safe transport overseas. I visited this same factory a total of six times for similar projects.

This project was to inspect the lashing of a jet engine to a shipping skid, which was then lashed to a low-boy truck chassis. Simple job, but someone had to take the responsibility, and that was me!

A long-term project was to inspect a total of forty (40), 40-foot containers, loaded with parts for a wheat milling plant in the country of Jordan. These components were manufactured at several factories in Nebraska. I learned a lot about all those cylindrical farm structures along our highways!

Another part of cargo inspection work is damage. Damage can occur in a ship from water leaking into the cargo hold, or cargo breaking its lashings in the cargo hold, on the deck of a barge, or in a container in a rail yard. After a huge Pacific storm had caused one of the largest cargo losses in history, when cargo containers broke loose and fell off numerous ships, all of the marine surveyors on the West Coast were busy. One of my insurance clients sent me to San Pedro, California, to inspect damage to the framing inside a ship's cargo hold, after machinery broke away from its lashings and "bounced" around in the lower cargo hold. Part of my responsibility was to determine the cause and estimate the cost of repairs.

On several occasions, steel imports into the Great Lakes arrived with damage. Although there are surveyors whose full-time job is just to perform cargo inspections, there are occasionally several parties involved, each needing a surveyor dedicated to their particular interests. When that occurs, the cargo surveyors have recommended my services. These inspections can be interesting, involving determinations of how and where physical damage occurred (usually lift truck damage). If water damage is the claim, then a determination must be made whether it is salt water (from leaky hatches) or freshwater (rain). Hatch cover leakage tests are typically performed once saltwater damage is confirmed. Determining when physical damage occurred, is usually a case of looking at the level of rust film on the damaged area. If still shiny, it occurred in Chicago during off-loading. If there is a rust film on the damage, it occurred at the loading port.

**STEEL COILS BEING UNLOADED IN THE SHIP'S CARGO HOLD**

**CRANE TAKING COILS OUT OF CARGO HOLD**

Damage from transit in containers is very common. One unusual job was inspecting broken jars of olives going to Whole Foods. The job included counting those jars that were unbroken, each type, and also counting the number of damaged labels if the jars were unbroken. Those jobs were worth avoiding, whenever possible! Very time-consuming for low pay.

**MARBLE SLABS 'EXITED' CONTAINER IN RAILROAD YARD**

One such job is pictured here, showing an expensive load of cut marble slabs, which had arrived from Italy in a cargo container. The train yard frequently "humps" freight train cars, letting them bang into one another.

In this case, they sent this car into the yard a little too fast, and when the rail car hit the end of the train being assembled, the marble inside hit the door of the container, breaking it open. My inspection showed the cargo was well restrained by heavy wood dunnage, but the impact broke through the wood. The marble then continued out the open door, damaging about half of the slabs. Surely some salvage buyer made a nice profit, buying the rejected cargo from the insurance company at salvage price, and selling it to less picky buyers!

There is a lot of imported furniture arriving from Europe and Asia, damaged during transit, which became a frequent survey call. Those jobs were much easier than counting olive jars!

One unusual cargo which was recently inspected was the steel grates for gas grills, sold by Weber Grills. Those cast-iron grills are imported and three containers of grills were heavily wetted during a storm during ocean transport, resulting in rusty pitted surfaces on the grills. I attended a joint survey with two other surveyors, to determine if the wetting was from freshwater or saltwater, performed by a chemical test using silver nitrate. The wetted areas turn white when silver nitrate touches salt water or remains colorless if it is fresh water.

On a few occasions, I have inspected imported cargo to determine quality, which was not visible without detailed inspection. In one such memorable project, the Chicago buyer of electronic parts was concerned with the dimensions of some cable connections, as well as quantity. There was a container shipment of three separate small parts, 10,000 of each part. There was no way to inspect 30,000 individual parts, so with some research, a MIL-SPEC was found, outlining how many samples were needed to determine the overall condition.

First, one had to determine how the random samples would be chosen, and each box contained 150 parts. The MIL-SPEC instructions (from memory, but may not be exact) determined only five boxes to be opened from different locations on the pallet, taking five parts from each sampled box, and again choosing pieces from the top, bottom, and middle of the box. Twenty-five parts seemed to be a small sample for 10,000 pieces, but the instructions were followed.

After measuring and performing other tests to determine whether or not the 25 samples of each part were acceptable, the results showed one part was 100% in compliance, one had less than 3% defects, and one had 30% defects. My skepticism made me perform another sample and inspection, using different boxes, and to my surprise, the results were identical. Whoever determined this sampling technique sure was a genius!

Then the determination of quantity was similar, taking sample boxes and counting the number of items in each box. This showed the number of pieces to be approximately .05% deficient. This is when I "cheated" because there were some boxes near the bottom of the pallet that appeared to be crushed. When those boxes were opened, the quantities were 25-50% less than the packing list showed. The shipper wasn't too smart, placing those boxes near the bottom, where the weight of the other boxes crushed those under-packed boxes. That fact was reported separately from the other results.

The client seemed happy and this was a great learning experience about imported goods and sampling techniques.

During the 2020 COVID-19 pandemic, there was a critical worldwide need for blood thinners to treat hospitalized patients. One of the well-known blood thinners is Heperin. I was asked by one of my marine shipping company insurance underwriters to attend the export of a huge shipment of the raw materials used to manufacture Heperin, which to my surprise, was the "slimy" internal coating found in swine intestines. I first attended the plant in Wisconsin, where the swine intestines were "stripped" of that substance. I had to count and verify the amount of plastic drums being shipped and loaded in the semi-truck. I then attended the Air France Cargo Terminal at Chicago's O'Hare airport, where I watched the truck being unloaded and the containers being lashed to air-shipping pallets. Once the pallets were sealed, I filed my report. I was told that this one truckload of those swine intestines was valued at around $3 Million.

## <u>An Unusual Request</u>

The large yacht in the following two photos, was the largest aluminum yacht in the world when launched, but it has been surpassed several times since then. The owner was a successful businessman in Singapore.

The vessel was built inside a large building, which was approximately ¼ mile from the floating drydock, where the boat was to be launched. My job was to represent insurance interests for the moving procedure from the building to the launch site. We had to level the roadway and lay steel plates on any soft areas to prevent the yacht from shifting on the heavy-lift carriers, which were self-propelled. The move took all day, but all went well.

LARGEST ALUMINUM YACHT, WHEN THIS WAS LAUNCHED

## <u>MY "DO-GOODER" CLIENTS</u>

There is no disrespect meant by the "Do-Gooder" comment! But for some reason, my personality seems to attract people who decide to buy and renovate old, historic ships, such as the two Bob-Lo Island steamboats, "Columbia" and "Ste. Claire", old carferries, and retired military vessels.

These owners and potential buyers are "lovingly" referred to as "Do-Gooders," because their intentions to preserve history and the "Lore of Maritime Vessels" are very commendable. However, they typically do not understand the huge expenses involved in preserving and improving the condition of a steel ship that is still afloat. They do not understand that the vessel will eventually sink if these expensive repairs are not performed. In most cases, these buyers expect large numbers of people to share their interests in maritime history. They also do not seem to understand the limits of the American public to pay for the experience of going on board a museum vessel. Funding from grants and other such sources is limited, and when that eventually dries up, the upkeep of the vessel will depend solely upon volunteer efforts and the money obtained from limited visitors. Before they realize their mistake, the project has become hopelessly in debt and is typically abandoned or sold to another group.

The small vessel below, the "Dixie," is a 100-year-old, small paddlewheel-driven passenger ferry, operating on an inland lake in the middle of Indiana. The original owner started the business to carry passengers from the residential area on one side of the lake, to the commercial, shopping area on the other side.

The vessel fell into disrepair and the State of Indiana condemned the vessel as unsafe. Because the Coast Guard had no jurisdiction over this inland lake, the State of Indiana agreed to accept my credentials for an evaluation of the condition and to recommend repairs. Because the vessel was riveted and not built according to traditional marine standards, there were a lot of repairs required. However, the Dixie did get back into service, and nothing more has been heard from them, which is a positive sign.

## Milwaukee Clipper

One of the saddest examples of such a ship is the "Milwaukee Clipper" which is now moored in Muskegon, Michigan, harbor. The Milwaukee Clipper was originally built as a passenger vessel named the "Juniata," which carried many immigrant passengers from Cleveland to various ports on Lake Michigan. The vessel was eventually converted into a car-carrying passenger vessel on Lake Michigan, which operated for many years and had many dedicated followers. The Clipper stopped operating in the early 1970s and my first experience with it was at Muskegon Michigan. The new owner intended to refurbish the vessel for sailing operations. A Coast Guard officer and I surveyed the vessel, and we advised the owner that the boilers were in very poor condition, and it was unlikely the vessel could operate again without major mechanical repairs, including an expensive retubing of the boilers. In addition, we found the owner was repairing the teakwood decks but had failed to repair the heavy steel corrosion beneath the wood, due to the owner's inexperience. The owner later realized his mistakes and the next time I saw the Clipper, it was moored at Navy Pier in Chicago as an attraction vessel, to be used for weddings and meetings.

The next owner still had intentions to make the ship operational, so when Navy Pier raised the docking fees to "discourage" such vessel tenants, he towed the vessel to the shipyard at Sturgeon Bay, where it was drydocked for hull repairs, to obtain a Coast Guard certification. Partway through the repairs, the shipyard asked for a partial payment, and then realized the owner did not have sufficient money to pay for the repairs already completed. Repairs were stopped, and the vessel was placed under U.S. Federal Marshal's control until the repair invoices were paid.

That owner finally realized his dream was unrealistic, and he sold the vessel to the city of Hammond, Indiana. Hammond did a great job refurbishing the Clipper as an attraction vessel, with no intention of making it operational. It had an old, Art-Deco restaurant, bar, and meeting rooms available for rental by the public. Being a member of the Chicago Chapter of the Great Lakes Shipmasters Association during this period, many of our meetings were held aboard the Milwaukee Clipper. However, the city of Hammond quickly changed its feelings toward the Milwaukee Clipper when Harrah's Casino proposed a large floating casino, which would be moored at the same dock where the Clipper was then moored. Again, my involvement was requested in the very lengthy and complicated moving procedures to get the Clipper out of Hammond (it had been permanently grounded on a bed of gravel). It was then temporarily moored in the Calumet River, while negotiations were made with a historical group located in Muskegon, Michigan, to take possession of the vessel.

**THE 'CLIPPER' BEFORE LEAVING HAMMOND**

The Muskegon group then requested my services to survey the vessel and help prepare it for towing from Chicago to Muskegon. The new owners were advised to complete the hull repairs, which had been started in Sturgeon Bay about 10 years earlier. Once the vessel was moored in Muskegon, it was clear to me they would never have another opportunity to make the expensive tow to Sturgeon Bay. The Muskegon group had no funds to make such repairs at the time, and they felt the city of Muskegon and private parties interested in the history of the Milwaukee Clipper would fund these repairs after several years. They were also advised to keep the ballast tanks full of water. Corrosion in freshwater occurs very slowly, however, in damp conditions, with the water removed, corrosion levels would be significant.

**THE 'CLIPPER' MOORED IN MUSKEGON**

To raise money, the Clipper's preservation organization sold the rights to use the vessel's staterooms to local contributors, if they would refurbish the staterooms to their original condition. This worked well for a time. However, the vessel had no security system and vandals soon boarded the vessel and damaged much of the refurbishment that had been accomplished, breaking into those finished staterooms, expecting to find valuables.

The Milwaukee Clipper has been visited several times at her mooring, but we never found them open, and it appears that the vessel is listing severely to starboard. It would be sad to see a vessel with this history be sold for scrap. However, these organizations never fully understand the financial implications of owning an old vessel that is in constant need of repairs. Most of these well-meaning groups end up in bankruptcy.

## Bob-Lo Steamboats

Both of the old remaining Bob-Lo steamboats have been one of my consistent projects for over 20 years. Bob-Lo Island is located on the Canadian side of the Detroit River, near Lake Erie. The two steamboats referenced here were operated from downtown Detroit to Bob-Lo Island, taking passengers to a very nice amusement park located on the island. Many Detroit residents still have fond memories from their childhood and young adult life, because of their excursions to Bob-Lo Island on these vessels. In fact, "yours truly" was one of those passengers several times, while stationed in Detroit during my Coast Guard years!

Once these vessels were permanently laid up, several smaller diesel vessels continued to carry passengers to the island, however, the island was eventually sold to developers for residential purposes. Those diesel vessels were also surveyed for potential buyers, once Bob-Lo Island was permanently closed to the public.

The S.S. *Columbia* was purchased by a man from New York, who had originally lived in Detroit, and he worked for many years to refurbish the vessel in hopes of taking it to New York. He intended to operate the vessel as a steamboat on the Hudson River. His insurance company would hire me to inspect the vessel on almost an annual basis, to be sure the vessel was safe in its moored position off the Detroit River, free from pollutants, and well protected from ice and vessel allisions. That owner, Richard, died about 10 years after he purchased the vessel, but the organization he started is still serious about the refurbishment. The vessel was first moved to Toledo, Ohio, where it was drydocked for repairs. My attendance on drydock was again requested by the insurance company, and this organization had done a good job to that point. The vessel has now been moved to Buffalo, New York, where further renovations are taking place, and I again inspected it there. So far, this organization seems to be well-funded and has employed a well-qualified marine consultant from New York. Let's hope this organization does well, and The Columbia can someday meet Richard's dreams, even though posthumously.

**S.S. COLUMBIA BEFORE LEAVING DETROIT**

The sister vessel of the S.S. *Columbia* is the S.S. *Ste. Claire*. After many years of lay-up in Detroit, the *Ste. Claire* was purchased by a couple from Toledo, Ohio, and converted into an attraction vessel. The vessel was even used as a Halloween "Haunted Ship" in order to fund repairs. Again, my services were used for several moves of the Ste. Claire from Detroit to Toledo, back to Detroit, and then to several mooring locations in the Detroit area. The *Ste. Claire* was purchased by a family in the Detroit area, with serious intentions of using the vessel for weddings, prom dances, and other such events. The vessel was moved to what would be a permanent and safe location on the upriver end of the Detroit River near Belle Isle, and their refurbishment continued.

However, in 2018, the vessel caught fire and all of the structure above the main deck was destroyed. Again, the vessel was surveyed for insurance after the fire. When called for this survey, I happened to be finishing a job in Toledo, Ohio, so it was an easy diversion up to Detroit, while on the way back to Chicago. The owners have stated it is still their intention to rebuild the vessel, and they have contacted a qualified architect to help them with this endeavor. They are very nice, sincere people, and I wish them well. As of 2021, the lower two decks had been replaced.

**THE STE. CLAIRE DURING RENOVATION**

**THE STE. CLAIRE AFTER THE 2018 FIRE**

Recent photos seen on Facebook show the rebuilding has progressed well.

## Submarines

The public seems to have a curiosity about submarines, which makes them a better candidate for a museum attraction. The German U-boat at the Chicago Museum of Science and Industry is one good example. There was a brief encounter with the curator of that submarine, but they decided not to use my consulting services after I pointed out that the U-boat's ballast tanks were still full of salt water. The water was dripping from the bottom of the submarine (before it was moved inside) and I verified it was salt water, apparently remaining since its capture during World War II. When the curator was informed the water should be removed, he kicked me off the project, thinking this would harm his prized possession! Hopefully, they eventually took care of the problem, but working with museum curators has not been one of my best moments!

There are three more submarine museums on the Great Lakes, the "Cobia" located at the Maritime Museum in Manitowoc, Wisconsin, the "Cod" located in Cleveland, and the "Silver Sides" located at the Maritime Museum in Muskegon, Michigan. Those three submarines are still afloat. The museums are responsible for maintaining the vessels in good condition, but drydockings are expensive. Many submarines were built at Manitowoc Shipbuilding during WW II, and they were towed to New Orleans on a barge, where they were launched. The Cobia served in the Pacific and has a great battle record.

My only experience with the submarine Cobia, at Manitowoc, Wisconsin, was related to an insurance claim made by the Museum after a runaway barge sideswiped the submarine after the barge broke away from a nearby loading facility. My representation was again for the insurance company of the barge owner, and a joint survey was organized with a surveyor chosen by the Museum. Our original notification of the claim was from an attorney representing the Museum, and his letter stated, "Your barge has struck and injured our prized possession." There was no question the barge had caused the damage, but we thought referring to such damage as an "injury" was quite dramatic!

The Museum curator was contacted on the day of the survey and he seemed to think I was his enemy. The surveyor who had been obtained by the Museum was also there, and his credentials were excellent, both as an experienced surveyor and an expert on military Museum vessels. We inspected the hull together and found no structural damage internally and only minor scraping of the paint externally. The only other damage was a bent tubular propeller guard at the stern of the vessel. Both the other surveyor and I agreed that the necessary repairs were minor and could be deferred until the vessel's next drydocking, which was in approximately 2 years. The Museum seemed to believe the cost of repairs should include their normal drydocking costs, however, these were denied, because the vessel was already required to be drydocked regularly.

SILVERSIDES AT MUSKEGON MARITIME MUSEUM

We also surveyed all of the museum vessels at the Muskegon, Michigan, Military Maritime Museum the following year. This survey included two old Coast Guard vessels and the Submarine "Silver Sides." This was a survey for their insurance company, providing what is generally known as a Port Risk Policy survey. My job was merely to ensure that the three vessels at this Museum were being adequately maintained to be safely moored at this site, that no pollution risks existed, and the vessels were safe from weather and other potential damage risks.

The Museum staff at Muskegon was very cooperative and friendly, as compared to the staff at Manitowoc. There was also a small damage to the propeller guard on their submarine, similar to what had been noted after the incident in Manitowoc. When asked how this damage had occurred, their curator said the submarine had been used to film a documentary, and during the towing operation, the tugboat struck and damaged the propeller guard. Thinking the towing company or the movie company should have paid for repairs, the Museum curator at Muskegon stated instead, "We don't want to do that, because we tell our visitors that this damage was caused in a World War II battle." It was comical that the two museums thought so differently about similar damage to their submarines. The Muskegon Museum is worth a stop if you get into the area!

## Submarine "Cod"

In 2020, I surveyed the U.S.S. *"Cod"* at its Cleveland, Ohio, location. The submarine had not been drydocked in over 40 years, and the light, outer plating of the ballast tanks had corroded to the point that leakages were developing. Temporary repairs were made by divers, but the *Cod's* management was able to obtain grant money to pay for drydocking and hull repairs at the Erie, Pennsylvania, shipyard.

**HIGHWAY 16 AT END OF COMMERCIAL SERVICE**

I was hired to survey the *Cod* and approve the tow to the shipyard. After the repairs had been completed in 2021, I also surveyed the *Cod* while drydocked in Erie.

The *Cod* is presented as an active submarine. The dishes are set on the table, family and girlfriend's letters and photos are posted next to the sailor's bunks, and other items are arranged to make you feel like the crew is still living aboard. I think this adds a lot to the museum's experience for their visitors, and it is well worth the visit.

## Highway 16

**HIGHWAY 16 AT END OF COMMERCIAL SERVICE**

The "Highway 16" was originally built as a World War II LST Landing Craft. In the picture here, you can see the large bow doors from the original military design. The LST was brought to the Great Lakes at the end of the war, and it was converted to carry newly built cars from Michigan auto factories and deliver those cars to Milwaukee. This saved a lot of money in rail and trucking costs. This use for the vessel finally came to an end, and the vessel sat idle for many years. The owner has now allowed a WW II History Museum group to use the vessel as an attraction, and it has been repainted to its original camouflage pattern. The vessel still requires insurance inspections, so it has been interesting for me to see the vessel change over the years during my surveys.

**HIGHWAY 16, NOW RENOVATED TO 'LST 393' COLORS**

## Carferry "City of Milwaukee"

One of the best-managed museum ships on the Great Lakes is the Carferry *S.S. City of Milwaukee*. Their secret is a good bunch of dedicated and maritime-experienced volunteers. They not only keep the ship looking good, but they also keep a close eye on the important maintenance, to keep the vessel from leaking, freezing, and overheating. This museum also includes the Coast Guard Cutter "Acacia", a 180-foot buoy tender/ice breaker. I had also surveyed that vessel to approve its tow from Chicago to the museum.

I originally surveyed the *City of Milwaukee* for its insurers, before the move to Manistee, Michigan, where it is now located.

My compliments to the great staff and their volunteers for a job well done!

## Fireboats

Fireboats have been another one of my "special attractions." Maybe because in my Senior year of college, our Naval Architecture design team used a Fireboat as our Final Design Project. Since then, I've had this attraction for fireboats. Several of these fireboat jobs were interesting, and several of them were in Chicago. Chicago had three good fireboats in the 1980s, all built around 1940, probably to protect WWII defense factories located along rivers in Chicago.

There was also a Water Department tug of the same basic design, used to service the water intakes offshore from Chicago. Until the 1980s, City employees were living out on those water intake cribs, 24/7/365, to maintain the pumps and valves, and this tug delivered supplies and changed the crews regularly. During a test of that tug, they took me out to a crib one day (now automated), and they were quite nicely outfitted! This Water Department tug had been well maintained, drydocked regularly, and as of 2019, it was still in service.

As the fireboats aged, the City got rid of two of them. It was not that a 1940 vessel is considered old on the Great Lakes, but a common problem with most Municipally owned vessels (other than the Water Tug), these fireboats were never drydocked for hull repairs. The machinery needed for pumping fire hose water was well maintained, but not the hulls!

On my first Chicago fireboat occasion, a frantic call came from a small Calumet River shipyard. They had drydocked one of the fireboats because the firemen were getting wet, laying in their bunks, which were located near the waterline. Upon arrival at the shipyard, the City's representative told me the amount of money he had to spend, which was minimal. Looking along the outer hull, there were maybe 200 small protrusions near the waterline. They explained that these were "golf tees," driven into the leaks from the inside. Each fireman had a box of tees to use for this purpose when leaks were found. It was hard to believe what they were saying until we started breaking them off!

This corrosion problem is known as "wind/water line corrosion because fresh water alone does not corrode the steel, but the oxygen needed to cause corrosion is mixed with the water at the waterline. The vessel had never been drydocked for repairs or repainted since it was built, and with no paint left on the hull, the waterline was severely corroding. The proper solution was to cut an 18-24-inch strip of steel around the entire vessel and make a properly inserted, welded replacement. The shipyard made a quick estimate of cost, and it was about five times the available budget. Our decision was a compromise, to make "lapped patches" over the worst steel, where the firemen's bunks were located, and "pad-weld" the remaining pit holes (just weld the pit itself), after the golf tees were removed! This was not a typical "Coast Guard approved" repair method, but luckily, the Coast Guard does not inspect Municipal-owned vessels.

After the repair plan had been laid out, we did a walk-around to see what the other conditions of the vessel might be. The propellers, which were cast iron, looked like a cob-web. There was a possibility that the propeller blades could break off, and if it occurred at the wrong time, the blade could pierce the hull and the fireboat could sink. Again, the lack of funds was explained, so my small company, A3Pi Services, purchased two new propellers for the City of Chicago to install on this tug. We could not let them go back into the water in that condition. The City eventually paid me back for them.

Eventually, one of these three fireboats became so bad, it was sold to a scrapper. The scrapper was paid by an ecological organization to remove all the machinery, paint, asbestos, oil, and other pollutants, so the hull could be sunk as a diver's attraction in Lake Michigan. That plan is on extended hold, and the vessel was lying on shore in Escanaba, MI, the last time I saw it.

The second fireboat was sold to a Chicago tour boat operator, who made repairs sufficiently to get Coast Guard approval as a passenger vessel. After that man's death, the boat was purchased by a tour boat company in Sturgeon Bay, WI, where it still operated as "The Chicago Fireboat." It was again sold to a Chicago-based operator in 2019, and it is now operating in Chicago.

LAST OF THE OLD, CHICAGO FIREBOATS

Finally, I was tasked with a year-long project, on behalf of the City of Chicago, which involved making a full rehabilitation of the hull, rudders, and propellers on the third of these old fireboats. What should have been an easy job turned out to be terrible as I tried to satisfy all the City Managers with no marine experience! That fireboat is still operating in Chicago. The City purchased a new, jet-drive fireboat, which was to replace the last of those old ones. However, the jet-drive cannot break ice as well as the old one and it does not have sleeping quarters for the crew, so Fireboat No. 58 is still in use. I also surveyed the new fireboat for insurance interests, since it came to Chicago.

Other than Chicago fireboats, there have been surveys on the Detroit fireboat, and a very interesting survey of a historic landmark in Buffalo, New York.

The "Edward M. Cotter" was built in 1900, but was still operating when I surveyed it in 2013. There was a struggle between a Historical Preservation group and the Buffalo Fire Department, and my services were requested to determine what maintenance needed

THE 1900 BUILT, BUFFALO FIREBOAT

to be done. She is a beautiful boat and for over 110 years old, it was in very good condition.

## Car Ferries

The car ferry, SS *"Badger"* is a good example of people's love affair with carferries. Many people rode carferries on the Great Lakes as well as New York Harbor, Seattle Harbor, and other such cities, and their fond memories continue for these vessels. My family rode them across Lake Michigan when I was a child.

THE CARFERRY BADGER, LEAVING LUDINGTON HARBOR

The Badger has been surveyed by A3Pi Services probably more than any other single vessel in my career! She is a beautiful ship and still coal-fired, boiler steam, reciprocating steam engine powered. It is a pleasure to cross Lake Michigan on the Badger, and we try to do so whenever possible.

TERRY MCKAY AND I, ON THE PERE MARQUETTE 41 DURING CONVERSION TO A CARGO DECK BARGE

It cuts off around 5 hours of driving over to Michigan, and it is a relaxing cruise, as long as the weather cooperates. Remember my motion sickness!

On the Great Lakes alone, in addition to the Badger, my company was involved with surveys on the carferries Viking, Arthur K. Atkinson,

Spartan, City of Milwaukee, and the Pere Marquette 41. The Pere Marquette 41 was converted to a cargo vessel around the year 2000, and many "lovers of Great Lakes carferries" objected to this conversion. The photo here is of my good friend, Terry McKay, a retired Coast Guard officer who supervised the conversion of the Pere Marquette 41. Don't blame Terry, as he was just doing his job!

**PERE MARQUETTE 41, LOADING CARGO**

These old steam vessels are difficult to preserve in their original operating form because steam is extremely expensive to maintain and difficult to meet EPA requirements. The car ferry Badger has spent millions of dollars to save and remove ash from the vessel, and to install computerized combustion systems on their boilers, to reduce exhaust emissions.

Without the viable business income that the Badger maintains, it would not have been able to make those upgrades.

The car ferry Viking was sold to a group in Canada, who intended to operate the vessel between Canada and Cleveland. The Viking was diesel-powered and did not have the steam-related expenses of most carferries. However, the Viking was "returned" to the United States when that buyer defaulted on their payments. It was held for a time as a potential Casino Boat but was eventually converted into a cargo vessel. It has not operated at all since the conversion. I mentioned "returned" above, but the Viking was actually hi-jacked in the middle of the night by a Captain & crew, hired by the car ferry's American owner. The Canadian buyer was not making payments on the purchase contract, so the owner just decided not to wade through a legal battle, and just "took it" in the middle of the night. Their Captain on that voyage got into trouble with the U.S. Coast Guard for violating a lot of regulations, but the owner got the Viking back!

SPARTAN, A.K ATKINSON & CITY OF MIDLAND          BADGER IN DRYDOCK (GRAVING DOCK)

The latest car ferry project on my project list was a very nice and sincere Chicago man who wanted to buy the car ferry Spartan. His intentions were good, but the owner of the Spartan wanted the propellers, propeller shafts, rudder, and other machinery removed to maintain repairs on their existing vessel. They would sell the Spartan if the purchaser would pay to have the Spartan drydocked, and to remove those major machinery items. The potential buyer did not understand the cost of drydocking and removal, and this purchase idea soon disappeared. He also found the City of Chicago did not want the Spartan moored in any of the Chicago harbors. Chicago had been home to both the "Silver Sides" and the "Milwaukee Clipper" at Navy Pier before they moved, and Chicago knows these vessels are not as popular as their owners think. Once the funding dries up, the conditions of the vessels deteriorate, and the vessels become an eyesore instead of an attraction. His only remaining option would have been Waukegan, Illinois, where the number of visitors and other income sources would have been limited. This potential buyer is still looking for another vessel but has not located the right vessel or a willing seller.

## Coast Guard Vessels

Several organizations have attempted to buy and preserve retired Coast Guard vessels. The Coast Guard Cutter on which I sailed for thirty months during my Coast Guard years, the CGC *"Bramble"*, was moored in Port Huron, Michigan, for many years as a museum after it was retired. The Bramble was purchased in 2018 by a man from Virginia, intending to recreate the 1950s circumnavigation of North America, through the Northwest Passage, which the *Bramble* had been part of. The crew even took it out into Lake Huron to break a little ice. The new owner contacted me for a survey, and it then sailed to Texas for drydocking. However, the owner went bankrupt and the *Bramble* was sold at auction to pay the shipyard. It is sitting idle, with no current plans.

**USCGC BRAMBLE, MOORED IN PORT HURON, MI, BEFORE LEAVING IN 2019**

The CGC "*Acacia*" is currently moored with the Carferry *City of Milwaukee*, in Manistee, Michigan, and appears to be doing well. The *Acacia* was surveyed for insurance and to approve the vessel for towing from Chicago to its first home, near Frankfort. I had not seen the vessel again until recently, at her new home in 2018.

It was great to recently survey the icebreaking CGC "*Mackinaw*", which was the largest icebreaker the Coast Guard had on the Great Lakes until it was retired around 2010. The *Mackinaw* has been used as a museum attraction vessel since it was retired and has numerous volunteers, and retired Coast Guard sailors who had worked on the *Mackinaw* during their years in the Coast Guard. The *Mackinaw* appears well-maintained but is certainly underfunded. The "Big Mac" is worth a visit for those who may be interested.

ICE BREAKER, C.G.C MACKINAW AT MACKINAW CITY, MI

There have been numerous calls over the years to assist in the inspection and potential purchase of Coast Guard vessels, and although I would try to help these individuals, it must always be pointed out that there are pitfalls and high expenses involved with owning a vessel of this kind.

## <u>Dredges</u>

One of the more interesting vessels to survey is a dredge. Dredges are used to maintain the water depth in our harbors and rivers, but one of the more interesting types of dredging operations is at sand and gravel pit companies. Most people never get to see the dredge equipment used at those locations, because they are generally hidden from view in rural areas.

One of my clients told me early in my career to buy any piece of property near a large city if the soil contained a large amount of gravel. He said it was a quick way to become a millionaire, by opening a gravel pit. I did not fully understand his statement until I saw the constant flow of trucks coming from these facilities, supplying raw materials for concrete and highway construction during urban building booms.

Some of these dredges are worth millions of dollars, while others are basically "homemade" pontoons holding a large dredge pump. All of my surveys of gravel pit dredge equipment have been on behalf of their insurance company, which carries the risk on this equipment. Most of my surveys for river and harbor dredges have also been on behalf of their insurance companies, however, an occasional pre-purchase survey would occur on behalf of their bank.

'HOMEMADE' SUCTION DREDGE IN A GRAVEL PIT, WITH FLOATING DISCHARGE PIPE

The insurance companies are not only concerned with the condition of the equipment but also need to know the consequences for salvage if the dredge should sink into a deep pit. Salvage of any vessel in a river or harbor is typically easier, due to limited water depths of 20-30 feet. However, gravel pits can easily reach depths over 100, even 150 feet, and would make salvage very difficult.

Dredge equipment used for harbor and river dredging tends to use clamshell bucket dredges or cutter head dredges.

*Clamshells are a typical crane-operated bucket that digs the material from the bottom of the navigation channel, one bucket-full at a time. The dredge spoils are then deposited in a hopper barge and hauled away to a land disposal area if contaminated, or can be dumped offshore if the dredge spoils are clean.*

TYPICAL CLAMSHELL DREDGE

CLAMSHELL BUCKET

*Cutter heads are large rotating devices on the end of a boom, which is lowered to the bottom of the harbor or channel. The cutter head is rotated either by a shaft from an electric motor on the surface or by a hydraulic motor adjacent to the cutter head. Behind the cutter head is a large diameter suction pipe, which is connected to a dredge pump on the floating portion of the dredge. The dredge pump sucks the loosened mud and small stones, which are dislodged by the cutter head. The dredge pump then discharges the dredge spoils to shore using a floating pipeline, which can be several thousand feet long. A booster pump is occasionally used when these floating pipelines are so long that the main dredge pump is not capable of pumping to shore.*

**LARGE CUTTER HEAD ON THE FRONT OF A GREAT LAKES HARBOR DREDGE**

**WALKING SPUD IN FOREGROUND, AND A SECOND, MOORING SPUD IN BACKGROUND**

These dredges can be moved by tugboats, but occasionally they will have spuds that moor the dredge to the bottom. One of the spuds may be referred to as a walking spud. This walking spud can be dropped at an angle from vertical and then used to pull the dredge forward.

Some dredges use anchors located off to the side of the dredge and then use winches on the deck of the dredge to move the dredge from side to side, over a larger portion of the channel.

**LARGE SAND PIT CUTTER HEAD DREDGE NOTE ANCHOR WIRES TO EACH SIDE**

**LARGE CUTTERHEAD DREDGE IN SAND PIT**

**LARGE BUCKET DREDGE WITH GANTRY IN PIT**

The dredges in a typical sand and gravel pit are similar to the dredges just described, however, some variations are required due to the extreme depths of the pits, and because it is necessary to separate the sand and gravel. In some cases, the dredge will include a rock crusher, to break down larger rocks into gravel-sized pieces.

The dredged material at most pits is typically transferred to shore from the dredge, using a long conveyor belt system. The conveyor belt is mounted on floating pontoons. However, some pits use a dredge pump and floating pipeline if they are using a cutter head. Sometimes the unseparated materials are deposited in barges, rather than using a conveyor or a long floating pipeline. The barges are then unloaded at a processing plant ashore.

**SMALL CUTTER-HEAD DREDGE USED IN MARINAS OR INLAND LAKES**

## Towing Vessel Client Kept Me Hopping

One of my good clients, The Great Lakes Towing Company, who was also one of my first clients, has continued to use me for most of their surveys from 1990 until the current day. They hired me to perform Condition and Valuation surveys for both their insurance companies and their bank, and unless I was unable to attend due to other commitments, they used me for all of their damage surveys.

The Great Lakes Towing Company has had operations on the Great Lakes as well as in Florida, Hawaii, and Puerto Rico. For many years, they had an ocean-going tugboat that they owned but chartered to other ocean towing companies. The on-charter and off-charter surveys of that tugboat were performed on almost an annual basis for many years.

*An On-charter Survey is performed to document the condition of a vessel before the contract is signed, between the owner and the charterer. Typically, there will be two surveyors involved in these surveys. One surveyor will represent the vessel owner and the other surveyor will represent the charterer.*

*At the end of the charter contract, an Off-charter Survey is required to determine any damages that may have occurred during the charter and to compare inventories of spare parts, fuel, oil, and other consumables.*

During the first on-charter survey of this ocean tug, the vessel owner had me in attendance and the charterer had employed another surveyor. The survey went very well and all parties cooperated. Both surveyors' reports are typically shared.

When again asked to attend the vessel off-charter on behalf of the owner, the charterer did not have a surveyor in attendance when the survey began. The representative for the charterer stated he was very satisfied with my detailed reporting during the on-charter and with my attempts to mediate any misunderstandings between the owner and the charterer. For this reason, he told the owner he would share my expenses and fees, rather than have two surveyors in attendance. That was a great compliment to be trusted by both parties!

This was the first time this occurred in my career, however, my reputation of being fair to both parties resulted in me representing both sides during many such surveys. However, the point was always made clear, both sides must agree to accept my "Third Party" status. This not only saved money for the owner and charterer, but it certainly gave me more business.

Such an arrangement to share one surveyor cannot be used during Damage Surveys between two vessels, because both insurance companies will require, their own independent surveyor representation. Several times, I had to refuse a damage survey for one of my clients, because I had already been retained by the other party.

Because this towing company client performed numerous vessel assistance tows in congested harbors, they would occasionally damage the vessel being towed, and sometimes bridges, or docks during those tows. Because of the unforeseen nature of these occurrences, calls were received at all hours of the day and night, weekends and holidays, requesting my attendance at a damage survey as soon as possible. In many cases, this adversely affected family plans, vacations, and many good nights of sleep.

This same client had four tugs in Florida, dedicated to a Navy base. Because of the good relationship we had, they would occasionally ask me to perform surveys on those vessels. Those trips were great because of the good food in the Florida Panhandle, and good sightseeing, such as the Naval Air Museum in Pensacola.

One of the best locations this client had was at Pearl Harbor, in Hawaii. They had several tugs located there, which were surveyed several times. The manager of their Pearl Harbor operation had become a good friend, and we always planned a nice dinner and sightseeing whenever the Pearl Harbor surveys were required.

On one occasion, we took a detailed tour of Pearl Harbor after one of their towing operations, and seeing the Arizona Memorial from the water and taking a land tour of the old airbase was a great experience.

Despite the nice trips to Honolulu, my favorite location for their tugboat surveys was Puerto Rico. Numerous trips were made to San Juan for this towing company, as well as trips to some of the smaller ports in Puerto Rico. The simple foods in Puerto Rico became a favorite treat, and we made several side trips to the El Yunque rain forest, El Morro (fully, Castillo San Felipe del Morro), and other sightseeing trips whenever possible.

On one occasion, one of this company's tugboats was exchanging crew members for a U.S. Navy submarine, offshore near San Juan. Because the

351

submarine was not allowed to stop while in sea conditions, the personnel transfer had to take place while both vessels were moving. The tugboat had thrown a mooring line to the submarine crew and the tug was being towed alongside the submarine. When the crew exchange was completed, the submarine crew prematurely threw off the mooring line. Before the tugboat could get underway using its own power, the tug was swept alongside the submarine and went through the propeller of the submarine.

The tugboat suffered minor hull damage when one of the submarine's propeller blades cut through the hull side plating, and the tug also suffered damage to its steering system. The Navy filed a claim for damage to the submarine, including hull damage and damage to their propeller.

The insurance company requested my attendance at a survey of the submarine, to be held at a Navy base in Georgia. One of my client's Port Captains met me at the Navy base and we were shown the submarine at its mooring, next to the dock. The Navy had divers in the water with cameras to show us the minor hull damage that had occurred during the incident, but the propeller had already been removed for repairs. The propeller was hidden under a large tarpaulin on the pier.

**DAMAGED SUBMARINE**

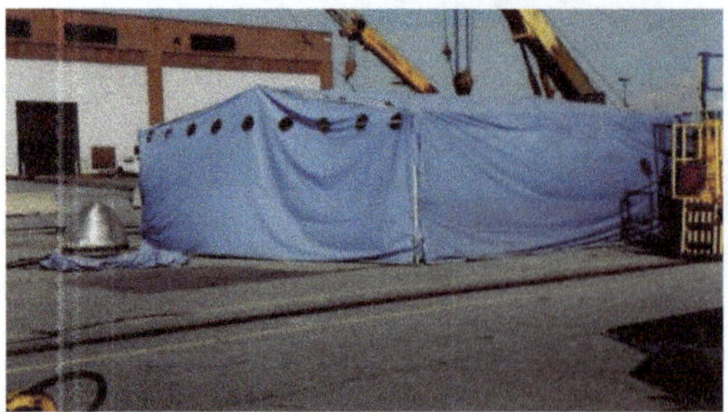

**CANNOT SEE OR TOUCH THIS PROPELLER**

We informed the Navy officer at the scene that we needed to see the damage on the propeller if we were to make a claim with the insurance company. We were told that the propeller was top-secret, meaning non-authorized personnel could not see it. We then asked the officer if he could let me feel the damage to the propeller, and again, we were informed the propeller coatings were also top-secret, and non-authorized personnel were not allowed to touch the propeller. I told the Navy officer, "If I cannot see or touch the propeller, I will have to report to the insurance company that no damage had occurred." The Navy officer replied, "Do you think the U.S. Government would lie to you?" I did not reply, but the smile on my face spoke better than words. The officer just smiled back.

This was all reported to the insurance company, and, to the best of my knowledge, the Navy never followed through with their claim. This incident occurred shortly after a serious submarine incident near Hawaii, totally unrelated to The Great Lakes Towing Company, but which had been widely publicized because it had resulted in several deaths. The Navy possibly felt this current tugboat incident occurred because the crew had thrown off the mooring line prematurely, which my report stated before the tug could reach sufficient speed to safely get away from the submarine. The Navy probably thought it was better to avoid publicity due to the Hawaii incident.

**OBSERVING AN ASSIST TOW IN THE CALUMET RIVER, CHICAGO**

## Vessel Sinkings

As we well know, vessels sometimes sink. The reasons may be due to damages caused by collisions with other vessels, allisions with other objects (docks, piers, bridges, etc.), running aground, or heavy weather. For this discussion, we will ignore sabotage or wartime actions. However, one of the major reasons for sinking on the Great Lakes is FREEZING weather.

Particularly as vessels age, the seawater piping in the vessel starts to thin due to rust and erosion, and this is hard to determine because it normally occurs inside the piping. The exterior of the piping (generally in the engineroom) appears sound because it is kept generally dry and well painted. Classification Societies will open the sea chests and inspect the sea valves every five or six years, and sometimes they will inspect the piping by taking thickness measurements in suspect areas.

However, most small tug boats are not inspected in such detail regularly, although recent Coast Guard Regulation changes are making small tugs (26 feet in length or larger) comply with similar requirements.

During my career, there were at least six sunken tugs and several sunken barges which I covered for the Insurance Underwriters. Each of the sunken tugs, except for one, was caused by the frozen pipes which were described above. Three of these sinkings were unusual, and worth some detailed discussion.

## Left Unattended

The "gory details" will be left out of this one because it caused two major lawsuits, which required my courtroom testimony. Most larger ships and tug/barge units are laid up in Winter, and there is a full-time shipkeeper living on board. Sometimes this shipkeeper even has his wife on board with him. Because of all the sea water piping in the engineroom, there are usually heaters running all winter. The alternative is to fill the sea chests with biodegradable grease, but this would mean the ship would have no fire water available if needed.

In this case, the ship keeper was living close to the ship and decided to go home occasionally, I assume without permission. While at home on one of those occasions, a severe Winter storm hit the area and the shipkeeper did not get back to the ship for several days. What he did not know, was the electric power was out during that period and the engineroom heaters had stopped. When he returned, the heaters had restarted, but he did not notice several pipes had frozen and fractured. The heat thawed those frozen pipes, and the sea water flooded the engineroom, sinking the tug at the dock. This is when the lawsuits started, and the tug was eventually sold for scrap. Many very long stories are involved, which cannot be told!

## Texting While Driving!

Another unusual sinking occurred while a tug was towing a barge near Chicago's Calumet River. It was a beautiful, sunny day with no heavy seas. Everything was going so nicely, this tugboat captain decided to call his girlfriend while he was at the wheel, in the pilothouse.

There is a phenomenon which occurs while towing, which is hard to explain, but barges which have no skegs (like rudders) on the stern, do not want to follow nicely behind the tug. The barge tends to "wander" and occasionally will actually come up alongside the tug. Tug Captains can better explain this, but when this occurs, the towline which now extends over the side of the tug, exerts a side force which can actually capsize the tug. This occurred in this instance, and because of the good weather, the engineer had left the engineroom doors open for better ventilation.

Before this captain realized what was happening, the tug was pulled over on its side and water rushed through the open engineroom door. The tug sank quickly, but all of the crew members escaped. The tug sank in only 20 feet of water and it settled on the bottom, sitting upright. When the Coast Guard arrived, the crew was standing on top of the pilothouse, wet but safe.

This salvage required hiring a team of divers, working offshore with a large floating crane. The salvage was relatively easy but very expensive!

## The Saga of the Tug "Ohio"

The tug "Ohio" was built in 1903 and had a venerable career. I surveyed the tug many times for Insurance Underwriters, Banks, and for Cargo Towing Approvals, on behalf of the owner, The Great Lakes

Towing Company. During my career, the tug "Ohio" escaped any real damage claims.

She was retired in 2017 and negotiations began to donate the *"Ohio"* to the National Museum of the Great Lakes, located in Toledo, Ohio. In November of 2017, the *"Ohio"* was towed to Toledo in preparation to hand over the tug to the Museum, but legal documents caused delays. One morning, the workers at the dock where the "Ohio" was moored, called The Great Lakes Towing Company to tell them her stern deck was going under, and the *Ohio* partially sank at the dock. I was called to represent insurance interests, and the picture below is what we found.

Because it was Winter, the ice created problems. We first had to contain the oil which was escaping. We developed a Salvage Plan and obtained approval from the Coast Guard to start raising the tug. A well-respected Diving Company was hired and they began sealing up the deck hatches, portholes, and any other openings in the hull and deckhouse. We then inserted suction hoses for three large salvage pumps, and began pumping on the second day. It appeared we would make some headway and the divers tried to access the engineroom to find the source of the water, but then the tug began to sink back again.

We called Joe White, the retired Shipyard Superintendent from The Great Lakes Towing Company, and he described the interior of the engineroom for the divers. Based upon Joe's advice, we had the divers close a hatch in the stern, which had gone unnoticed, and then they rearranged the suction lines for the salvage pumps. On the third day, the pumping began again. I had not eaten all day, so the crew told me to go to a late lunch, and sure enough, while eating lunch, the crew called me to say the tug had suddenly popped up!

The result was, we found a small pipe on the sea chest, which had frozen and burst during the cold weather.

## <u>Drydock Certifications</u>

Because of the experience gained during my three Drydock Certifications in Guam (see Chapter-13, "I Really Loved Guam"), similar certification inspections were performed on other floating drydocks and graving docks. Most of these inspections were routine, however, there was one very interesting inspection of a large graving dock in Boston, Massachusetts. The large cruise vessel, *Queen Elizabeth 2*, had been damaged due to a minor grounding off the East Coast of the United States, and they wanted to drydock the vessel in Boston to inspect the damage and make temporary repairs. The graving dock in Boston had not been used in several years, and the maintenance was in question. Therefore, my services were requested in Boston to report on the condition of that graving dock.

The major concern in a graving dock is the condition of the gate (or caisson), which holds out the water after the graving dock has been pumped dry. Serious accidents have occurred at poorly maintained drydocks around the world, when these gates have failed. The other concerns in a graving dock are the condition of the machinery, mainly the pumps used to remove the water.

My first day in Boston was spent examining the interior structure of the large floating gate (caisson) for this graving dock (see Chapter-11 on Panama for more details on caissons and sills). Some minor repairs and additional strengthening were required, but the gate was in otherwise good condition. The next step was to insert the gate into the end of the dry dock and to pump the graving dock dry. This not only tested the condition of the machinery, but we also were worried about the condition of the seals between the drydock gate and the sill, located at the bottom of the drydock entrance. We determined that the seal was in adequate condition with only minor leakage, and the small "stripping pumps" were able to adequately pump the leakage.

During my inspection, the condition of the concrete in the walls of the graving dock were noted, and although they were not in any dangerous condition, it was an area of concern if the drydock was to be used on a regular basis.

The *Queen Elizabeth 2* was drydocked about a week after my departure and the drydock reportedly worked flawlessly. One of the irritating things about my job is I seldom get to see the end results of my work.

# CHAPTER 25

## AN ARRAY OF INTERESTING SHIPS

There were just some ships that were too interesting to leave out of this book. The stories were not as dramatic and exciting as some of the others, with around-the-world trips, nor were they done in exotic places, but they should certainly interest those who like ships!

### <u>Keewatin</u>

The S.S. "*Keewatin*" was a Canadian passenger steamboat, built in 1907, and was laid up for many years in Douglas, Michigan, near Saugatuck. It was surveyed several times for insurance, port risk policies, and once for a potential buyer. It was purchased by a group in Port McNicoll, Ontario, Canada, but recently moved to the museum in Kingston, Ontario.

It's too early to know whether or not they will be able to maintain the vessel. The woodwork is amazing, and the sample shown in the photo is just

one example of the wood artistry in this ship.

This unusual barge, called "The Music Barge", was originally built as a River Hopper Barge in the United States. The man who purchased it built a complete symphony orchestra stage on the deck, and the cover over the stage was raised hydraulically to form a backdrop for the orchestra. There were office spaces, galley, and even some accommodation spaces for the crew. The old hopper below the stage was a museum. The barge operated in Russia, along the Volga River for many years but was returned to the United States. My survey was made on the Illinois River, where the last concerts had been held on the barge, near Ottawa, Illinois. The survey was to report on the condition, for a potential buyer in Buffalo, New York.

North Atlantic.

Most of the Staten Island Ferries look similar, so it is impossible to tell which one this may be. This photo was taken on one of my departures from New York to Bermuda. Two ferries were built in Marinette, Wis, and delivered to New York via the St. Lawrence Seaway and the

### An Array Of Interesting Ships

My job for insurance purposes was to recommend any modifications and safety precautions needed to deliver the ships without damage. To this end, the shipyard was instructed to build a temporary bulwark around the opening at the bow, where the cars would normally drive aboard the vessel. Although the shipyard thought this was excessive on my part, the temporary bulwark reportedly became necessary when the delivery crew encountered heavy seas near Canso, Nova Scotia.

I received the following account of this Staten Island Ferry delivery from Chuck Cart, an excellent Chief Engineer whom I've known for many years. Chuck made the delivery trip on that ferry. I include this story to show just how crazy the maritime business can get!

*"We departed (the builder's) yard with the (ferry) in early December and made our way to Detroit, where we tied up at Nicholson's for minor repairs. From there we proceeded across Lake Erie and stopped in New York for the same issue. The transit through the Welland (Canal) was smooth, as was the passage out St. Lawrence until we got to Quebec City.*

*"At this point, we were running in brash ice, and as these ferries are not designed for this, we were having difficulties with plugging of the cooling water strainers. We never were in danger of losing the plant, but I was dumping strainers as quickly as I could pull them. (One crew member tried to help by directing a hot water hose against the strainer housing but all he succeeded in doing was filling my boot with tepid water).*

*"The Pilots were aboard by this time, and being aware of the issue, they requested that we have a tug as a preventative measure, should we find ourselves in trouble in the narrow channel under the bridge. (As an aside, that was the shyest tug skipper I've ever seen, we chased him around the river for quite a while trying to get a line and we finally threw one of our hawsers to him!).*

*"Once past Quebec we let the tug go, de-boarded the snooty Pilots and made our way out into the Gulf of St. Lawrence. Here we were met with some pretty good seas, which we were taking on the "bow". Your bow-plate and anchor rig were working well enough but we were still taking water over it, and the vehicle deck was sometimes awash with a foot or so of water. I was watching this, and was afraid we would lose one of the*

*big soft-lines stowed there, which perhaps could foul the wheel. We managed to get everything secured, after which the Captain decided to alter course and run with the seas to the SSW. The bow-plate was not in any danger of being carried away and I don't remember any weld cracking or other issues even as it was being heavily tested.*

*"About this time, the Captain told me we had received a radio call from the Canadian Coast Guard requesting that we return to Quebec. My understanding is that the towing company had filed a salvage claim against the vessel for assisting in prevention of a grounding or allision with the bridge. Dean told the CCG that with the sea-state we were in he wasn't comfortable with returning. They understood and directed us to stop at the Canso canal where we would be met. Our original course was to take us east of Cape Breton Island. During our transit, the CCG kept frequent radio contact and over-flew us a number of times to ascertain our location and presumably our intentions.*

*"As an interesting bit of rumor, it was said that the towing company had lost the bid for the delivery of the ferries under tow and were taking the opportunity to get a slice of the pie. I was surprised, as I understood them to be a subsidiary of one of the big towing outfits in New York harbor and annoying the City would seem to me to be a bad decision.*

*"Once we arrived in the (Canso) canal we tied up across from Port Hawkesbury, where the "Mounties" met us (I was disappointed that they didn't have bright red coats and pencil mustaches). We were there several days, long enough for us to rent a car and tour Cape Breton Island anyhow. The captain was working with the attorneys for the builder's yard, the Canadian government, the U.S. government, The City of New York, etal.*

*"After a couple of days, the Captain was able to get permission to move the ship to a sheltered berth in Shelburne N.S., where we arrived at night, in the fog, just before Christmas. We spent Christmas there in Shelburne and the people were great! The crew were all invited to share Christmas dinner with families in town, and some went and said they had a great time. I had the watch, so stayed aboard.*

## An Array Of Interesting Ships

*"I'd like to point out here that we've been aboard now for about three weeks, aboard a ferry designed for a twenty-minute passage, with no galley (we had three second-hand refrigerators, two electric skillets, two crock-pots, a toaster, and a microwave oven), and no staterooms. As a Senior Engineering Officer, I had the luxury of removing several hundred life jackets from their large locker, giving me a room tall enough to stand in and wide enough to stand next to the cot, which only hung out the door to mid-calf, but in a sleeping bag it isn't a problem (some folks didn't even have a cot) Plus it had a light with a switch!*

*"We left Shelburne a couple of days after Christmas as I recall, and made our way south and west to the Cape Cod Canal, down the East Coast, into Chesapeake Bay and then on to Colonna Shipyard at Norfolk with no incident other than some heckling by the Boston fans who were incensed by the orange painted vessel with NEW YORK painted on it as we passed through the Cape Cod Canal. We left the ship at Colonna's for final preparation before delivery to the City of New York. I was not involved with the final leg of the trip."*

So, getting this story from a seasoned Merchant Mariner, you may be able to understand why some of my adventures became so "unusual"!

### <u>Columbia Yacht Club "Abegweit"</u>

These two pictures of the "Abegweit" in Chicago Harbor show the current, dark hull, and the light blue hull from its early years in Chicago. The Abegweit was built as an ice breaking passenger car ferry in Canada.

The Yacht Club purchased the vessel and turned it into their club house. The vessel has a

**M/V ABEGWEIT IN CHICAGO**

beautiful restaurant, bar, and office spaces in the superstructure, and the car deck is used for classes, sail lockers, showers, etc. It was surveyed several times for insurance interests.

The *"Quest"* was originally built as an oilfield supply vessel (similar to the orange one in the small photo). The owner of a large United States hotel chain bought the vessel and converted it into a well laid out, ocean fishing "facility", carrying its own, 40-foot fishing boat. It also had extra passenger quarters built on the two lower decks, and beautiful owner's suite behind the pilothouse, plus it typically carried a helicopter and a diver's propulsion unit for underwater exploring.

The purpose of my survey was to make a determination of the vessel's condition to meet SOLAS requirements. The vessel was a private fishing vessel, and therefore did not require SOLAS (Safety of Life at Sea) certificates. However, the owner intended to offer the vessel to a charitable research organization at no charge. This organization was requiring SOLAS approvals to assure their volunteers would be safe.

The interesting part of the charter agreement was that the fishing boat and owner's suite were not part of the charter. The Captain on the *Quest* always contacted local fishermen wherever the vessel was located in the world. If the fishing was very good in that area, the Captain would call the owner, and the owner would fly to the airport nearest to that location. The helicopter would fly to pick up the owner, take him back to the *Quest*, and he would be fishing, while the charterer went about their business. The crew had shown me the fish tackle room on board, which had over 50 rods, even more reels, and thousands of lures and other supplies. Amazing ship!

The Westcott Boats are famous in Detroit! They are known as "The Mail Boats," delivering mail to the freighters passing through the Detroit River. The Westcott Company actually has their own Zip Code! When my Father was sailing, our letters were typically mailed to him, C/O the Westcott Company, Detroit, Michigan! The ships would hang a leather bag or bucket over the side and the Westcott Boat crew would drop the mail inside for the crew to pull up.

The photo above was taken during my survey, which followed a tragic accident. Occasionally the Westcott Boats would deliver a Great Lakes Pilot to a passing foreign flag vessel, typically during an exchange of pilots. In this case, the *J.W. Westcott* was pulled against the side of the ship and lost control, capsizing and sinking. The pilot survived, but the Captain of the *J.W. Westcott* was trapped in the vessel and drowned.

Five of these Navy tugs, pictured here, were purchased by a Great Lakes operator, hoping to run rail barges and rail car ferries across Lake Superior and down Lake Michigan, combined with using railroad cars across the Upper Peninsula of Michigan. Three of these retired Navy tugs were laid up in Norfolk, and two in San Francisco. My surveys were performed each time the vessels were moved, to ensure they were safe from weather and any possible striking by other vessels. This type of survey was called Port Risk by the insurance companies, which was done frequently on various types of vessels which were laid up for long periods.

## <u>Passenger Excursion Vessels</u>

Because my experience included both design and building of small passenger vessels in my early career, inspections of small passenger vessels were done on a regular basis in my surveying business. These excursion vessels are used for sightseeing and for dinner cruises around almost every major city harbor in the United States. They tend to carry between 100 to 400 passengers and typically will be 60 to 150 feet long. Some of the larger excursion vessels are similar to the casino vessels, which were described in the chapter on Gaming Vessels. In some cases, gaming vessels are converted to dinner cruise vessels or vice versa, which was a good source of business over the years.

Most of these passenger vessel inspections were made for insurance companies, however, some pre-purchase surveys were performed for potential buyers.

The toughest part of these surveys is to determine a Fair Market Value, because each vessel design may limit the demand. Factors such as age, size, and number of passengers are easy to compare with other vessels. However, other factors such as food service spaces and food preparation equipment, and the interior decorations, are much harder for comparison purposes. Some dinner cruise vessels use catering for their meals, so they are not willing to pay extra for a vessel that has a full galley, etc.

These larger passenger vessels, used in the dinner cruise business, carrying from 150-400 passengers, were a very frequent survey for insurance Condition and Valuation. They were usually Coast Guard inspected as well (except a few on Inland Lakes), making my job much easier.

Some years there were as many as 50 small passenger vessels surveyed, of various types.

Another type of small passenger vessel was like this one at the Wisconsin Dells. Insurance companies worry about the maintenance being performed, in areas which are not under the jurisdiction of the U.S. Coast Guard, as well as the safety equipment the owner has on board.

**PADDLEWHEEL EXCURSION VESSEL AT FRANKENMUTH, MI**

This is one of the many small, paddlewheel passenger boats surveyed over the years. Because of my experience in designing and building this type of vessel, early in my career, these jobs seemed to come up regularly. This one is in Frankenmuth, Michigan, which is known for their stores selling Christmas decorations, year-round.

The "National Geographic Explorer" was a very interesting survey. The ship was built as an ice breaker and converted to passenger service. National Geographic intended to operate the vessel in both the Arctic and Antarctic Passenger Service. She was beautifully outfitted and had every conceivable way to experience the natural surroundings, with dive gear and underwater cameras displayed on the ship's TV channel. I even had a chance to meet and speak with Bob Ballard, the man in charge of the expedition to find the "Titanic." Great all-around job!

The S.S. "Independence" is a very interesting story. She was delivered in 1950 as the "Independence", then sold and renamed the "Oceanic Independence", then the "Sea Luck I", and finally the "Platinum II" before being sold for scrap. But I saw it when she was laid up in the late 1990's, at the M.A.R.A.D. Reserve Fleet Facility, in Suisun Bay, Benicia, California. ABSTech requested me to attend a survey with an architect working for the City of New York in 2003. The City of New York intended to use the vessel as a floating hotel for homeless families. The idea was a good one, however, the cost of improving the vessel to meet fire and other safety requirements, as well as the removal of asbestos in the vessel, made the cost of this project prohibitive.

The Brig "Niagara" is a replica of the ship used by Oliver Hazard Perry in the Battle of Lake Erie during the War of 1812. This replica is a working sailing ship and is very active in various Tall Ship Festivals around the United States. My services were centered around a couple drydockings of the vessel, where a stability study was needed to safely drydock her. Otherwise, I only went aboard her at the museum in Erie, Pennsylvania, where she is moored when not sailing.

This Showboat was surveyed while sitting on blocks. The hull was in poor condition, and the owners were trying to determine if it could be refurbished sufficiently to be refloated. Some vessels are just too far gone to be economically feasible!

This is an aquatic plant harvester owned by the City of Milwaukee. They were purchasing a new one and needed to obtain a Fair Market Value to sell this older model, or to negotiate a trade-in value. Because of my experience with the manufacturer of this equipment (described above, in the "Closer to Home" chapter), they used my services to perform a Condition for Valuation.

Government vessels were not typical work for me, although there were surveys of retired Government vessels, as described above.

This adjacent photo looks like a ship, but in fact, it is a mock-up of a ship. The mock-up is inside a building at the Naval Training Station, Great Lakes, Illinois. It is used to train Navy enlisted men on the use of deck machinery, and it needed to be certified to meet Navy Safety requirements. In addition to this mock-up, I had earlier certified a set of cargo cranes at Great Lakes, also mounted at a shoreside installation. Interesting jobs!

However, there were occasional Government surveys on a few small Coast Guard vessels, and the Army Corps of Engineers would ask for On-Charter and Off-Charter surveys, when they chartered privately owned barges.

There is one shipyard on the Great Lakes which builds a lot of equipment for the U.S. Navy, and their insurance underwriters have required surveys on many of those vessels.

Some towing approvals are made to move Government vessels. One large contract had me inspecting barges at the building yard in Wisconsin, then waiting for them to reach either New Orleans or Mobile, through the River system.

The barges would then be loaded onto a large, ocean barge, for transit to East Coast yards for use on Navy vessels. The reason for these two inspections was to look for damages, and to determine where the damages occurred. If damage was noted in Mobile or New Orleans, the River towing company was held responsible.

This same shipyard also built two large Barracks Barges for the Navy. Those barges are used to house the crew of a large ship, while the ship is in drydock, undergoing repairs. The shore power supplied to the ship in drydock is not sufficient to power the air conditioning and other "hotel" services in the crew accommodations. Therefore, the crew stays on these Barracks Barges until the ship is ready to return to service.

The insurance carrier for this shipyard was worried about the delivery trip from the Great Lakes, with one Barracks Barge going to Norfolk, and the second barge going all the way to San Diego, by way of the Panama Canal. My biggest worry was the "slamming of the barge in heavy seas, and the large, chain towing bridle hanging over the bow. We placed temporary steel covers over the doors and windows on the front of the barge, but the heavy chain, laying on the steel deck and bow rake knuckle, was bound to cause damage. Again, this shipyard (the same one objecting to the Staten Island Ferry delivery modifications), objected to any additional expense. However, the insurance underwriter understood my concern and demanded the shipyard make the temporary modifications in my recommendations.

The steel deck in the area where the chain bridle would be rubbing was 3/8" think, but we welded another ½" plate over the area where the chain would be rubbing. The tow made it to both Norfolk and San Diego without any problems, but I never heard the result of my extra "doubler plate" and whether or not it was necessary.

A few years later, there was a survey of an unusual Navy barge, which was on drydock in Norfolk, which I will discuss next. However, in the drydock next to the one on which we were working, there was a nuclear aircraft carrier going through a refueling of its nuclear fuel rods. Because the carrier had no electrical power, the Barracks Barge, which I had modified, was actually sharing the drydock where we were working, so the crew could be close to their ship during the drydocking of their "home." Looking up at the bow of that Barracks Barge, there was my "doubler plate" modification, still in place!

One of the Navy Shipyard crew working with me was familiar with the Barracks Barge, so when the story about the doubler plate was shared with our crew, he told me the doubler had been worn nearly half through between the Great Lakes and Norfolk, and he remembered hearing the barge heading for San Diego, the doubler was worn nearly through after a rough trip in the Caribbean. That was a relatively inexpensive modification and worth the extra safety factor, using those doubler plates.

So, the unusual barge, which was the reason to be in Norfolk, was an old, World War II tanker, which had been modified to hold nuclear waste. The aircraft carrier next to us, was removing their spent fuel rods, and those rods were placed in this barge. The interior of the barge had been modified and modernized, but the hull was still the old, partially riveted, WW II structure. It was my riveting experience which brought my services to the attention of the Navy. They had trouble understanding which rivets were in serious condition and which should just be left alone. In some cases, we needed to make welded inserts in the hull, and we developed a plan to eliminate rivets in those areas.

Because much of my inspection needed to be done internally, I had to wear a radiation dosimeter, even though I was quite far away from the actual radioactive waste. They also had me sit through a short training video about radioactive safety, which was quite interesting. This barge spent most of the time sitting in drydock, next to the ship discharging the waste, but it did need to be refloated occasionally to be moved to another drydock, so the Navy treated this old ship's hull very well!

The Pollution Control boats, owned by the Chicago Metropolitan Water Reclamation District, were a fairly regular job over the years. They needed a vibration analysis one year, ultrasonic thickness readings of the hull another year, and once they hired me to inspect a new vessel being built at a small shipyard in Escanaba, Michigan. They were always interesting and challenging projects!

# CHAPTER 26

## EXPERT WITNESS WORK

Part of the responsibility of a Marine Surveyor, is to provide testimony for both depositions and trial, if necessary. This responsibility usually applies to those projects on which the Marine Surveyor has performed a marine survey. In such cases, the surveyor's reports and records related to the lawsuit will be subpoenaed by the opposing attorney. The opposing attorney will typically then subpoena the surveyor himself, to obtain his testimony, which would be used during a trial. During my career, approximately thirty such depositions were given and court testimony occurred approximately six or seven times. If a surveyor has written a good report, and the opposing attorney sees that it would be difficult to "trip up" the surveyor during his courtroom testimony, the cases tend to be settled out of court, rather than take the chance of the surveyor/witness damaging their case.

However, if the surveyor develops a good reputation as an expert in certain types of ships, or certain technical areas, he is occasionally called upon to investigate and report upon accidents and equipment failures, for which he was not originally involved. This type of testimony has been requested approximately seven or eight times during my career and this requires a large amount of preparation, including the review of numerous depositions, reports, and background material. All of that is billable time, of course.

The best way to describe this type of testimony is with some examples:

An attorney in San Diego, California, contacted me about two shrimp trawlers, which were converted to tuna fishing vessels at a shipyard in the Gulf Coast of the United States. The vessels proceeded through the Caribbean, and then the Panama Canal, in order to proceed to the tuna fishing grounds in the Pacific. While in transit, one of the vessels suffered the loss of its rudder. The other vessel towed the damaged vessel to the nearest port for repairs. While the first vessel was being repaired, the second vessel was examined, and it was found the rudder on the second vessel was also suspect, due to poor welding.

A damage claim was filed with the vessel owner's insurance company. However, the vessel owner not only claimed the repairs for the vessel that lost its rudder but also included the repairs for the vessel that had not "yet" lost its rudder. The claim for the repair of the second vessel was denied by the insurance company. All of the records and testimony were reviewed and my report was submitted to the underwriters. The central point in the case was insurance covers loss, but not a potential loss. In this case, the rudder of the second vessel had not fallen off and was being repaired to prevent future damage or losses.

The defense attorney for the insurance company had prepared me well for my testimony, and the jury was interested in hearing what I had to say. All of the other witnesses had been giving testimony about cost for repairs, but no one had testified about the technical issues in the case. The attorney for the insurance company called me to the stand, reviewed my background and experience for the jury, and emphasized my frequent work in the tuna fishing industry.

For some unexplained reason, the opposing attorney had failed to request my deposition within the allowable time set by the court, and that attorney had not seen me until my appearance on the stand in the courtroom. This attorney apparently had no experience in the marine industry and she tried to question my qualifications. Because many expert witnesses spend most of their time doing research, rather than actual surveys, she asked how many surveys I performed in a typical year. I answered, "I am now, semi-retired and only performed 100 surveys in the past year, however, I typically performed over 300 surveys per year." The smiles on the faces of the jury members showed they did not like the attorney's lack of preparation. She then asked how much of my survey experience was on fishing vessels, and I recounted the numerous tuna vessel damages which had been surveyed, and overseen for repairs, during the last 20 years.

When she saw that her case was falling apart because of my testimony, she said, "That's enough Mr. Ojala, you are excused." At that time, the trial judge said, "Remain on the stand Mr. Ojala. I have some questions for you."

The judge proceeded to ask questions about how a shipyard works, who is responsible for quality, and whether an owner typically has a quality inspector at the shipyard.

It was evident to everyone, including the judge, the shipyard which performed the work in the Gulf of Mexico, was responsible for the poor workmanship, and apparently the owner had not inspected the work before taking possession of the two ships. Expecting the insurance company to pay for repairs to poor workmanship that would eventually have failed, is just not how insurance works. Despite the poor workmanship, the insurance company had paid for the loss of the first rudder, but they were not responsible to pay for repairs to prevent a potential loss. Our client won the defense case and apparently sued for legal expenses because this was considered a frivolous lawsuit.

## Injury Cases

Another example of a frivolous lawsuit, which never went to trial, occurred when a tug boat crewman was injured while breaking ice in a Great Lakes harbor. He was in the engine room, and had hurt his shoulder when the tug boat lurched in heavy ice. His employer paid for his medical bills and rehab, but an "ambulance chaser" type of attorney talked him into filing a lawsuit for damages.

After I filed my report, the attorney subpoenaed me to give a deposition regarding this injury lawsuit, and I was representing the towboat company. My research was done and the case file reviewed before the deposition. The opposing attorney started asking me questions about the tug boat, which had been used to break ice. He stated his assumption that this tugboat was not designed as an icebreaker, but I then produced copies of three drawings from the original construction of the tugboat. The title block of the main structural drawing was entitled "Great Lakes Icebreaking Tugboat" and a subsequent drawing showed details of framing in the bow, entitled "Intermediate Ice Frames". In addition, a third drawing was produced, which was entitled "Stainless Steel Icebreaking Propeller."

The attorney obviously saw his case slipping away and he then made a statement that inferred this tug, where the injury occurred, was too small for the job. He then referred to another tug in the fleet by name, which he said was larger. He implied, using the "larger" tug would have prevented injury to his client.

Recognizing the name of the second tug to which he referred, I stated that both tugs were the exact same size. The attorney then said, "That is impossible, because the first tug is 98 tons and the second tug is 150 tons." I asked him if the tons to which he referred had the letters "GT" behind them? He answered, "Yes," and then I then asked him if he knew what the letters "GT" meant? He answered, "No, but I have a feeling you are going to tell me!"

I then proceeded to explain to him that "GT" referred to Gross Tonnage, which is not a measure of weight or hull size but of the cargo-carrying capacity of a vessel for tax laws in the United States. Both of these vessels had the same hull and machinery, however, the 150 gross-ton vessel had a small deck house with a galley, which theoretically could be used to store cargo. This produced a higher gross tonnage (GT) on one vessel, but the vessels' hulls were identical.

It has always amazed me how poorly prepared some attorneys are for their lawsuits. My work has been with several excellent lawyers, most of whom were trained as Admiralty Attorneys. Most of those "good attorneys" will ask me to research specific areas in which they do not feel qualified, so that they can properly question the opposing witnesses, and use the proper language to avoid embarrassing mistakes.

Occasionally the opposing attorney is good at his job and does ask good questions. In several of these instances, those attorneys have followed me out of the courtroom and thanked me for my honesty and good testimony, even if it hurt their case. In at least two such occasions, I was later asked to provide testimony in a different case by that opposing attorney. That is a huge compliment!

One of the occasions in which I was approached by the opposing attorney after a trial, I was testifying against a State Government, representing a vessel owner who was suing the State. During the preparation for the trial, my impression was that the State used a poor defense position due to the details of the case. My testimony was truthful, and my client won his case. However, the States Attorney met me in the hallway after my testimony and asked if I would work on their behalf on another case, not mentioning the current lawsuit. My response was, "I will work for anyone as long as I'm allowed to state my opinions honestly." About a year later, the State called me, and as suspected, they were preparing a countersuit against my original client. Luckily, my testimony was not required in court on that case, though I did file a report for them.

In one recent case where my services were being used by a very good, Detroit Admiralty Law firm, they asked me to inspect some equipment on a large piece of marine dredging equipment, which failed while chartered by a marine contractor. There were several insurance companies involved, and the challenge was to determine which insurance carrier was responsible for the claim.

The equipment appeared to have been in poor condition before the charter, and numerous failures occurred, both before the equipment was put in operation, and then more failures during operation. The charterer reported these problems to the owner, and the owner recommended mechanics and other services, so the charterer expected the owner was going to pay for repairs, seeing the problems existed before the charter started.

The bills started to come to the charterer, not to the owner, and the owner told the charterer he should read the contract, which basically stated, "The Charterer takes the equipment AS-IS, but must return the equipment in good condition."

Common sense and ethical business practices seem to dictate this was not a fairly written charter contract, yet both parties signed it. Obviously, the Charterer had not read it, or he just assumed the owner would not give him a piece of faulty marine equipment. We seldom read rental agreements for cars and home repair tools, assuming the contract was fairly written. This is now up to the attorneys to prepare the case, and for a jury to decide.

My services included the inspection, as well as reading hundreds of pages of repair records, invoices, depositions, and E-Mails between the parties involved. I then summarized the pertinent details and wrote a lengthy report.

What made this case even more interesting is the fact I have had several run-ins with this same equipment owner in the past, all as a Third Party, and all of these instances involved rentals of faulty equipment, or equipment not suitable for the work being performed. He continues to operate because most of "us" just trust that the "other guy" is being honest. The lesson here is to be aware that such people exist and not everyone is honest!

In another case, my Condition & Valuation reports were subpoenaed for a case where two owners were parting company and one owner wanted his share of the assets in cash. My valuations for their equipment were being used to justify higher values than realistically possible. We arranged a phone conference call with the attorneys from both sides, and my first question to them was to read the first paragraph in my reports, which stated, "….performed on behalf of the vessel's underwriters." As described in a previous chapter on such C&V surveys, the reported values done for insurance companies tend to be higher than those for banks, and much higher than those done for pre-purchase. I told the attorneys I would be happy to testify, but that would be my testimony. No call ever came to give a deposition, and I never heard the result of the suit.

# CHAPTER 27

## COLORFUL PEOPLE IN THE MARITIME BUSINESS

Part of my attraction to the maritime industry was the people. First, I had my father, who had sailed the Great Lakes ore carriers ("Lakers" to those living up there) for 32 years. Then I experienced 4 years aboard a ship with some great people during my Coast Guard enlistment. After college, I worked in a shipyard and eventually found my career in marine surveying (ship inspections). However, it was the hard-working, dedicated, honest (generally) people I came in contact with who made me stay in my profession because I enjoy it. I have never retired from working because I'd miss the people too much!

Some older readers may remember a series of old, black-and-white movies centered around a character called Tugboat Annie. She was a tugboat captain in New York harbor, who seemed to be too wild and crazy to have been a real person. Well, some of the tugboat owners/operators I've come across in my career made Tugboat Annie look tame. Nevertheless, I learned a lot from these people, some of which made me a better ship surveyor.

**Dennis Egan was a tugboat owner in Lemont, Illinois.** The "dog eat dog" nature of running a successful tugboat company requires owners to be different from the rest of us. Dennis was, however, very misunderstood by outsiders, even though he turned out to be a loyal friend to those who knew him well. He had been a Will County, Illinois Sheriff before we met. When we met, Dennis had already moved to Lemont where he partnered with another man along the Illinois Waterway to form Service Welding Marine Shipyard in Lemont, Illinois. I first met Dennis when I was still with ABS. We (ABS) would inspect barges on the homemade drydock at Service Welding, which could only pick up one end of a barge at a time. This drydocking method made it difficult to see the middle of the barge bottom because it was never fully raised out of the water. Dennis devised a method to solve this problem, which he called the "submarine."

The submarine was a cylindrical tank that had small pontoons on either side. The tank stood vertically in the water and was weighted on the bottom so only 12 inches of the tank was above the water. The inspector was expected to stand in the tank and the shipyard crew used ropes to pull the submarine under the barge so the inspector could see the center area of the barge.

On one of those drydocking days, the Coast Guard inspector was in the submarine and I was in Dennis Egan's office on the second story of their office building, which overlooked the shipyard harbor. The harbor was an old stone quarry off the main channel of the Chicago Sanitary and Ship Canal (better known as the Illinois Waterway). His office had a door that opened out onto a balcony. We heard some loud chattering on the radio in Dennis' office and without any warning, Dennis pulled out one of his pearl-handled 45-caliber pistols from his belt, walked out on the balcony, and started shooting at a small tugboat that was "barreling" into the shipyard's harbor.

I was shocked, for sure, but held my composure. I asked Dennis what had just happened and he explained in "very colorful language" that the @#&*#!! tug was coming into the harbor too fast, creating a @#&*#!! wake and the guy in the "submarine" would have had his head jammed up into the bottom of the barge. The warning shots from Dennis' 45-cal. hit the pilothouse and the tug quickly stopped and turned around, leaving the harbor.

Such incidents gained Dennis a very colorful reputation. He was a big, red-headed Irishman who usually wore an open shirt that showed his hairy chest and gold chains. At some point, he stopped wearing those 45-cal pistols, but he always had a pistol in his desk drawer.

After leaving ABS to start my own business, Dennis was one of the few Great Lakes area Marine Industry contacts that called to give me work. Dennis was a real "ideas man," and he had some great projects that he wanted to see on paper. He would call and ask me to come to his shipyard to discuss a project. Once I arrived, I would listen to his ideas and create drawings, which we would then revise numerous times. There were maybe ten such projects from Dennis for which he paid well for my time, but he never built any of them. Years later, it dawned on me that Dennis knew I was struggling in those first years, and those projects were his way of keeping me going. It was not just charity. He knew he would need my surveying services, and if I did not make it in my business, he would lose a good resource.

I did a lot of marine surveys for Dennis, but the most memorable one was a grounded asphalt tanker in the St. Lawrence River. I was at Dennis' shipyard one day, and he was in a long phone conversation when I got there. When he got off the phone, he said he wanted me to fly to Canada with him to look at a tanker. I thought he meant later that week, but then he said, "No, I mean right now!" I did not have any clothes or travel essentials, but Dennis said we would buy them along the way. Luckily, this was before the days of needing a passport to travel to Canada. Dennis had already chartered a plane that was meeting us at the small, local airport. I called my wife to tell her what was happening, and we were on our way.

**RE-BOARDING THE PLANE AT MONTREAL MONTREAL, WITH MY NEW JACKET**

We stopped in Montreal to clear Customs/Immigration and because I did not have a jacket, Dennis bought me a nice leather one. We then headed to Anticosti Island, near the mouth of the St. Lawrence River, and arrived at night. The airport was closed when we arrived, so our pilot made a pass over the airport to send a radio signal that turned on the lights. He then made a second low pass to scare the deer off the runway (seriously, and there were many). Finally, we could land on our third approach.

There was a rental car with keys in the car, waiting for us at the airport. With only 250 inhabitants on a huge island (nearly 150 miles long) with few roads, nobody had reason to steal a rental car.

Anticosti Island is a hunter's paradise, we were told, where Canada's wildlife organizations beg deer hunters to come and take deer. There was only one hotel on the island, adjoining its only restaurant.

The next day, Dennis "held court" in the restaurant with some of the locals. We needed a helicopter to fly us out to the stranded ship, so the Canadian Coast Guard arranged for us to fly out there. We flew out to the ship and back, after which Dennis held a meeting with the ship owner's insurance adjuster.

Dennis had a lot of experience with asphalt and had recently cleaned up a huge asphalt spill at an oil refinery, so his idea was to get the asphalt in the ship removed by circulating hot asphalt in the now-hardened cargo tanks. We could tell that the insurance guy was skeptical.

We left the island, flew back to Chicago, and repeated the trip back to the island one week later. We brought along a Mechanical Engineer friend of mine, John Goss, to assist in the discussion with the insurance adjuster about getting the stranded ship off the island. Even though everyone else was convinced that our method would work, the insurance company decided to cut the ship into pieces and scrap it. We understood that the clean-up of the asphalt around the island, although hardened, became very expensive. Having the best idea, but a very innovative and unusual one does not always win everyone over!

Dennis later tried to get some work to clean up the oil in Kuwait after the first war in the Arabian Gulf. He wanted me to go with him if he got the work, but I was secretly hoping it wouldn't happen. Not one to avoid some reasonable risks, but going to Kuwait seemed a bit too dangerous for me at the time.

Dennis died in 2017 from Diabetes. I never had a chance to thank him for the help he gave me to get started. He would never have allowed me to say thank you when he was healthy, but I didn't hear about his impending death until he had lost consciousness. I think God will look kindly upon him. He knew the real meaning of charity, despite his crusty exterior!

**Gerry Bernardo was one of the best friends I've had in my life**. He was a certified marine chemist and a part-time marine surveyor. I referred to Gerry in my chapter about the tanker explosion in Trinidad when I called him for advice. Although the other marine surveyors on the Great Lakes and Rivers thought of me as a competitor, Gerry Bernardo immediately came to me and asked me to help him with survey work. He had a lot of contacts in the Marine Insurance Industry and was respected by everyone on the Great Lakes.

Gerry covered every Port from Duluth, Minnesota, to Toledo, Ohio and, because of this responsibility, Gerry was on the road 6 or 7 days a week. He wore out his cars every 18 months and had reward status on several airlines.

Gerry was still working with his mentor when we met, but he had already been certified (maybe in more ways than one!). Gerry was one of those people who always started every conversation with, "Have you heard the one about............?" and then he told at least three jokes before we went to work, and they were always "clean" jokes. These were the days before the Internet, and I never heard a joke from Gerry that I'd heard elsewhere. Who knows where he got them all?

Gerry knew I was struggling at the beginning of my business, so he subcontracted a lot of survey work to me. I was not able to do Marine Chemist work, but Gerry shared many Safety Audits and large Condition Surveys in every Great Lakes shipyard and most of the large marine construction companies. Eventually, he just handed over many of his Insurance Company contracts to me, for which I was always grateful.

Gerry Bernardo also gets credit for extending my life. Like many of us who spend too much time in cars, airplanes, hotels, and eating at restaurants with our clients, Gerry was a big man who was quickly becoming overweight. One day in Milwaukee, Gerry climbed a ladder up the side of a large ore carrier. He got to the top and had a massive heart attack. I knew I would probably suffer the same fate as Gerry if my lifestyle did not change, so the following week, I joined a health club and lost 25 pounds in a few months. Weight control is an ongoing struggle for me, but I am much healthier now than I was when Gerry died. I still miss our lunch meetings, his sound advice, and his great jokes! Thanks, Gerry!

**In Escanaba, Michigan, it was Dan Kobasic**. Dan Kobasic was the owner and President of both Basic Marine Shipyard and Basic Towing Company in Escanaba, Michigan. He got his start in the marine business as a crew member on cargo ships serving Viet Nam during that war. Dan came back to his home and started a pizza business with his brother, Claude, who Dan called his best friend.

Dan could not get that marine business out of his system, so he bought some abandoned property along the Escanaba Harbor, where he started a small shipyard. He also started his "collection" of tugs. Dan would keep a close eye on Government surplus sales and auctions for tugs and barges, buying many of them as well. He even sank a tug he'd purchased on the East Coast while trying to tow it back to the Great Lakes. Dan used his shipyard to fix the tugs, and he often repowered them with engines he obtained from Government surplus sales.

We first met at his shipyard when I went there to survey a tug that a different owner was working on, using Dan's new floating drydock. Dan yelled at me because he thought I was just a nosey local intruder. I yelled back at Dan and started to leave, but he stopped me. The fact that I yelled back gained his respect, and it started a friendship that lasted over 28 years.

Because I spoke my mind and would even admit I was not an expert on every subject, Dan trusted my opinion. We worked together on numerous large cargo towing projects, delivering large European-built engines around the Great Lakes.

CARGO TRANSFER TO KOBASIC BARGE DAN KOBASIC AT BASIC MARINE 2006

Whenever Dan was in the Chicago area, he would call me to share a drink and/or dinner, and in October 2017, he called me on one of those occasions. I was on my way to the hospital for surgery when he called, so Dan just said, "Next time then." I did not realize at the time, why Dan had called and wanted to meet, but it turned out he had just received word from his doctor, and he wanted to tell me he was dying from pancreatic cancer. By the time I found out, Dan was non-responsive and his brother, Claude, didn't want me to see him in that condition. Dan died just over one month from the time he'd called me.

Because Dan was outspoken, many people disliked him. But he was extremely honest and the work done at his shipyard was some of the best on the Great Lakes. I would always tell people to go to Escanaba for honesty and quality, and "just yell back if Dan yells at you." It worked for me, after all!

**In Chicago, the "River Pirate" of the harbor was Captain Ed Barnaby**. Ed was one of the "crustiest" individuals I ever met. He ran the largest towing service on the south end of Lake Michigan with almost no competition because people feared competing with him. He never earned my respect because he only seemed to think about money. Making money is necessary for business but not when it hurts other people. In my opinion, Captain Barnaby only thought about money, and he stepped on everyone in his way, including his children and other family members to get it. My only contact with him was through ABS, and after starting A3Pi Services, I would occasionally see him when I was representing an insurance company on a damage survey of one of his tugs. I would have refused to accept a job paid for by Barnaby himself.

When Captain Barnaby died, his business was split among several people. He left the business to his second wife and daughter who were unable to run it and eventually sold it to **John Kindra**. John had previously run a very successful barge cleaning service near Lemont, Illinois. That towing business is still operating under John Kindra, who is considered a real gentleman in all his years in the tugboat business, and he hasa good reputation.

Captain Barnaby's son, Tom, from his first marriage, tried to set up his own tugboat business. He was a hard worker and was doing well. However, Tom found himself with some serious criminal issues that he was unable to deal with. He ended up taking his own life.

**Glenn Dawson, with his wife, Holly,** set up a competing tugboat business in Chicago after Captain Barnaby's death. Glenn had been a tug Captain for Ed Barnaby when he was young and did consulting work for him until Barnaby died. I knew Glenn and Holly well and did a lot of survey work for them. They reported several damages within a short timeframe and blamed them all on one of their tug captains. That captain eventually lost his license and got into legal trouble with the Coast Guard.

Glenn Dawson grew up in South Chicago and knew the local Aldermen. He ran errands for the Aldermen and other Chicago politicians before he eventually became an Illinois State Representative. Glenn also was Captain of one of the Chicago Fireboats when I met him. He ran some passenger party boats for a while; I surveyed them for his insurance companies. In the early years of Navy Pier, before it became a tourist attraction, Glenn was the Director of Marine Operations there.

Despite all of these connections, Glenn and Holly had a lot of legal issues with the City of Chicago, issues that eventually resulted in their divorce. Their previously successful marine towing business went bankrupt after the divorce. Glenn acted as a private marine consultant for various contractors until he died in 2021.

**Another boat captain** owned several small passenger party boats that operated in Chicago harbor. He "stiffed" almost everyone who invoiced him for services, He owed me some money, so I always refused to do his work until he finished paying me for the last job. One day, I received a phone call from a Chicago Marine Police Officer who was a friend of mine. He wanted to know if this captain owed me any money. I told him he still owed me about $500. "Well, you won't ever see that money because our captain friend got WHACKED last night!" We suspect he cheated the wrong people. When they found him, he was in a kneeling position with several bullets in the back of his head!

The last colorful individual that was part of the **Chicago marine towing industry was John Selvick**. John came from a long line of family members in the tug and barge business on Lake Michigan. His father, Curly Selvick, was well known on the Great Lakes, but I only had occasional contact with Curly. I will cover the rest of the family when I get to the section on Sturgeon Bay.

John was a rough individual with a reputation for being the best boat handler on the Great Lakes, even among his competitors. John picked up some old vessels and started his own business. Early in my A3Pi Services career, I surveyed most of his equipment for insurance after one of his tugs sank. John was running on a tight budget back then, and he was not happy with the numerous repairs I recommended to his insurance company. However, he made those repairs, and despite his grumbling, he did not seem to hold any grudges.

I had become a certified auditor for American Waterways Operators (AWO), which required their non-Coast Guard inspected member companies to comply with AWO rules, nearly as strict as the Coast Guard. John wanted to become an AWO Member, which was required by many of the larger cargo shippers, like BP Oil, so he asked me to be his AWO auditor. However, because I was so aware of the problems he had, I offered him an alternative, which was for me to prepare his tugs and crews before the AWO audit. This turned out to be a great training experience for me, plus his employees all seemed to like my training style, from which they said they learned a lot. The result was great, and John's company passed its AWO audit. The company has maintained its certification, which shows how well John improved his company, despite his constant complaining about the cost!

John Selvick died young from pancreatic cancer in 2016. His company was split between his wife, son, and daughter. Two of John's trusted employees remained part of the business, and they are now part of the ownership. That outcome has worked well, and the company is still successful.

**In Detroit, the "Legend" of the Detroit River was Bill Hoey.** Bill ran a marine towing business in Detroit and a company of small passenger excursion boats. His base of operations was on the Rouge River, downriver of Detroit, in a very industrial part of town, surrounded by oil refineries and steel mills. When the Rouge River caught on fire back in the 1960s, it spurred the city of River Rouge to get that river cleaned up.

I first met Bill Hoey when I was surveying one of his old tank barges. One of my clients wanted to buy it for refueling ore carriers in Ashtabula, Ohio. This was not very long after I left my ABS job. Dressed in my white, ABS coveralls, with a flashlight in one hand, and carrying a large piece of railroad chalk in the other hand, I headed toward the barge. Bill asked me what I was doing with that piece of chalk and I told him I intended to use it to mark up any damages and broken welds seen in the barge. "If that's going to happen, you need to buy the barge first," Bill said to me and held out his hand. "Either hand me a check or hand me that chalk." I must have looked confused because Bill went on to explain to me that if I marked up those problem areas, and my client decided not to buy the barge, he would be unable to sell it to the next potential buyer once they saw my markings.

# Colorful People In The Maritime Business

I learned a good lesson from Bill that day: there was a big difference between my old ABS Surveyor job, where I had authority, and my new role as an independent marine surveyor, contracted by the vessel owners, where all I could do was report my findings to my clients. I no longer had the authority to demand or recommend repairs, just to record and report what I found.

**In Sturgeon Bay, Wisconsin**, Curly Selvick's two daughters, Susan and Sharon, are affectionately called "The Girls." Those who dislike them call them the "Dragon Ladies," but everyone still respects them as being in full control of their large fleet of tugs. They grew up in the tugboat business and can swear better than any tugboater when they need to. Having done a lot of work with Susan and Sharon, I respect them too. They are honest but can be tough and, most importantly, they've never asked me to do anything unethical. Working with them was great unless they were mad at you.

Susan and Sharon are identical, and part of a set of triplets. However, the third child is a boy. Steve is one of the largest Marine Risk Insurance brokers on the Great Lakes. He is also the Insurance Agent for many large marine accounts and was the agent for his sisters' business.

Susan and Sharon eventually sold their business to a local tugboat captain called Don Sarter. Don was working as a captain for a local marine construction business and was planning to retire at the end of the year when he tragically drowned while working on Lake Superior, just months before his planned retirement. His wife tried to run the business for a few years but finally had to sell the business in 2022.

**In Buffalo, it was Tommy Dawes**, who had a small fleet of tugs when I first met him in Buffalo. We were loading boilers to be delivered to a plant on Lake Michigan, and I was doing the Lashing Plan and Towing Approval for their insurance company. What made Tommy interesting was his friendship with "Papa Doc" and "Baby Doc," the two dictators in

LOADING BOILERS IN BUFFALO WITH TOMMY DAWES

Haiti. Tommy owned a home in Haiti and operated a towing business in the Caribbean when he lived there. After those dictators fell out of power, Tommy spent most of his time on the Great Lakes, working for other towing companies.

I cannot forget to mention **John Larkin** and **John Greenwood**. The reason they are mentioned together is that John Greenwood called me to assist in some projects he was doing for John Larkin.

John Greenwood was a very respected business consultant in the marine industry. He had worked for one of the largest iron ore companies in a business capacity and, by the time I met him, he was well-established as a consultant. John was also a publisher and is best known for his Greenwood's Guide to Great Lakes Shipping. That Guide was (and still is) a "bible" for information on the companies on the Great Lakes, including each ship with their important particulars, each owner with addresses, phone numbers, and important contacts, plus services to the marine industry. My A3Pi Services company had a full-page ad in the Guide for many years.

John Greenwood asked me to meet John Larkin, who was trying to deliver newsprint paper from Canadian paper mills to the newspapers in Milwaukee and Chicago. He owned a small railroad in the Upper Peninsula of Michigan. The plan was to move the cargo in rail cars across Lake Superior by ship, then use the Escanaba & Lake Superior Railroad to move the rail cars to Menominee, Michigan, where they would again be loaded onto a ship to complete the trip to Milwaukee and Chicago.

John Greenwood and I accompanied John Larkin on inspections of numerous old rail-car ferries on the Great Lakes, which he purchased. He was also able to obtain five Navy tugs, two in Norfolk and three in San Francisco. On one trip to Norfolk to inspect those tugs, John Larkin rented a Lear Jet from one of his friends, picked me up at Meigs Field in Chicago, and then flew to the Lakefront Airport in Cleveland, where we picked up John Greenwood. We spent a half day in Norfolk, then back to Cleveland and Chicago.

I even surveyed a surplus, icebreaking cargo ship in the Texas Reserve Fleet for John Larkin, which was destined to break the ice on Lake Superior for this project. Due to lawsuits with competing railroads, this project never materialized, but it really would have worked and saved money for everyone, other than the railroad that sued.

Another project John Larkin planned was to disassemble and move a taconite iron ore loading facility from Canada to the Upper Peninsula of Michigan. We inspected the facility in Canada for its condition and viability, and then the negotiations started with the owner of the loading facility, which was a major oil company. John Larkin again used the Lear Jet to pick up the oil company president and fly him to Ontonagon, Michigan, where John Greenwood, John Larkin, and I met the plane. John owned several beautifully refurbished, classic, antique rail cars. The four of us rode one of those trains to Menominee, Michigan, and then back to Escanaba. We ate lunch and dinner in the formal dining car and relaxed in the "smoker car." In my opinion, this treatment was "over the top" even though I certainly enjoyed the trip. As it turned out, the oil company president was against the project.

JOHN LARKIN (RIGHT) ON HIS TRAIN INTERIOR OF RESTORED DINING CAR

John Larkin still owns several of the rail car ferries and tugs he bought, but those projects seem to be on his "back burner" now. In 2015, John Greenwood died. His Greenwood's Guide still lives on!

**In Croatia, Davor Jurum** was one of the first Environmental Officers I met on an "extended cruise ship audits" job I worked between 1999-2008. Davor was a licensed Marine Engineer and the cruise line needed him in that position to get their program started. He had intended to go back to his Engineering job after a year, but he took the Environmental position seriously and dedicated himself to making his ship the best! In the chapter on Cruise Ships, there is a picture of Davor with his fist in the air. He had just heard at that dinner that his ship completed our Environmental Compliance Audit with zero deficiencies. This was a very unusual accomplishment in the first several years of our audits. Although most findings in our audits were not considered serious, having zero deficiencies was something the ships were proud to achieve.

I maintained my friendship with Davor after the audit period was completed, Davor helped me find my home in Croatia. I continue to keep in touch with Davor to this day. This photo below was taken in 2016 in Pula, near Davor's home in Croatia.

**MY GOOD FRIEND, DAVOR JURUM**

**Melvin McLaurin** is one of the best people I have met in my entire life. I met him during my short career at the Army Corps of Engineers, shortly after I started working in the Chicago District. Melvin was a crane operator for the Corps of Engineers, and he and I planned the removal of several large piles of concrete at Chicago's Calumet Harbor.

Melvin was impressed with me because he said he had worked for the Army Corps for over 15 years, and not once had he been asked for advice during a project. Although Melvin was a trusted crane operator, he hadn't been promoted beyond the level of a crane operator. That changed during the time I worked with him. Feeling valued motivated Melvin to get involved. As a result of his getting involved, the USACE promoted him to a level of authority, and he blossomed!

Crane operators are normally criticized for damaging barges when unloading large rocks (up to 7 tons each), but Melvin received compliments from the towing companies for never causing damage. Melvin was also the best boat operator I ever worked with, and he made everyone feel safe when he was operating a boat.

Melvin and I took several long road trips together. We talked about anything and everything during those drives, including our upbringing and early childhood experiences. Melvin said he got his work ethic from his mother who did not allow any excuses. I even met Melvin's parents.

We often greeted each other with a big bear hug, and I think we trusted one another completely. I often told Melvin teasingly that he must have been my long-lost brother! Whenever Melvin walked into my office, we just gave each other a knowing smile.

Melvin was only a few credit hours away from his Bachelor's Degree and I was trying to talk him into finishing it. With that degree, I told District Management that Melvin was better qualified than anyone to take over my job at the Lock. Management agreed. But he could not take over from me without that piece of paper (his degree),

In 2017, Melvin became excited about a potential short-term project in Alaska. I remember Melvin coming to my office at the Lock, very excited and telling me he was going to Alaska. I reminded him of my August retirement and wanted to be sure he planned to be at my retirement party. Melvin promised he'd be there.

In Alaska, Melvin was operating a construction roller when a bee entered his space. He was allergic to bees and always carried an EpiPen. It is believed Melvin, to avoid being stung by the bee, caused the roller to run off a berm and was crushed and killed. The Chicago District (and I) were devastated by Melvin's death. He will be deeply missed for years to come. The new Field Maintenance Building in Calumet Harbor is now named after Melvin.

On the next page, I share a picture of Melvin. He is wearing a sweatshirt that reads, "Respect is Earned." Melvin lived by that philosophy; it's what made him the great caring person he was. He was also a huge University of

Michigan fan. He never fully explained why that was, but being a U-of-M grad myself, it was OK with me!

# CHAPTER 28

## SO, WHAT'S NEXT?

The career described in this book started in 1989 when I left the employ of the American Bureau of Shipping (ABS) to start my own business, A3Pi Services, Inc. (now A3Pi Services LLC). Over the years after college, I dabbled in things on the side, always thinking I would have my own business. At first, because of my Naval Architecture degree, it seemed like it had to be designing ships, mainly small passenger boats, tugs, and barges. However, as more design jobs came along, the more it became evident to me that sitting behind a desk was just not going to make me happy! Luckily, the ABS job came my way, which provided me with a way to experience working aboard ships and working side by side with the crew. It also provided a way for me to combine my Engineering background with field survey and inspection work.

Surveys keep coming my way even now, and many of my clients tell me, "You are NOT ALLOWED to retire!" Luckily, I love my work and enjoy working with most of the people in the Maritime business. For example, while vacationing in Aruba, making the final edits for this book, I told one of my insurance company clients I would be out of the country for a few weeks. He asked me where I was going, and when I told him it was Aruba, he said, "You wouldn't mind working while you're down there, would you?" Sure enough, he had five passenger vessels to be surveyed in Aruba, and I enjoyed meeting the people in this Aruba maritime operation, and it helped out my client while earning some extra money. My work is part of my life, and I enjoy it!

Because my career has been so active, boredom sets in easily when there are no ships to survey, so writing has become the next thing to keep me out of mischief!

If you enjoyed the stories in this book, my next book is more Autobiographical, starting from my "Early Years" with a father that sailed, my Coast Guard experience, my College Years in Naval Architecture, and my first jobs out of college, which prepared me for my Independent Marine Surveying career.

Then there was a short stint (7-1/2 years is short?) of working for the Army Corps of Engineers, which could be an entire book in itself! They were good enough to allow me to keep my business going during the 2008-17 recession, working my A3Pi surveys on weekends and vacations. The Army Corps was also a great experience in many areas. I had never worked in Lock Operations, breakwall repairs, flood control, and heavy construction equipment, but I was able to do that in the Army Corps.

My seventeen years working for ABS were critical, and that experience, tied with my Naval Architecture degree, landed many of the interesting jobs described in this book. For example, the trip to Kwajalein was because I was a Naval Architect, not because I was a Marine Surveyor. Having those two major things on my Resume' made the difference in landing many of those interesting jobs, numerous times over the years. Then my Great Lakes experience with riveted ships landed my project in Panama, repairing their caisson and lock gates.

If you are interested in the "colorful side" of the maritime business, there is a Chapter in that next book called, "Colorful People in the Maritime Business" which will make you think these people could not exist! But trust me, they did exist, and some became my very good friends!

After that book, Autobiography of a Ship's Marine Surveyor, I put together a book, Sweetwater Sailors, which started out about the life of a Great Lakes Merchant Mariner, based upon my father's 32 years of sailing. It ended up being a compilation of great, real-life stories, told by about eighteen sailors. I also have a sequel coming for that book. My writing style is practical and full of examples and pictures, so it should make those books interesting as well.

Now I am writing novels, based upon characters I have known during my career. GOOGLE me, Bob Ojala, and see all my books!

## *So, What's Next?*

Keep reading my books and keep me off the streets!
Thank you!!!!!!!

# ABOUT THE AUTHOR

Bob Ojala has a BSE in Naval Architecture & Marine Engineering from the University of Michigan, Class of 1970. Bob spent four years in the U.S. Coast Guard, 17 years with the American Bureau of Shipping, and 7-1/2 years with the U.S. Army Corps of Engineers, in addition to 35 years in his own business (including the time while with the USACE). Bob is still active in marine surveying and consulting.

Bob is a Wisconsin native with Finnish roots. His father was a Merchant Mariner for 32 years, giving Bob the interest in the Maritime Industry, but not the desire to be a sailor.

Bob worked as a Naval Architect, designing small passenger vessels, tugs, and barges after graduation. However, Bob found he enjoyed working in the shipyard, with the workers, more than sitting in the design office.

When the opportunity came to join the American Bureau of Shipping, working as a Field Surveyor, inspecting ships, and equipment going into shipbuilding, Bob thought this was what he was looking for.

Eventually, Bob started his own Marine Surveying & Consulting business. Because Great Lakes clients were slow in changing loyalties, Bob began traveling the world, surveying (inspecting) cruise ships, tankers, drydocks, and even some warships. Bob also conducted investigations of accidents, pollution incidents, and several accidental deaths.

Although he lost track after a while, Bob visited over 70 countries and worked in at least 58 of those (he kept track!). Bob sent home E-mails with his observations of the cultures he experienced during these travels, in addition to the more interesting parts of the work he performed. This book tries to give his impressions of the people he met, both good and bad, as well as descriptions of the vessels he worked on and the accidents he investigated.

Bob Ojala's books include:

- Autobiography of a Ship's marine Surveyor
- Sweetwater Sailors (non-fiction, real-life stories from Great Lakes mariners)
- Sweetwater Sailors – The Rest of the Story (Wives, women sailors, and "Unusual" sailors' stories)
- A Tugboater's Life (Contemporary Romance based upon a family working in Great Lakes Marine Construction)
- The Tugboater Family (stand-alone, but the characters continue from A Tugboater's Life)
- Crew's Shop Affairs (Life on a large cruise ship, BELOW the passenger decks)
- KIDNAPPED – A Tugboater's Tale (Human Trafficking in middle-America)
- UNDERCOVER AGAIN – Fighting Human Trafficking
- COMMERCIAL FISHERMEN – GREAT LAKES STYLE (non-fiction, real-life stories from Great Lakes Commercial Fishermen)